ANDROS ODYSSEY
The Return
1940-1990

Stavros Boinodirs PhD

iUniverse, Inc.
Bloomington

ANDROS ODYSSEY - The Return
1940-1990

iUniverse books may be ordered through booksellers or by contacting:

iUniverse
1663 Liberty Drive
Bloomington, IN 47403
www.iuniverse.com
1-800-Authors (1-800-288-4677)

ISBN: 978-1-4620-1994-6 (sc)
ISBN: 978-1-4620-1995-3 (hc)
ISBN: 978-1-4620-1996-0 (e)

Printed in the United States of America

iUniverse rev. date: 06/10/2011

Table of Contents

Table of Figures

COVER PAGE: 2009 Photo of the Village of Kalivarion at the island of Andros. Across the straights, you can see the mountains of Southern Evia.

Introduction

Word-of-mouth Tradition

My father Anthony was a man who had the gift of a good memory. He also liked the excitement of a good story. He talked a lot, narrating stories of what he knew, what he heard and what he read. He had a booming voice and his whole face became part of the story. Most of the people around him would characterize him as religious, with high moral standards. He would always do manual labor as he was chanting church hymns. He also had a meager education – he did not complete elementary school education- but he loved to read. Although his education was meager by his standards, elementary school education in those years was at a different standard than today's schools. Along with Greek and Turkish, the children of his school had to learn French and Arabic.

Those that really knew my father would characterize him as a highly energetic person, to the point of hyperactivity. At times, he could start dancing, because he felt like doing so. He also was highly emotional; he would be the first to start crying in a sad situation. He was a rather impatient individual and often got in trouble by making impulsive hurried decisions. He had the great fortune though, to marry my mother, also born at the birthplace of my father, a diplomatic woman that I can characterize as the Gibraltar of my family. My mother had the capacity to remain cool and decisive, even in the most adverse situations; in such situations, she would bring balance to my father's impulsiveness, thus saving the day.

When my father reached his sixty-second birthday, he retired as a grocery store owner. He became a gardener, growing produce until his seventieth birthday. Yet, his mental energy was at the fullest, always entertaining his guests with his stories. It was then, that I decided to channel this energy, by asking him to start writing his memoirs. By the time of his death, my father had hand-written ten notebooks.

It took me several years before I started reading them. I was surprised by the style of his writing. Although disorganized in the order of events, his memory-derived dates and sources of information were very accurate. In comparison to him, my memory of dates and events is very poor at best. I have to rely on notes, encyclopedias, computers and other means to remember historical events, medical appointments and other daily schedules. My father could remember the names of Turks he met in Mersina seventy years earlier, a person that he did not see since then. Some entries, which I had heard before in his stories during my youth, were especially surprising this time, after I paid the proper attention to what he was saying. The excerpt below is from a translation from the fourth book of my father:

"In this notebook I am recalling what I have been told and what I remember from my childhood. I am recalling political and religious events, from the time that I started remembering events until now. My name is Anthony Boinodiris and I was born in the Old Kalivarion, or Karvali *or* Gelveri *as the Turks called it then, located in Nigde of Akserai in Cappadocia of Asia Minor. The name of the village today is Guzelyurt.*

Based on a word-of-mouth tradition, transferred to us by our grandparents, our origins are from the island of Andros. Our suspicions are that there is a relationship somehow between the names of our village to Kalivarion of Andros, a small community of the northwestern part of that island, but I have no concrete proof for that. Our ancestors told us that we immigrated to Cappadocia under some unknown circumstances, at an unknown time, lost in the memories of people that preceded us. Our ancestors also told us that other immigrants from islands near Andros ended in locations near ours. Our ancestors identified that the people of Haskoy, a village to the northwest of Guzelyurt came from Naxos; and the people from Kalecik, a village to the north of Guzelyurt came from Lemnos.[1] I was told that our immigration is linked, but I was not told how."[2]

It was a challenge for me to shed some light on my father's biographical data of the 20th century to that of the historical past. I had to find

---

1   Andros, Naxos and Lemnos are Aegean Islands.
2   A. Boinodiris, Book 4, Cover Entry.

what events in history were hiding behind the Andros migration to Cappadocia. When and how did all that happen?

Going Back In Time: Return to Andros
(East Coast of Attica, July, 1997)

It was a hot day in July of 1997. My wife Despina and I arrived at Andros on the ferryboat from Rafina. The trip took about two hours and was very pleasant. A number of tourists were chatting loudly on the deck. A band of Greek Americans from the Chicago area were speaking in English and arguing whether the United States could use wind power, as in the Greek islands. Several windmills were visible on the top of the mountains of Evia. The tourists were looking forward to a good time at Myconos.

The ferry landed at the small port of Gavrio and started unloading cars and trucks, including my car, a 1967 Toyota Corolla. I drove this venerable car up to an almost deserted mountainside, which according to my father may once have been the stomping ground of his earlier ancestors. What struck me was the architecture of the numerous slate houses, most of them deserted, or used to house animals.

At the village called Kalivarion, there is a church, a cemetery and a handful of populated houses. The cemetery is full of Venetian-sounding names, a reminder of who populated the region after many of the Greeks departed. The place is ideal for "kalives," or sheds, used by shepherds herding animals. Thus, the name remained as "Kalivarion."

We boarded our old Toyota Corolla and drove to the city of Andros. Some of the people of Andros have distinct characteristics that are recognizable in the Kalivarion, or Karvali clans that now live in New Karvali, near Kavala, Greece; men are rather short, stocky, with rough faces, and heavy eyebrows. Cartoonists used these same heavy eyebrows in depicting the ex-Prime Minister of Greece, Constantine Karamanlis; his name also suggests that his ancestors may have come from Cappadocia. Women are well rounded. The people are frank, direct and shrewd.

A woman, sitting in front of her house, near the ruins of the Venetian castle (Kato Kastro) of Chora, told me about its recent history during World War II: "When the Italians declared war against the Germans, they mounted a small 'fart-cannon' on the fort, to defend the city. The Germans sent a boat over and they blew them to smithereens, causing a great deal of destruction to our homes. We had to rebuild many of the houses in town. So, what you see of that fort is what was left after the Germans were done with it."

"My father believes that our ancestors come from Andros," I said.

"Really?" she responded. "The Andrians now have three roots; the old Andrian, Italian roots and Albanian roots." She paused. "Which roots do you come from?"

Despina looked at her and smiled.

"Stavros thinks that he may have come from the old Andrian people that left this island many centuries ago, before the Italians or Albanians arrived. He is still trying to find out when and how."

She looked at me with a puzzled look and smiled. We got directions from her to the public library, but unfortunately, it had closed for the day. We left Andros and planned another trip. A year later, we entered the library. "Can I help you?" the librarian asked.

"I would like to see Mr. Dimitris Polemis please," I replied. Dimitris Polemis is a known historian from Andros and the supervisor of the local library. The librarian led me to the library office. She pointed to a man sitting behind the office.

"I am Stavros Boinodiris. I called you yesterday."

"Yes. Have a seat. How can I help you?" I told him about my father and his notes.

"My father claims that the original people of Gelveri in Cappadocia came from Andros. They specifically name Kalivarion as the source. There is also a connecting heritage for some locations in Asia Minor, which have links to Lemnos and Naxos."

"This is interesting. I happen to know Gelveri in Cappadocia. Have you been there?"

"No."

"You must go. I did." He looked at me intensely. "I have no historical evidence that Kalivarion existed before the Albanian migration here. The only known ancient place nearby is that of Amolochos. Even then, this island is quite a distance from Cappadocia. It does not look likely that people from here would simply travel to Cappadocia. Do you have any other historical evidence?"

"No. That is why I came to you. One possible source may be that of Theophanes the Confessor, dealing with the period of Kosmas."[3]

"I studied Theophanes. There is not much there about Kosmas. Theophanes does not talk much of Andros."

"Are there any other possible sources?" I asked.

"I suggest you read some of the literature of other immigrants from that area. There is a Center of Asia Minor Studies in Athens. They published a book, titled: 'Religious Life in the Region of Akserai −Gelveri.' I believe we have a copy here." He walked out, towards the bookshelves, as I followed. "Here it is."

I thanked him after he handed me the book, got a copy of the front page and started scanning through it. It covered the recent century with details of religious life in Cappadocia. My mind started wondering. *"Is it possible that the stories propagated from generation to generation on the journey of these Andrians are true?"*

---

3   The first section of this book covered the "Kosmas revolt," an event of 725 AD.

I signed the library visitor's book and departed. My mind was still spinning, as I boarded the ferry, going back to the Greek mainland at Rafina. *"Suppose that these people were trying to tell us their story starting from their beginnings in this island. Why is there no record of this? There are three possibilities: either it did not occur, or it occurred and the information was lost, or someone had tried to suppress this information from the historians of that time. "*

My research had just begun.

It was summer of 1998, when I sat at my computer at Schinias, a coastal resort area near Athens. I was wondering how to explain the ten, handwritten notebooks that my father Anthony left to me. He scribbled the books in Greek on regular notebooks, jumping from fact to hearsay, from one war to another and from one disaster to another. My father had facts describing his own experience, or the experience of people he talked to on occasion. Many times, he repeated his story. Yet, he was consistent. He always explained how and when he experienced what he wrote. In every instance, where his information was hearsay, he reported how he received it and from whom.

I had two choices, regarding the content of his work:

Write only the facts experienced by my father and others, and scrapping any unsubstantiated stories. This would be a purist approach, loved by historians, like Mr. Polemis.

Write about the facts experienced by Anthony and others, but include the stories passed down to us. To avoid offending purists, I felt that I had to warn the reader when I was presenting information based on word-of-mouth tradition.

I chose the second option. In addition to my father's data, I added my own memories and those of my mother's. To distinguish facts from fiction, I used some different text formatting as follows:

All **fictional characters**, added to build up the story I present in bold text, as shown in this sentence. I ask the reader to treat such sections with such bold entries as fiction.

These books are an attempt to connect the real experience of a few families, burdened with an unwritten tradition, passed on from generation to generation. It is a testament to the human endeavor to survive and create their own way of life in the face of forced migration, wars, hunger, oppression and violence. It takes place over a period of 1300 years and on four continents.

The purpose of this book is threefold. First, to shed some light on this mystery of the Greeks of Kalivarion, or Gelveri; second, to shed some light into this not so well-known time and place of human history; and third, by viewing a story in terms of a very long period, in relationship to world events, to experience how slowly humans have evolved. It shows how many of the issues that our ancestors dealt with are still with us. As Dr. K. Wright said, "... it is depressing to see how slow our progress has been. Youngsters reading this book must be very frustrated, as they have a gleam in their eye in improving the world. Human behavior is changing, not in terms of months or years, but in terms of centuries, over many generations of youngsters, with the same gleam in their eyes."

Human progress has been slow, if someone does not look at history with the right lens. During the four million years –give or take a million years- of human existence, we have come a long way and should be proud of it. Humans, like most other species cannot evolve faster than evolution permits. We need time to alter our primitive instincts and tendencies to violence through rational thought. The 1300 years covered in this series, is just an instance in the evolutionary timescale and it should not depress us. We simply cannot experience human progress in a single lifetime. Human progress can occur only through a long term planning, involving multiple generations. We can see this, only by looking at history with the macro-lens, used in the Andros Odyssey series. We must see how our ancestors worked out multi-generational planning. To achieve this goal, "ignorance of our past is by no means bliss." Unless we know how we dealt with our problems in our own historical past, we and our youngsters cannot plan correctly. Our "success in surviving as a species as long as possible," must be widely supported and be a patient, multi-generational process.

This definition of success may seem simplistic, but that is what our own human history and our accumulated knowledge of our environment tells us. We know that no matter how much effort we place in our survival and progress, all we can achieve is a minute step forward, as this step compares with the bigger picture of human survival. Besides that, we are one of many living organisms on this earth, most of which became extinct trying to survive. The mighty dinosaurs that ruled the earth for millions of years vanished in this inhospitable environment. According to the best scientists, our own earth and our solar system have limited life span. Our own universe is doomed to oblivion. Yet, no human, from birth to death thinks of doing anything else but be part of the Human Odyssey, because we are driven by some strange evolutionary laws.

What evolutionary drive makes us be who we are?

Are we driven by survival and pleasure of life, over which we have no control? Are we driven by curiosity on the mystery of life (thirst of knowledge on how things turn out, no matter what the outcome)? Are we ignoring the long term demise of our species with the hope that somehow a miracle would save us? Are we driven by a belief that somewhere there is a Supreme Being with a reason for all this and that there is another dimension of life, after our departure from this world?

No matter, what your beliefs are, be patient. You are part of a Human Odyssey. Enjoy every minute of it. You are programmed to do that by evolutionary instincts. The way we can best observe these evolutionary instincts, is to pay attention to children. Children think neither of their past, nor of their future. They concentrate on things that grownups seldom do: enjoying the present.

Andros Odyssey is a tiny part of my Human Odyssey. Whether you know it or not, there is a good chance that your Odyssey probably relates to mine, even in the not so distant past. Chances are that some of your ancestors are part of the millions of Byzantines, mostly Greeks who, between 1200 AD and the 1900s made their way throughout the globe.

The evidence of Byzantine Greek influence is all around you. The Greek roots in the English language, or other European languages are by no means an accident. Neither is the way of Western thinking, as it compares with the thinking of other civilizations. People can learn a lot, by simply observing and questioning some common occurrences around them.

Dedication and Acknowledgements

These books would not exist without the heritage passed to me by my parents. My father worked on his notes for twenty years, until he could not write any more.

Thanks to all of my friends and relatives in North Carolina and in Greece for their encouragement and help. Special thanks to my wife and my niece, Dr. Kathryn Wright, both of whom contributed to the enrichment of the book.

This book is a heritage to my children Phaedra and Ismini, and grandchildren Athena, Sebastian, Persephone and Zander, passed in a manner similar to that exercised by my ancestors throughout the millennia. I am proud to be part of that tradition.

Stavros Boinodiris
February 2007

Prologue

Summary of Andros Odyssey: Byzantine Kalivarion

During the evolutionary years of Christianity, as the religion was embracing a multitude of nationalities with idolatric backgrounds, Byzantium struggled to unify and defend its people from the Islamic onslaught. Several ethnic and religious rebellions forced Byzantine emperors to take drastic measures.

One of the many religious rebellions involved icon worship in the Greek Islands. After a rebellion by Kosmas, a leader from the Greek Islands, Emperor Leo the Isaurian, himself an immigrant from a region of northern Syria, decided to put a stop to all this by secretly dispersing all the rebellious icon worshipers from the islands of Andros, Lemnos and Naxos. The forced exile was secret, to avoid further internal rebellions by the other followers of icon worship. In this manner, this event went unnoticed by historians of that period. In that edict for a forced exile, shipping part of the Psellus family to Cappadocia, together with many of the inhabitants of Andros.

The exiles from Andros established Kalivarion, a Cappadocian colony, naming it after their own home village in Andros. They built a community in caves, utilizing techniques used previously by the local population there, but by adding their own architecture, known from the islands. The people of Lemnos and Naxos formed similar colonies near-by, with the exception that they were established in open, fertile plains and unprotected from invaders. The exile split the Psellus family into two branches, one in Cappadocia and the remaining in Andros.

Both branches of the Psellus family survive four centuries (700-1100 AD) of Byzantine turmoil and struggle. The Cappadocian branch of the Psellus family married into a family from Amorium. When the Arabs destroyed Amorium, part of the Cappadocian Psellus family ended up in Constantinople, working around the Palace. As cooks, instructors, servants and officials they experienced the struggle between

Christianity and idolatry and between faith and superstition that took place during that period. They also experienced the ambition, intrigue, treachery and murder plots machinated by the people running the Byzantine Empire.

The Andrian branch of the Psellus family became well known because of Michael Psellus the Elder (780 AD-862 AD), a famous scholar and teacher of the Andros Academy. After repeated attacks by Saracen pirates on Andros, the Psellus family migrated to Constantinople, where they also found work near the Palace. Eventually, in the 9th century, the families reunited.

One of the Psellus family members from Andros participated in the expedition by Emperor Nikiforos Focas to liberate Crete, in 960 AD. Among the liberated Saracen slaves was an illegitimate son of a Greek slave girl. He was adopted by another slave, who took his name, namely **Stravolemis**. The **Stravolemis** family was established when this slave boy, after a profitable raid into Syria built up his wealth as an Arabian horse trainer and dealer. He married into the Cappadocian Psellus family and settled in Kalivarion, where he took over some of the family property.

The Psellus family went through its brightest and darkest period between 970 and 1070 AD. They were now closely involved with the Palace, during the reign of John Tsimiskis, Basil Bulgaroctonus, Basil's brother Constantine VIII and the destruction that followed, after the battle of Manzikert, when in 1071 AD the Seljuk Turks defeated the Byzantine Army. [4] The one that came closest to running the political machine of Byzantium was Constantine Psellus. Young Constantine and a number of his friends collaborated with each other.

Constantine Psellus became Consul of Philosophers. Because of him and his friends, Emperor Constantine Monomachos endowed the Chairs of Philosophy and Law at the University at Magnaura. The University opened the door to many in a renaissance of learning, because education at the University was now free and available to all who had the ability. Constantine Psellus soon entered the Imperial service where his quick

---

4   Manzikert is today's Malazgirt, Turkey, north of Lake Van in Asia Minor.

intellect and profound scholarship enabled him to be promoted to high posts. Constantine Monomachos and many other emperors admired his eloquence. He became a Secretary of State, Grand Chamberlain and Prime Minister. He led the delegates to present the throne to Isaac Comnenus, a task that required extremely high diplomacy. He composed the accusation against the haughty Cerularius, who as Patriarch had rebuffed a Pope and brought the final blow to the schism between the Churches of Constantinople and Rome.

Suddenly, everything fell apart for Constantine Psellus- also known as Michael Psellus. He joined the monastic life and changed his name to Michael Psellus. Yet, he still carried the burden of his obsession to be faithful to his friends in the government, no matter where that was leading him. He secured the deposition of Romanus Diogenes and made sure that his friend Michael Ducas took his place on the throne, betraying Romanus and causing the disaster at Manzikert. Then, all his friends gave up on him, even Michael Ducas, who sought his demotion. After his seclusion, Michael Psellus ended up writing the history of those trying times. As a historian, he wrote events, which he not only experienced, but also frequently helped to shape and control. In his historical works, he was so extremely observant in detail, that he could bring a character to life with a few words.

After the disaster at Manzikert, most people saw Michael Psellus, not as a distinguished historian and politician, but as a person, who led the Empire to ruin. As a result, the whole family changed their name to **Megas** to avoid humiliation.

Summary of Andros Odyssey: Byzantium under Siege

The saga of the **Megas** and **Stravolemis** families continues as the families faced the insanity and destructive forces of the Crusades. The holy wars of Islam, which expanded through war and forced conversions led to the Crusades, after the Normans appeared in Italy.

Early Muslim expansion was always by the power of the sword, but the Byzantines held. Then the Normans, a new expansionist force from the West appears, with eyes to the riches of the East. After relentless attacks on Byzantium from the West, the Muslims in the East weaken the Byzantines to the point that they cannot face the attacks. They ask from some help and they get the invasion of the Crusades.

This invasion was initially a series of holy wars to counter Islam. The Byzantium-based families from Andros suffer during the crusader attacks. Crusaders of the Armenian Kingdom of Cilicia raid Kalivarion as they try to escape from the Byzantine army of Manuel Comnenus. In that raid, the son of the crusader ruler violates a local girl, before they capture him and kill him. News of the girl's bastard son reaches Thoros, the brother of the rapist. He helps the boy by giving him a name (**Leonides** or Leo's offspring) and opportunity to expand a trade business in Cilicia.

The **Megas** families of Constantinople survived the crusader occupation between 1203 and 1261 AD and some of their members participated in counter-attacks against the crusaders under the leadership of the epileptic Emperors of Nicaea. By the time Constantinople is liberated, the Byzantine state was in ruins. In spite of the situation, the Byzantines, now primarily consisting of Hellenic background counter-attacked in the Aegean and regained control of some territories. The Cappadocian families are living in their caves in a defensive posture against Turks, Mongols and crusaders alike. Many other Greeks from the Pontic Mountains find refuge there, after repeated Mongol attacks, which subjugated the Seljuk Turks. The only ones that were thriving were the **Leonides** family in Cilicia, doing business, which had extended its borders and trade into Cappadocia under Mongol protection. The **Leonides** family soon finds itself trading and helping their relatives in Kalivarion. They are soon involved in trade with the Lusignan and the Ibelin families of Cyprus. In their trade business and because of their links to the King Hetoum of Cilicia who was a Mongol ally, they become knowledgeable of Eastern caravan routes to China and meet with Venetian traders like the Polos, who use their valuable knowledge. In an attempt to stop western aggression, the Byzantines were by now actively seeking the reunification of Churches. Under pressure from the Turks, the **Leonides** family retreated from Cilicia into the caves of Cappadocia. After the Turkish re-occupation of Cappadocia, the

Leonides were renamed the **Aslanoglou** family and the **Stravolemis** were renamed the **Boyun-egri-oglou** family.

As the Turks reoccupied Asia Minor, Constantinople became a battleground between Genoese and Venetian business interests. In spite of repeated pleas to the West for help and a humiliating submission of the Byzantine Emperor to the Catholic Church, help from the West came too little, too late. Even after the Mongol intervention by Tamerland, which resulted in a temporary defeat of the Turks, the West refused to help Byzantium, resulting in the fall of Constantinople to the Turks. Several male members of Megas families in Constantinople were involved in the defense of the City, after sending their families to the Princess Islands in the Sea of Marmara. Some of these men fought and died with their City under the rumble of a new, terrible weapon: the cannon. As the Greek, Genoese and Venetian galleys retreated, the survivors became a source of spirited search for freedom and determined source of resistance against the Turks. One Greek-Genoese family from Chios, the Colon family, became raiders against Turkish ships and advanced their knowledge and skills in navigation to the art of exploration. Among the retreating men of the **Megas** families, there were two, whose families survived in the Princess Islands as fishermen. Under the Turkish occupation, the families of these men had to change their names to the **Magioglou** and the **Meroglou** families.

The families in these islands and in Cappadocia survived under a very repressive Ottoman occupation. Almost everything was stacked against them as they tried to retain their identities, but they held fast to their Hellenic culture and their insatiable thirst for knowledge.

Summary of Andros Odyssey: Under Ottoman Rule

The families, after the fall of Constantinople experienced the Ottoman oppression. The Turks, as conquerors treated them as their slaves and forced their children to convert and become Janissaries (converted soldiers) through well-established methods of abduction and conversion. Millions of Greeks from Byzantium continued to escape abroad. They dispersed into Europe and from there to other continents, spreading their knowledge, expertise and solidifying the effects of Western European renaissance, which they initiated after the crusades. As the effects of mass exodus were felt, the alarmed Sultans became smarter in dealing with minorities, by trying to stop the mass exodus of Christians, by curtailing slavery and corruption and by trying to reverse it. The only success in the reversal of the population loss came through the enticement of other suppressed minorities abroad, like the oppressed Jews of Europe and the rich rewards of government-sponsored piracy to entice men of fortune to become Barbary pirates.

Meanwhile, through continuous Islamic pressure for conversion, a significant portion of the remaining Greeks converted to Islam, whether coerced by the better life, or by force. They, together with other minorities became a major contributor to the power that drove the Ottoman Empire to expand its borders from Venice, to Persia and from Africa to Austria.

The remaining Greeks within the Ottoman Empire endured a very patient waiting game using education as their only weapon. While they waited, they used their skills to make themselves indispensable for the Operation of the Empire as interpreters, functionaries, educators, political analysts, bankers and sea merchants. They also drove the legal reorganization of the Ottoman Empire from the Shariah law to Cannon law. These skills placed them in positions where they were aware of all the intricacies within the Ottoman system of government. Through small, but calculated moves they prepare secret alliances of the Greek minority with the Pope, Venice, Austria, England, the Dutch Protestants and finally Russia.

External powers, at different times offered some means of pressure on the uncontrollable mistreatment by the Sultans of Christian populations within their Empire. One power that played a major role was Venice, who held major portions of Greece at various times. Their struggle to hold their power helped the Greeks of the islands to maintain their identity, but at the same time their self-centered tactics caused the destruction of the Parthenon on Acropolis.

The stark difference between the mistreated Christians who were de facto slaves by conquest and the invited Jewish minorities remained for centuries. Their competition was utilized by the Ottomans to divide these minorities within the Empire and to check any tendencies for rebellion. Educated Sephardic Jews competed for the same posts as Greeks. Some of them, like Joseph Nasi, the Duke of Naxos, established the first autonomous Jewish ruling authority in Tiberias, Palestine for many centuries. Christians saw with jealousy the Jewish alliance with the Ottomans, causing a further rift between Christian and Jewish Ottoman minorities.

In spite of their internal controls, the rebellion against absolute and corrupt rulers came from abroad, after the American and French Revolutions. Greek sailors and students abroad brought in new ideas on how to achieve independence. In spite of the suppression of Patriarchal authority a network of monasteries and secret schools started operating under a new national movement. Through a low key, coordinated effort the naval skills of the Greeks are transferred to Russia. After a long struggle and in spite of English opposition, Russia manages to emerge as a major naval power in the Mediterranean. The Russians got support from the West, including that from John Paul Jones of the American Navy. Finally, Russia became a de facto protector of all Orthodox Christian minorities of the Ottoman Empire.

Meanwhile, the rest of the world, including the Americans, fed up with the Sultan's state-supported policy of piracy within the Mediterranean, embarked on an all out attack on the Barbary Coast. The first Americans to die on foreign soil died in the Middle East, fighting pirates, supported by the Ottomans.

Under the Russian protection and the indispensable position gained within the Ottoman Empire, the enslaved Greeks emerge as opportunist merchants who broke through naval blockades, pirated enemy vessels and competed effectively with some of the best navies of that period. With every year that passed, progress was rapid. Greek seafarers made a lot of money but they also gained further knowledge and experience and they sought to advance and refine their ships and their men in warfare against the pirates, as they had no navy to protect them. Their new, revitalized spirit made the Greek seamen feel free; the growth of their merchant fleet gave them confidence; their success in fighting off pirates and others to reach their destinations with loaded ships made them feel more independent. Through that spirit of independence and after several failures, they prepared themselves to gain independence, while at the same time they undermine the Ottoman Empire.

The Greek struggle for independence began in 1821 and lasted seven years. Besides sacrificing all they had, they borrowed 2.3 million pounds, expecting that the entire Hellenic nation of about seven million would become responsible and pay off the loan under a solid government of their own. From that, less than one million pounds reached the Greeks. In desperation, they negotiated the loan as "a hopeless affair" at the exorbitant rate of fifty-nine and fifty-five-per-cent. They spent this sum immediately in the purchase of materials for carrying on the war. When the war ended, a little more than one-fifth of the people who had hoped for freedom received it and a little more than a third of the territory fought for was freed. Less than a million people found themselves responsible for the payment of a debt which had been contracted by many millions. This raw deal was compounded by the fact that Greece was excluded from the money markets of Europe and had a difficult task to become self sufficient, under the disadvantages of a small territory and sparse population. About a fourth of the population lived by agricultural pursuits on a very small, mountainous and ravaged land. Her merchant marine was engaged in the trade with ports of the Aegean, which Turkey taxed and controlled. The poverty of her people, the feeble resources, the influences of old customs and habits failed to fulfill the unreasonable expectations of enthusiastic Philhellenes.

The liberation of the small piece of land below Thessaly did not mean prosperity for the remaining, much larger Christian population under the Sultan. These people now were under very strict scrutiny, sometimes looked upon as spies and enemy supporters by the Turks. Initially, as the war of independence raged on, fanatic Turkish elements attempted to exterminate them, a village at a time, so that they become invisible to the eyes of the protecting Russian Czar. Other Turkish elements, sensing a weakened Sultan, began to plan the formation of their own independent states, like Ali Pasha of Albania. Many Christians took to the mountains and became bandits, to escape persecution from the chaos, which characterized the Ottoman Empire of the 19th century. In Constantinople, the prosperous Magioglou family was now out of a job. They could no longer be trusted to serve the Porte as interpreters and advisors. The people of Kalivarion of Cappadocia were under attack from rogue Ottoman generals who hated Greeks. What saved them was their location, their skill to negotiate at the highest level and sheer luck.

In spite of the difficulties, within thirty-five or forty years of freedom, Greece doubled her population and increased her revenues five hundred per cent. They founded eleven new cities on deserted sites. They rebuilt more than forty towns, reduced to ruins by the war. Some roads replaced the foot and saddle paths that were the sole avenues of communication under the Turks, and telegraphic communication were extended over the kingdom. Eight or ten ports were been cleared, deepened and opened to communication. Meanwhile, the Russians defeated the Turks and the Treaty of Saint Stefano of 1878 began to bring added pressure on the Sultan by liberating more Balkan nations.

As Greece was recovering, the first modern Olympics are established, bringing in international focus on this small part of the world and helping the people of Crete and some islands achieve independence. As the Sultan turned his attention away from Greece and towards his numerous problems at the East and with Russia, one member of the Magioglou family of Constantinople is involved in the modernization of the Ottoman transportation system, using railroads. Eager to regain trust and fame within the Ottoman circles, John Magioglou puts himself to work on the railroad, even at the cost of his family and heritage. This causes internal family problems which will continue into the Magioglou saga of the 20th century.

The families, starting from before 1800, are now real, documented people, with biographical excerpts, covered by the written material of the author's father. Thus, the latter part of this book is no longer a historical novel, but a historical biography of a group of people who lived and left their mark, as the world was about to enter the 20th century.

Summary of Andros Odyssey: Liberation

The saga of the Andros Odyssey families continues into the 20th century, as the world events unfold around them. Evanthia Magioglou escapes from a dysfunctional family environment by getting romantically involved with George Boyun-egri-oglou and forcing the issue through her pregnancy. This pregnancy produced a little boy, Anthony Boyun-egri-oglou.

Anthony grew up during troubling times. Even though he had aristocrat maternal grandparents, he felt the bitter taste of being disowned by them. The dysfunctional family dissolves after the son, Pandelis escapes to America and his parents die soon later. Anthony saw very little of his father, who left for Constantinople and went to Russia, when Anthony was very young, to escape from being drafted in the Turkish army. He grew up in the shadows of the Ottoman Empire as it was going through major revolutions and wars. He experienced the Armenian Holocausts (1909 and 1915), the Balkan Wars (1912-1913) and the Turkish-Italian conflict in Libya of 1911. He also experienced the prejudice and brutal treatment by the Turks on the Greek minority. This mistreatment became more intense as Turkey faced Greece and other countries in the Balkan Wars, after the Young Turks took over the government from the Ottoman sultans (1908-1909). The First World War (1914-1918) then befell upon them, causing shortages and anguish on Cappadocian Greeks and Turks alike.

Meanwhile, the Aslanoglou family departed from Cappadocia for Selefkia in 1914, where John Aslanoglou established a thriving trade business. Meanwhile, Pandelis Mayoglou enlisted in the American Navy. As soon as the First World War ended, the Greco-Turkish War began, causing a flood of refugees, lack of schooling for children and more persecution of Greeks by the Turks. John Aslanoglou became one of many victims and in 1922 was forced to escape to Greece. The politically erroneous reasons upon which Greece launched the Greco-Turkish War (1919-

1922) ended up in disaster. The Turks rallied behind Mustafa Kemal, who after receiving aid from almost all countries that were previously fighting against Turkey, routed the Greek army from Asia Minor and East Thrace with Greek civilians paying for that error. The Greek and Armenian death toll rose into over a million. In the ensuing truce, Greece and Turkey agreed to an exchange of populations, whereupon (with some minor exceptions) all Christians in Asia Minor would move to Greece and all Turks from Greece would move into Asia Minor.

The uprooting (1924) of the Boyun-egri-oglou family involved a trip that lasted three months, involving rail and ship transports. It started with the venting of hate by Turk refugees, the bitter struggle to get on a transport and the uplifting feeling of liberation, as they departed from Asia Minor towards the Greek mainland, leaving almost twelve hundred years of history behind. A history that began from 730 AD, when the Byzantine Kalivarion was first established.

The Boyun-egri-oglou family, now arbitrarily renamed Boinodiris, settled in Drama, a town in the region of Macedonia, Greece. There, they met the Aslanoglou family, who although came earlier, was struggling, like most refugees, to find a shelter and to survive. In that initial struggle, John Aslanoglou and Paul Boyun-egri-oglou die. Greece, devastated by a series of wars, had become inundated with refugees. The new refugees consisted of 20 percent of the new population of Greece, added to another 20 percent that came within the Greek jurisdiction after the Balkan Wars, only a decade earlier.

The struggle of the refugees is recounted by Anthony very graphically. Anthony went through quite an ordeal, as he tried to provide for his mother and sister. Just before he was drafted in the army, he met and fell in love with Elisabeth Aslanoglou. He also received news from his father from Russia and his uncle from America. His father, having had enough of Russia during the Communist revolution, returns to Greece. His homecoming brought Anthony's economic disaster and made Pandelis a lifelong enemy. In addition, Anthony found out that his father George was a bigamist, leaving another family back in Russia. In spite of that, he married Elisabeth and with her help started his recovery all over again. In his struggle to survive, he faced trouble with a nemesis, lost his temper, got into trouble with the law and landed in jail for a two year sentence. After his release from jail, he began for the third time his struggle to recover.

Anthony barely managed to build his own house, when he loses his mother. He and Elisabeth then take over the upbringing of their son and Anthony's young brother and sister, finally realizing that Anthony's father George had serious shortcomings. In 1940, as they started recovering from all these events, Greece enters into war with Italy, turning such a recovery into an impossible dream.

World War II (Anthony's Memoirs)

Figure 1 Prime Minister Metaxas

"NO!" (Greece, 28th of October, 1940)

The Italians declared war on Greece on October 28, 1940. When they requested the virtual surrender of Greece, Prime Minister Metaxas responded laconically: "NO." By then, the Italians had already penetrated the Greek borders through Albania. [5]

With an almost non-existent Air Force and modern equipment, Greece depended on the harsh, winter weather and the mountains of Albania for defense. The Greeks deftly used their mule-mounted supply trains, mule-mounted artillery and machine gun teams to fight the Italians. Italian tanks were useless in the goat trails of Albania. Greeks did not have, or

---

5   A. Boinodiris, Book 1, p. 51.

1

even know mortars until they captured some from the Italians. They used grenades instead. Italians used mortars very effectively, especially small, personal units firing up to one-kilometer range, causing many casualties on the Greeks. The heavier, more accurate, mule-mounted 75-mm artillery of the Greeks also caused heavy casualties on the Italians. One of the major factors for winning this conflict may have been the re-supply line. The Greeks did not need to re-supply from any foreign power. Local industries, like those of Botosakis Athanasiades, a refugee who came from Bor, [6]Cappadocia[7] provided all needed weapons, which were carried to the mountains using trains and mules. The Italians blew up bridges, but the mule trains kept on coming through the ravines. Even after the Italians blew up train after train in their stations, the Greeks had stored local supplies in mountain depots, which enabled them to go on for many months.

The entire country was under general mobilization orders when war was declared between Greece and Italy. When I was called to report, I was a 35 year old reservist. I ended up in the Bulgarian border, while my partner Basil fought in the Albanian border, fighting the Italians.

Everyone was called in. Even the Moslem minority of Thrace was drafted to provide support units. Approximately 13,000 Greek Jews also participated in that fight against the fascists. Many of them were receiving upsetting news about the posture of fascism on Jews.

---

6   Bor is the location of the ancient city of Tyana.

7   **Bodosakis was an orphan, adopted by Thomas Athanasiadis, who made linen in Tarsus and Adana of Cilicia. His adopted son was well educated in languages. After the exchange of populations, he took over his father's business (what could be survived) and after marrying a German lady he expanded it. He created many factories in Athens, Piraeus, Thessaloniki and Cyprus for the production of glass and cement, including several mines. (A. Boinodiris, Book 1, p.52)**

Figure 2 Map of the Greco-Italian Campaign of 1940-1941

German Attack (Greek Front, April, 1941)

I was ordered to report into my unit on the 28th of October, 1940. Both, my partner Basil Dimitriades and I left our store to our wives and joined the army. Elisabeth had the tough burden now to provide for the three children, my son John and my two orphan siblings, which we raised. The orphans stayed in our home, raised with their nephew John as brothers and sister, until they became adults and started working. Unfortunately, my father did not help even a little with their expenses.

Late in 1940, when the Allies fought against the Italians in Africa, the Greeks were fighting the Italians in Albania. De Gaulle organized the Free French force, consisting of about 7,000 men from French colonies. The English and French fought in North Africa under General Alexander.

Metaxas was now the Greek president, called dictator by most Greeks, because the King assigned him to this post since 1936. He was quite opposed to the Italians but was pro-German. He did not want to get

Greece involved in a fight with Germany. The Royal family of George II was pro-British and knew of the beliefs of Metaxas.[8]

The Greek front was doing poorly for the Italians. Instead of advancing into Greece and in spite of their superiority, the Italians were losing ground. Soon, the lowest one third of Albania was in Greek control. The Italian high command was changing generals one after the other, fearing a total disaster of being captured. Hitler saw that he had to act, in spite of objections from his staff. The Germans were preparing to attack Russia early in the spring of 1941 and the generals knew that any delay could cost them lives, because of the Russian winters. Hitler, in spite of their objections, decided early in 1941 to re-deploy in the Balkans to save the Italians. He feared the Russian winter, but thought that he could finish with the Greeks early enough to achieve both objectives.

The Germans negotiated with Hungary and Rumania, who joined them, in fear of being destroyed. Yugoslavia's turn came next. The Slovak-led party of Yugoslavia was to join the Germans. The other party, friendly to the Greeks, took control and refused to join on the side of Germany.

Bulgaria's turn came next. Bulgaria had King Boris. A right-wing president, named Filov negotiated with Germany, but with some gains. Hitler was to transfer the Greek Eastern Macedonia and Thrace as well as the Yugoslav part of Macedonia (later to be named FYROM) to Bulgaria, after the Germans won against Greece. Several elements of the Yugoslav part of Macedonia secretly collaborated with the Germans and the Bulgarians to gain access to the lands that their forefathers had abandoned after the Balkan Wars. The member of the opposing Bulgarian party, a communist named Dimitrov escaped to Russia."[9] He later would be instrumental in liberating Bulgaria from the Nazis and moving the country into a communist regime.

---

8   A. Boinodiris, Book 1, p. 94.
9   A. Boinodiris, Book 1, p. 76.

As the Germans negotiated with the Bulgarians, around January, or February of 1941 we found out that Metaxas is dead. Korizis, who also was opposed to fighting the Germans, took over. In two months he also died. Rumors were rampant that British agents assassinated them both, to prevent a pro-German presidency from taking a more passive stance with Germany against the allies. [10]

All these preparations took time. Hitler's attack on Greece came on the 6th of April 1941, a crucial time delay, which, coupled with the stubborn defense by the Greeks contributed to the destruction of his forces in Russia later on.

I was sent to the front, as part of the Supply Corps, since I had such training in my regular army service in the period from 1929 to 1930. My training in handling and equipping mules and horses at that time was as valuable as being an engine mechanic in the 1970s.

In 1940, during the Greek-Italian and Greek-German campaign, I served in the Bulgarian border, against the Germans.

My section commander was Papadomarkakis. My Major (4th Brigade) was Michael Stavrakakis.

My Lt. Major was Elias Koufaliotis from Lamia. My Lieutenant was Tziftoglou from Fotolivos, Drama. My Sergeant was George Techlemtzis from Horisti, Drama and a good friend. My corporal was Spiro Gerocostas from Lamia.

The Greek Army had very few vehicles then. Most of the supplies were moved by mules. Horses were used by the commanding officers of the Corps. I was trained in 1929 to equip animals with all sorts of leather reigns and saddles. I also had to know how to take care of these animals, including veterinary first aid and make them do what we needed doing. Each platoon of the Corps had one saddle maker and one veterinary nurse. I was the saddle maker of the platoon of Ioakimides. To avoid detection, all of our movements were made at night, in total darkness. We were to take supplies from the local depots to the front in one night

10   A. Boinodiris, Book 1, p. 94.

by foot, walking next to the mules and return during the day riding on the unloaded mules. We were supposed to take a short nap at noon, load in the afternoon and repeat the process again the next night. These supplies consisted of all sorts of ammunition, food, medicine, clothes, etc. for the men of the fortifications of the Metaxa line. Our corps was assigned to the fortifications of Volax, on the Bulgarian front.

Our great delight was receiving mail. The mail carrier was a man from Nea Karvali, called Leonidas, who was so good to me that he brought my mail all the way to the front fortifications. Occasionally we received a package. My wife Elisabeth- I call her Eliso- managed to surprise me with such precious gifts. One winter day I was delighted to receive a six-kilogram can full of a variation of grape jam called RETSELI.

We were delighted. I shared the can with the soldiers in my squad. Two of them spoke Bulgarian, but they seemed to be all loyal Greeks from Petrousa.Their names were Efthimiades and Nikos Nembis. For his effort, Leonidas got a good portion of retseli too. [11]

Our local depot was at Strana. The brigade commander was a Cretan named Papadomarkakis. Our battalion commander, also a Cretan, was named Stavrakakis. Our company commander was Ilias Koufaliotis from Lamia. Our division commander was Zoiopoulos, who, as I found out had German wife. Most of the men were from Crete or Macedonia.

We were all armed with rifles, guarding the supplies from enemy patrols that occasionally seeped through, trying to disrupt our supply lines.

On Sunday, April 6, 1941, Volax and the western fortifications of Skra faced for the first time the German war machine. We were only 40,000 men, guarding a large and mountainous Bulgarian border, from the Yugoslav to the Turkish frontier. Yet, our morale here as well as in the Albanian front was very high. We knew that the Germans had more men and better equipment, especially in aircraft and tanks, which we had none. To beef up our morale, we were told that another line was formed behind us, made up from British, Australian and New Zealand troops.

---

11   A. Boinodiris, Book 1, p. 90.

In the morning of that day, I saw two German reconnaissance aircraft overhead around the St. George position of Volax, where we were. One of our antiaircraft guns managed to hit one of them, forcing it to land slowly in the plain of Prosotsani outside of Kokinogia. The second plane went north, towards Bulgaria. [12]

Soon, we received the brunt of the German attack. German Stukas planes started dive-bombing Greek fortifications and supply lines. Many of our Greek soldiers remember the unnerving Stukas dive bomber noise in their nightmares, not because of their bombs, but because the mules became so wild and uncontrollable after they heard them, that many soldiers died after being thrown into deep ravines. After the Stukas, German artillery started pounding us. The fortifications started firing back with our own artillery, only to get further bombing from the German artillery. Soon after, we saw infantry advancing on foot. They had up front a battalion of infantrymen (which we called donkeys), walking in open, unprotected field, non-dispersed, in bands in order to draw fire. These sacrificial lambs were probably Bulgarians, Rumanians or Hungarians, drafted by the Germans to do their dirty work. The Greek crossfire sent most of them to the other life. Soon after, more of them appeared in the same manner and were wasted by the Greek fire, throughout that day. Then came night-time; our real enemy. At night, the German infantry penetrated to the first Greek villages, like Chrysokefalos. Small Greek bands were attempting to defend these villages, having some significant loses in that process. More enemy infiltrators were seeping in every night for three days, and more Greek defenders chased after them from village to village, trying to eliminate them. Finally, the infiltrators were wiped out and under orders from the local battalion commander the Greeks counter-attacked and pushed back the enemy all the way to the Bulgarian highway, where they held, with the help of the German mechanized divisions. These divisions came in support of the infantry, but were also under fire from Greek artillery, positioned at higher ground. Many vehicles sent to recover their infiltrating infantry were destroyed, before they could withdraw.

---

12   A. Boinodiris, Book 1, p. 77.

We were still afraid of night infiltration, but we knew now how to deal with them. We were becoming veterans.

On Tuesday, 8th of April 1941 I was supplying material to the troops on the hill of Holy Spirit, which still had snow in gullies and shady spots. Stavrakakis, our battalion commander, used this hill as an observation post. He was at a perch, watching with binoculars the action below. After finishing my duty, I asked for and he agreed to let me use his binoculars to view the scene below. At a distance of about 10 kilometers below the hill, I could clearly see the destruction that we caused to the German armored convoys.

After viewing the scene, I asked. "Commander Sir, how do you think we are doing?"

He replied: "I know now for sure that the Germans will not pass through this front. They may pass from somewhere else, but not from here."

On Tuesday, eighth of April we loaded ammunition, mostly crates of grenades and rifle grenades on ten strong mules. The crates had scull bones on top of them and the warning: "DANGER, DEATH." The night was very dark and the load was heavy. The mountains were rugged and dangerous. The trails, made by herds of goats over high cliffs had destructive effect on the mules, because of the spiny bushes and the sharp rocks. We proceeded in silence and darkness not to be detected by any infiltrators. None of us were issued even a flashlight, to make sure we walked undetected in silence. We followed the senses of our mules, feeling, rather than seeing our footsteps. Our main fear of detection was if a mule fell down. The explosion, caused by a grenade with a dislodged firing pin, could blow us all up or bring the enemy upon us. The only noise was that of "crack, crack, crack," of the crates, as the ropes squeezed them at every step that the mules took on the trail. We slowly brought our load down the ravine into a brook, near the village of Livadista.

On Wednesday, ninth of April we again loaded ammunition. This loading was done in the afternoon and at around 6 P.M. we are on our way. As we travelled in the darkness of the night we hear the "crack-

crack" of another convoy. We heard, "Halt and identify!" Passwords were exchanged in low voices. This went on a few times, with other mule teams joining ours in night convoys to the same destination: the front fortifications.

On the morning of Thursday, 10th of April and the last day of our fighting, the password assigned was "Gravia." We did our routine the night before and we were returning in the morning, riding on the mules.

I was so sleepy and tired, not having slept almost at all for five days that I started falling asleep on top of the mule. [13] On a turn, I found myself on the ground, having fallen from the mule. Fortunately, I was on top of grass, rather than being dead on the bottom of a ravine. Another soldier came to me with his canteen, helping me to recover from the shock of the fall. After recovering and somewhat embarrassed, I washed my face, jumped on the mule and followed the convoy. It took us another three hours from where I fell to reach our base. Our base was on the middle of a mountain saddle, chosen so because it had plenty of water and a shed, made out of tree branches for the mules, called "AMBRI." The AMBRI was positioned between four firs. It had a roof, made out of poles, pierced through the tree branches. More poles on top of them held ferns and dirt. We had there also our tents, on top of the hill. Each one of us had prepared a bed out of tree branches and dried leaves. We joined with our sergeant, George Techlemtzis, a lively and hard working patriot. [14]

George had responsibility of three groups of men, driving three mule convoys. He entrusted these convoys to team leaders. I was one of the

---

13 "I had a tough time sleeping during the day, especially in view of the preparations that had to be done for the following night. Saddles had to be fixed and animals had to be fed and patched up or replaced, before they are ready to be loaded again." A. Boinodiris, Book 1, p. 80.

14 "Sergeant George Tehlemtzis was a refugee from Matentzi, a Cilician village of Taurus Mountains. He lived in Choristi, a small village, about 5-km south of Drama. He was killed in 1978 from an automobile accident. He ran a coffee shop in that village and served as the village president before his premature death. He was younger than I was and quite healthy and active until his death. "A. Boinodiris, Book 1, p. 81.

team leaders; the other two were Dimitris Kougioumtzis and a smith, expert in shoeing mules, called Angelomatis.

Our company happened not to have any Cretans. All men in our company were from Macedonia, most of them refugees from Asia Minor. The local Macedonians were under scrutiny at that time, from fear of being spies. Some, among them were Bulgar-friendly and we had to separate them from those that were Greek Macedonians. Those that were Greeks were more Greeks than we were. Petrousa is a village, NW of Drama. The old, Bulgarian name of that village was Plevna. Many of these people were with us at the front and although spoke Bulgarian they fought hard against the Bulgarians for many generations. We were watching our back from those that were marked as suspicious, so that they do not harm us. Even a few could cause a great deal of harm. If one ran to the enemy and gave our ammunition positions, we could be hit by their aircraft or artillery and blown to bits.

That morning of April 10, after we drank our hot drinks (coffee, tea or milk) I fell asleep on my bed of leaves, exhausted from lack of sleep.

A soldier awakened me: "The pot is ready." This meant that we were ready to eat. The cook had prepared food, typically beans or lentils. As I was eating, we received the bad news: the Germans had invaded Greece and they were heading for Thessaloniki. It was accomplished by entering through Yugoslav Macedonia, through the Peles Mountain range and Lake Doirani. Based on the reports, the "Macedonian" elements of the Yugoslav army (later to be called FYROM) betrayed the Serbs and helped the Germans and the Bulgarians bypass the Serb and Greek defenses. The Yugoslavs could not hold them and the Greeks had no troops there to do anything about it. Everybody fell into depression. The Germans showed their appreciation to these traitors, by placing them at key posts within the Bulgarian occupational forces.

In the afternoon, while we were waiting for our orders for delivery of a new load, we received the news for cease-fire.

That same day, we were told that our troops would be returning from Albania. As all this transpired, we were here guarding a panhandle of

Greece, while the Germans were overrunning the rest of the country. Some officers were crying. Others were furious, blaming the Yugoslavs and our Allies for betrayal. Few of us were talking about staying in the mountains and conducting guerilla warfare with the weapons and the ammunition in our possession. Finally, they could not agree what to do. Therefore, not having any higher orders, they agreed to disband. Later, I would feel bitter for not having the sense to unite at that time. In hindside, we should have started organizing guerilla warfare, right then and there, since the Germans would have brought the Bulgarians one way or another. We should have done so. We had all the necessary tools for this guerilla fight, right there. We had food, fuel, ammunition and weapons to fight an extended guerilla battle that would have made a difference in our future and would have brought Germany to her knees sooner.

I attribute this failure to realize this opportunity to the lack of leadership and our ignorance of how brutal these invaders would turn out to be. We would pay dearly for that mistake in the years to come.

The Retreat (North of Drama, April 1941)

Figure 3 Greek Retreat[15]

---

15   Greek soldiers are leaving their positions after the surrender of the Greek Army in Macedonia. In the front, a Greek and a Bulgarian soldier support a wounded Greek.

On Friday, 11th of April 1941 we, who were about 60 soldiers started going back towards the highway for Drama using horses and mules for transportation. Our sergeant Techlemtzis stayed back, under orders by our company commander Ilias Koufaliotis. We were a little worried that the enemy could penetrate at any time and take us prisoners which would prevent us from having the option of any opposition.

As we were passing a hill, we saw the remnants of a camp, used by a mountain artillery battalion, without any men in it. We were saddened as we saw the artillery pieces, staring towards the sky with their barrel mouths open and with the shells in the breach, while stacks of shells were strewn around, all abandoned on top of the hill. We saw 40-mm antiaircraft guns with the cartridges of shells mounted, pointing aimlessly at the sky. We saw the big pot of the mess area, still containing hot food. We saw blankets, still in packages, cases of soap, underwear, military winter overcoats and other material, used by the army. We saw about 12 sacks of freshly baked bread, still hot, suggesting that they came in during the night. Seeing all this, I came up with a bright idea, which I immediately shared with the rest of the men:

"Come on guys, let's get down from the mules and load them up with supplies, including the bread. We can walk home, but I have a sense that we will need this bread in the days to come."

A corporal (whose name I forgot) loudly objected, by pulling the horse closer and shouting:

"No. We have orders not to touch any other unit's material."

I jumped down from my horse.

"Whoever gave you those stripes must have been completely blind. You are a jackass who cannot think to save your skin; forget about thinking for a company. The orders you had no longer hold. They are now obsolete. Metaxas also told us that we must face surviving starvation by planting wheat at all window planters."

I took my rifle off my sling and pointing it at him, I shouted:

"You want to stop me? You will have to do it now."

At that time, some of the men around me pulled their horses between us, facing the mounted corporal. "Anthony is right," one said. "I suggest you back off."

He pulled the reins of his horse and rode away.

We loaded the mules with all useful supplies, from bread to blankets and started again our descent from the mountain riding on the horses. About 3 kilometers from the camp we left we pass by a brook. On the opposite side of the brook we see another corporal from the infantry, fallen down, with his backpack still on his back. When he saw us, he waved and shouted:

"Please help me men!"

I dismounted and after I secured my horse, approached him, still on my side of the brook. The rest stayed on the trail. He looked awful.

"I am sick and have no strength to move. If you leave me here I will become food for the wolves."

His accent was Cretan. I thought he had malaria. It was a common occurrence. When it hit, soldiers had no strength to stand up, forget about walking twenty kilometers to their homes. This one did not have the strength to unbuckle his backpack. I waved at him to stay calm and walked back to my horse. I got ready to cross the brook on foot.[16]

"Where are you going Anthony?" said another soldier.

"I am going to put him on my horse. He is sick."

"You are stupid. I bet you he is faking. That means that you will walk all the way back."

"That's OK."

---

16   A. Boinodiris, Book 1, p. 83.

I climbed carefully down a precipitous bank next to the ravine, which was formed by the brook. I jump two ditches near the corporal and saw him up close. He was sick, but not with malaria.

Smiling I asked him:

"What's the matter with you corporal?"

He smiled back.

"I am very happy you stopped my good man. I know you may think I am pretending, but I am not. I have hernia. Even though I am ashamed to show you, I must do it."

I knew now that he heard all the ridicule I had to bear from my companions.

He took down his pants. The area around his genitals was swollen and blackened. He told me that he was assigned in the counter-insurgency teams. He must have had a tough hike, running from village to village chasing intruders.

"Will you please pull up your pants? "

I took his backpack off and slowly picked him up and placed him on my shoulder. I had to cross a very abrupt ravine with the corporal on my back, without killing him, or me. After a few minutes of climbing, I was next to my horse. I mounted him as carefully as I could, judging from his groans, whether I was doing it right and started walking fast in an attempt to catch up with the remaining convoy of troops.

On the way, he told me his story. He was indeed from Crete. He told me that he had a small hernia at the start of the hostilities, which was enlarged with all the lifting and walking he was doing.

Then I asked him.

"Why did your own company abandon you so?"

"We were in the infantry, up to the front and sick. When the news of disbanding came, all the transport vehicles of our company were far in the rear and did not come to pick any sick person left behind. Those of my company were simply too tired to carry me on their backs on foot over mountain ranges. They also wanted to save themselves from being captured. So I was left in the hands of God."

We finally reached the convoy. After a few kilometers, the animal convoy reached the highway. As we rode on the highway, the corporal with whom I had a confrontation brought his mount close to me, as I walked next to my horse, which needed rest.

"Mr. Boinodiris. You are a good soldier. You have saved this corporal from Crete because you are good-hearted. Yet, are you aware that what you did for a few loaves of bread can put you away in jail after a military court-martial?"

I responded:

"Corporal, you are a corporal until we reach Drama. After that, everyone tries to survive on our own, because we do not know what future is in store for us. A few days from now you may be thanking me for sharing that bread with us, instead of letting it be wasted."

On the way to Drama, we joined up with a platoon of infantry, led by a lieutenant from Fotolivos, named Tsiflikoglou. They walked next to us, planning to disband when they reached Drama.[17]

Near Petrousa, the battalion commander Stavrakakis had gathered the troops around him next to the road, as they were making their way to Drama. We joined them also, and we were told to wait. We needed the rest anyway. I lowered from my horse the sick Cretan with the hernia to the ground.

As we were resting, Stavrakakis climbs on his horse to be seen and starts talking:

"Officers and soldiers of the Greek Army; why are you having your heads low? You are not losers. We did what we could do on our side, not allowing them to have their way. In our sector, we stopped them

---

17   A. Boinodiris, Book 1, p. 85.

cold on their tracks. You have not lost. You must hold your heads high. The Axis powers did not win over us. This is just the beginning of this war. One day the Axis powers will be destroyed. This is only a small piece of the action. We are not alone in fighting this war and the rest of our allies will not stop. I am certain that we will win over these evil invaders. Good luck to all of you and God Be with you."

The trip to Drama resumed and I was full of thoughts. We were not losers, but in the meanwhile, we had to survive an occupation. How are we going to deal with this occupation? All of us, refugees from Asia Minor knew about living like slaves under the yoke of the Turks. How are the Germans and Bulgarians as occupiers? How do they compare with the Turks?

When we reached Drama, I went to the Municipal Hospital, which was a building next to the old church of St. Panteleimon. This building was later converted to a High School for girls. There, I delivered the sick Cretan corporal to the hospital staff.

"Efharisto poli patrioti, kala nase" he thanked me and wished me well.

"I hope you get well soon. Good luck on your return to Crete."

I turned north and rode to my home, armed with my rifle on my shoulder. I met some of my neighbors on the street. They told me that there was looting going on in the city, in all warehouses of the army. One warehouse was an Elementary School, called Ekpedeftiria. Some of them were carrying food supplies in their shoulders. One had a sack of flour another had two cans of olive oil.

Then it dawned on me. What if I was seen taking the rifle to my home? Who would be after me, when the occupiers come? Would I have someone blackmail me with threats of telling them what they saw?

Therefore, I changed direction, and rode away from my home. I went to the regiment headquarters and left all my weapons there. I took the blankets and the bread on my horse and then I came home. My wife and my nine-year-old son John greeted me and helped me unload. They also took care of the tired animal.

While the Germans were pursuing the small British forces that came to help southwards, the southwest movement threatened the rear of the bulk of the Greek Army (14 divisions), which was facing the Italians at the Albanian front. The Army belatedly began retreating southwards, first its northeast flank on April 12, and finally the southwest flank on April 17. The German thrust towards Kastoria on April 15 made the situation critical, threatening to cut the Greek forces' retreat.

One week passed since the disbanding of the army and around April 18, 1941, I heard the news that the Germans ordered all soldiers to appear at the regiment headquarters to receive our discharge papers. When I went there, I found that that place was an asylum for all soldiers who came from other parts of Greece. I sat in line for some time. A Greek officer, sitting next to a German, behind a table checked his book, finding my name and unit. When he found it, he issued me a German discharge document. As I was leaving, I saw the sick Cretan corporal that I carried on my horse laying on the floor, together with other Cretans, many of them officers.

After greeting me, he turned to his compatriots and said:

"This is the KOPELI (good man) that saved my life."

Several men from around him shook my hand.

"This effort was a worthwhile one, in the face of God and a fellow man," said one.

I thanked them. The Cretan kept on thanking me as I was leaving. Years later I thought about him and felt badly for forgetting his name. I wonder how he fared in his life. [18]

Within ten days, we heard news that a new, pro-German government has taken over, under Tsolakoglou. Several generals, under the leadership of Lt. General George Tsolakoglou mutinied on April 20, and took

---

18   A. Boinodiris, Book 1, p. 87.

matters in their own hands, signed a protocol of surrender. The very same day in Athens, Lt. General A. Papagos resigned his office as Supreme Commander while the King and his government embarked for Crete. Finally, that same day we were told that the English and Anzac troops in Thermopylae were defeated and are evacuating. The Commonwealth forces had decided to make a last stand at Thermopylae before their final retreat to the ports of Peloponnesos for evacuation to Crete, or Egypt. German troops had seized the Corinth Canal bridges, entered Athens on April 27, and completed their occupation of the mainland and most islands by the end of April.

Figure 4 Occupation of Greece by Axis Powers

Betrayed by a Friend, Saved by an Enemy (Drama, April, 1941)

Easter day, 25th of April 1941 the Bulgarians invade Eastern Macedonia, after the German command agreed to let them occupy that region. It was ready food to eat, without Bulgarian sacrifices. Their goal, under the leadership of their fascist president Filov was to change the makeup of that region by expelling, or eliminating all Greeks and turning it into a Bulgarian province. To achieve this, they offered all sorts of incentives to Bulgarians to move into this newly conquered territory. The transition from German occupation to Bulgarian occupation took several weeks.[19]

One day of the last week of April, when Greeks were still running the city hall jointly with Germans, Anestis Zoumboulides and I went there and got a license to sell charcoal. Then we went to Livaderon, loaded charcoal, packaged it in sacks and we sold it in Drama. Charcoal was the primary fuel for cooking at that time.

The second time, I had agreed to receive a load from Theophilos of Kranista. Kranista is a mountain village that (at that time) could have been reached only by horse or mule. He agreed to bring the load to the highway at Mokros[20] by mule, so that I could load it on my cart. He was late. I spent two days at Mokros, waiting for him. Finally he came. After I loaded and started my way to Drama, I passed a village called Taxiarchis (old name Sipse). As I was exiting the village, a young man in a Bulgarian uniform of forestry police stopped me.

"Tsakai," he said in Bulgarian, meaning "halt."

I immediately recognize him as my friend Nikos Nembis from Petrousa, the same that we shared food and fear and the same one who ate the RETSELI that my wife sent me at the front. Petrousa is a village near Drama, where most of the people spoke Bulgarian. It was therefore nicknamed as little Sofia.

---

19   A. Boinodiris, Book 1, p. 35.
20   Another name for Mokros is Livaderon. It is located at 41°17′N 24°13′ E.

"...Hello, Nembis. Congratulations on your promotion."

He became angry, and started yelling to me in Bulgarian, which I could not understand. Finally, frustrated he starts in Greek:

"Show me your license."

I did as he said. After reviewing the Greek license he said:

"This land is not Greece any more. It is Bulgaria."

"OK Nembis, next time I will ask for a Bulgarian license. This is what was issued to me for the time being."

"The charcoal is being confiscated," he said as he was looking at my load.

I knew the village very well and most of the people would have bent backwards and helped me. He was unarmed. I could beat him up senseless and escape from the village.

"You know me very well Nembis from the army"; and after a pause: "Do you really think you can steal my charcoal?"

He started taking off the ropes of the charcoal bags, throwing one of them down. I jumped on top of him. He fell on the ground shocked and I started hitting him on his face repeatedly.

"When did you manage to become a Bulgarian, you bastard? Traitor; a couple weeks ago, you were fighting next to me. I will kill you and whatever comes, let it come."

My heart was beating hard, praying that he was alone. Nembis was bleeding from my repeated hits on his nose and mouth.

Some women heard my shouts, and (to my good fortune) rushed around me, pleading me to stop. I recognized them. As I was trying to recover from my anger, I heard the distinct noise of a motorcycle. I rose and then saw the rider. He was a German soldier, dressed in full uniform with his helmet and goggles on. He had a submachine gun on his side, in addition to his pistol. I froze, next to Nembis, who was still lying down, beaten up, with a bloody nose. The German stopped and took off his goggles, looking at me. I thought that I was a goner. Suddenly he turned at Nembis and yelled in German. To my eternal surprise, instead of attacking me he starts kicking Nembis. Nembis took off like a rabbit and disappeared in the gully below.

The German slowly pulled his motorcycle under a tree on a hill and started smoking a cigarette. [21] I picked the charcoal from the ground and pulled my cart up the hill. I parked it near him. He looked at me, smiled and offered me a cigarette. I tried to communicate through signals, asking him where he was going. His response was "Africa, Africa."

As we were trying to communicate, a platoon of seventeen Bulgarian soldiers appeared from the gully, in which Nembis disappeared. They had rifles slung in their shoulders and carried in their hands large bunches of onions. They wore field shoes and as they were coming from the fields, they were pulling onions from the crop fields of the village. When the German saw them, he stood up, picked up his machine gun and started firing over their heads. They dropped all they carried and raised their arms. He beckoned them to approach. When he saw that some of them had bulging pockets, he signaled them to empty them. The contents of radishes and other garden goods dropped to the ground. He ordered them to move to the bank and showed them to stand at attention. Then he turned to the village women that watched the whole scene, beckoning them to pick up all the goods that the Bulgarians dropped. Then he turned to the Bulgarians and started yelling. I could not understand what he was saying and I believe neither could the Bulgarians, but from his hand and eye movements I gathered that he was chastising them for the barbarian attitude, shortly after they came. He was telling them that getting few onions may be OK, but pulling the whole crop out could starve the village. After that, he fired one more burst in the air and pointed them to leave, in a direction away from their rifles. Seventeen Bulgarian soldiers started running like rabbits.

---

21   A. Boinodiris Book 4, p. 79-82

He then approached the women and children who were picking up the onions. I followed him. He offered a chocolate to a toddler. He then pulled out a photo of his family. He had small children and a wife whose name was Piccolo (I will not forget that). He said, pointing to the direction of the Bulgarians:

"Bulgar nix good, politic good."

Then he pointed to us: "Grec good, politic nix good."

He signaled to me to go. He also assured me of safe conduct, by pointing to the Bulgars and waving his hands, then pointing to his machine gun.

I left towards Drama. While passing Livaderon, I hear his motorcycle. He passed me, turned back and waved at me. He was patrolling the road, making sure I was OK. When I was at the outskirts of Drama, near the barracks of heavy artillery, I heard him again. He followed me until I reached Chrysostomou Street, namely my destination.[22]

Regarding Nembis, I found out that he was with the 17 Bulgarian soldiers and that he was sure to get my charcoal. Naturally, if I knew that there were 17 Bulgarian soldiers with him, I would have never attacked Nembis. Even if I killed him, I would not have escaped the platoon, which would have surely killed me. Therefore, I owe my life to that German soldier. Nembis brought the soldiers up, but did not tell them that they were dealing with an armed German, who took the side of the Greek. They thought that they had to deal with only an unarmed Greek upstart. As a result, they were unprepared for him, and he surprised them with his submachine gun.[23]

German Customers (Drama, May, 1941)

While the Germans were in Drama, they did not hurt us, nor did we hurt them. At that time, the only currency that was usable was the German occupational mark. We did not know this currency. The

22 A. Boinodiris, Book 1, p. 93 and Book 4, p. 79-82.
23 A. Boinodiris, Book 1, p. 91 and Book 4, p. 79-82.

German soldiers were issued many marks and they used it for shopping. Each commander had the equipment to print his own currency, which they used it as an IOU for all things that they "bought." They bought everything good that they liked, sending it back to their families in Germany.

I had a small grocery store since 1937 with a partner whose name was Basil Dimitriades. When we came back from the war, we found it in shambles. I spent about a month (until the end of May 1941) helping my brother-in-law Michael Aslanides who was selling cold-cut meats. The Germans were good customers, eating lots of salami and sausages.

The Germans had a good time in Drama, so good that they were sad when their orders came to depart and leave the regional control to the Bulgarians. We did not realize it at the time, but these Germans that we hosted were some of the best trained paratroopers of the Third Reich. As they were leaving, we asked them where they were heading. They responded: "Creta."

Most of them were depressed, saying that they did not expect to survive this attack. The battle of Crete was raging between May 20 and May 26, 1941. News of the fighting arrived sporadically. We knew that the Germans that were our guests in Drama were attacking Crete. We later found out from their comrades that survived, that many of these Germans died there.

To conquer Crete, the German High Command prepared "Unternehmen Merkur", the largest airborne attack seen to date.

The attack was launched on May 20, 1941. The Germans attacked the three main airfields of the island, at the northern towns of Maleme, Rethimnon, and Heraklion, with paratroopers and gliders. The Germans met stubborn resistance from the British, Australian, New Zealand and the remaining Greek troops on the island, and from local civilians. At the end of the first day, none of the objectives had been reached and the Germans had suffered around 4,000 casualties.

During the next day however, through miscommunication and failure of the Allied commanders to grasp the situation, Maleme airfield in western Crete fell to the Germans. With Maleme airfield secured, the Germans flew in thousands of reinforcements and overwhelmed the western side of the island. This was followed by severe British naval loses due to intense German air attacks around the island. After seven days of fighting, the Allied commanders realized that the hope of Allied victory was gone. By June 1, the evacuation of Crete by the Allies was complete and the island was under German occupation. In light of the heavy casualties suffered by the elite 7th Flieger Division, Adolph Hitler forbade further airborne operations. General Kurt Student would dub Crete "the graveyard of the German paratroopers" and a "disastrous victory."

Figure 5 German Parachutists Attack Crete

The Massacre of Drama (Drama, Greece, 1941)

In the early months of occupation, walnuts, chestnuts, honey, eggs, cheese, butter and eggs were still available at the villages, but not in the city. When the Germans left, the market was depleted of food. All the food products were redirected to the axis powers. The local buyers, mostly tobacco workers, now had to scrounge for food to avoid starvation.

The plan for Greek extermination was set in motion by the Bulgarian fascists. It was partly as a reprisal for the defeat of Bulgarians in the period of 1912-1915 and partly to assure that there is no future opposition to a continuous Bulgarian annexation of Eastern Macedonia and Thrace by the resident Greeks.

In 1912, Drama was a village of 10,000 people with only 1500 Greeks in it. There were 8000 Turks and 500 Armenians and Jews. In 1941, it was a booming town of 35000, mostly Greeks from Thrace, Bursa, Pontus and Smyrna. All Asia Minor migrants experienced in cultivating tobacco ended up in this area, because Drama had the right land and climate for it.

In the summer of 1941, the Bulgarian fascist leadership planned to exterminate these new upstarts who came and took lands that the Bulgarians wanted for themselves after the Turks left. It seems that, those days, in the axis circles, extermination of troublesome minorities was in fashion; a fashion made acceptable by the arrogant speeches of the top exterminator, Adolph Hitler.

Preparation for Ethnic Cleansing (Drama, Summer of 1941)

The first step taken by the Bulgarian leadership was to put out a proclamation, replacing all priests with Bulgarian priests. All priests were sent to Thessaloniki.

Next, all school, bank, police, village and city public servants were disbanded, replaced by Bulgarians, speaking only Bulgarian. As the president of the village of Xiropotamos was leaving for Thessaloniki, he sold me his goat, which we named Marika. This left the common people without any voice, support or protection.

Next, they infiltrated tobacco factories, urging the leftist elements to revolt. Bulgarian communists played a major role in the infiltration, pretending to oppose the current Bulgarian fascist regime. Around the third week of July, some men appeared in my neighborhood, while I was trying to bring food from mountain villages into the city.

They came in the house of Charalambos Kertikoglou, a known communist who invited all the men of the neighborhood to listen. There were about 40 men in that house. Among these men was my other neighbor, John Charakopoulos. From the minute I stepped in, the house smelled of Stalin.

"Good day comrades. I am here to ask you to join me in our struggle against our fascist oppressors. At a warehouse, next to the railroad station we have amassed weapons. The weapons are those taken from the stores left in the field by the retreating Greek army. They are adequate to arm many men. Weapons can be stored inside the smokestacks of the homes, so that they cannot be found. We want volunteers to help us distribute these weapons to houses in each neighborhood. Each neighborhood would have a group leader. In your neighborhood, Charalambos will be your group leader."

"Our central leadership is equipped with a wireless communication, capable of communicating with Stalin's government in Russia. When we get the signal, we must join our Bulgarian communist brothers and fight against the fascists. This attack must be coordinated with a Russian attack, upon which time thousands of Russian parachutists will drop from the skies to join us."

I kept my mouth shut. As I was getting ready to leave, one of them stopped me.

"What do you think comrade? Can you help us?"

I hesitated. The speaker stopped speaking and he joined the man that stopped me.

"I would very much like to know your opinion," he added.

I paused, looked at the floor and then raised my eyes to the speaker. "You asked my opinion, so I will tell you. I was part of the Greek army. We had weapons and organization and fought hard, but the fascists managed to win this battle, because they were more prepared than we were. However, winning a battle is not the same as winning the war. We sacrificed ourselves, but we managed to buy time for our allies." I paused, trying to decipher their facial reactions. They listened with a blank look. I decided to continue.

"You are in too much of a hurry to lose your head, if you think that with these meager weapons you can win at this time. The Bulgarians have brought in Eastern Macedonia and Western Thrace 100,000 soldiers of their regular army. Patience must be our weapon. We must give time to the allies to get ready to fight this war. This war will be with us for several years."

Some of the men nodded their heads. John Charakopoulos, who joined the rest assumed a sarcastic look and a wry smile:

"Go to hell Anthony. You are a blood-sucking merchant who always looks after your profit. A revolution would prevent you from profit making, by scalping poor workers."

I ignored him and turned to Charalambos:

"I implore you to stop this insanity. You are being duped into this. The Bulgarians want an excuse to kill innocent people and you will provide them with the excuse they need, to prevent any international outcry. Stop being callous heroes and think about the innocent lives that will be lost and you will have in your conscience eternally."

With these words, I turned around and left.

September 22-27, 1941

Two months after that meeting, around the third week of September, my father and I spent a whole week (September 22-26) in the mountain villages gathering food. I remember that my greatest find was four cans of honey from the village Pepeles. We brought the merchandise to the village Kerasia, near the animal shelters of the Sarakatsanei.[24] There we met with Thanasis Tsartsalis, one of the members of that tribe. We

---

24 Sarakatsanei is an ancient Macedonian Christian nomadic tribe, herding animals in the mountainous regions.

bought meat, eggs and cheese from him, but we could not carry our entire load so we left the two cans of honey in his shelter, to be picked up later. [25] We returned to Drama on Saturday, September 27.

Sunday, 28th of September 1941

Sunday, the 28th of September I took little Paul (now 13 years old) on the horse and took off to retrieve the honey. We were planning to return on Monday. We were loaded with 5 kilos of salt and a few kilos of grapes as part of the trading payoff for the Sarakatsanei. On my way, I had to pass in front of the house of Charalambos Kertikoglou. He sees me and rushes outside to stop me.

"Anthony, stop. Where are you going?"

"We are going to pick up some of my stuff from a village in the north."

"Don't go today. Today we received the signal for the uprising. Today, the shit will hit the fan. I don't want you to get caught in the middle of the killings."

I looked at him.

"When I came out of the house, I said my prayers as I crossed myself. With God's help, we can make it back. "

"You have three children to support Anthony. It is not worth risking your life for some stuff."

"We are all in God's hands Charalambos."

I proceeded towards north, with a bit of apprehension. I reached near Vathilakos, where I met a woman from Perithalpsi.

"Where are you going Anthony?"

"To the Sarakatsanei shelters..."

"What is going on, Anthony? I saw many armed Greeks, passing from this place and heading to the mountains."

25   A. Boinodiris, Book 1, p. 242-243.

"I don't know, but thanks for the information."

I immediately decided to change my plans. As I approached the shelters, I looked at a thicket of birch trees on the side of the mountain, near the faucet and saw metal shining. The picture of one or more of the armed men that the woman saw, brandishing his metal gun in the sun came to mind. We hurried up and went to the shelter of Thanasis Tsartsalis. Thanasis' people had slaughtered a wild boar and cooked it on a skillet. We gave them the salt and grapes, had wild boar for lunch and I started loading the horse for the return.

"Where are you going Anthony? We have prepared your beds for tonight."

"Thank you, Thanasis. I do not feel comfortable in staying here any longer. If you look at that thicket over there you may see some brainwashed armed men, who may be planning something very stupid."

He looked towards the direction I was pointing.

"You be careful Thanasis, especially in the next few days."

I loaded the honey, more eggs, cheese and some of the wild boar meat. In addition, I loaded the horse with a sack of birch leaves for my goat, which I purchased from the president of the village of Xiropotamos. [26] On our return through Vathilakos, I stop by Apostolis Papadopoulos. He offered to sell me 30 Oka[27] of walnuts.

"I do not have money to pay you now," I said.

"It's alright," he said; "you are good for it. You can pay me another time."

I loaded my animal to its ears; it was a strong horse and did not give me any trouble. As I was passing the village, named Monastiraki, I met a leftist man, named Thanasis, who was considered a mental case. He was swinging a large staff with his hand and shouting.

"Long live Stalin! Kill all the fascist pigs!"

---

26   A. Boinodiris, Book 1, p. 244.

27   Oka was an old weight measure, used during the Ottoman Empire. 1 Oka is about 2.75 pounds, or 1.28 kilograms. It was used in Greece until the 1950s.

Without saying a word, we passed by him and went silently on our way.

"Even the mentally retarded communists are revolting," I said to Paul, when we were beyond listening distance.

Finally, we arrived at home safe. As I entered my home, I sensed that I was followed by a couple of tobacco workers.

"What goodies did you bring for us Anthony?"

I told them.

They followed me home to purchase some food for their families. They were joined by the handsome 26-year-old Basil Bostantzoglou, my newly wed neighbor. We became such good friends, that I was his best man in his wedding.

"God Bless you Anthony. Since you manage to get us something to eat from the mountains, we do not mind the occupation."

I heard a loud voice coming from 10 meters behind Basil.

"Don't worry Basil. It will not be long now. By tomorrow, the Russian parachutists will be here to rid us of these leaches."

It was my neighbor, John Charakopoulos.

I turned my back at him and whispered to Basil.

"I have never seen such a blockhead as this man in my whole life."

Rumors that Kill (Koudounia, Sunday, 28th of September 1941)

As I was traveling that Sunday, the communists, stupidly duped by the Bulgarian communists went on a regional revolt. They shot five Bulgarian police officers and six village presidents that day. They also destroyed the electrical generation facility of Drama, sinking the whole city into darkness. This stupid move became the cause that killed 17,000 people in the days that followed. [28]

---

[28]   A. Boinodiris, Book 1, p. 246.

Anestis Tselepides was a young man with communist parents. He was a marked communist since he was in high school, since he was an avid propagandist. When he joined the army, the government could not trust him with a weapon; so, the army made him a shepherd, herding livestock used to feed the army. He was stationed at the village of Koudounia and knew all the villagers there well. On September 28, 1941, he went to Koudounia and started his own little stupid war of lies.

"Why are you sitting here? Drama is occupied by Russian parachutists," he yelled at the villagers.

Some of them believed him. They gathered outside the Bulgarian village president's home and arrested him. Some wanted to kill him. The two Bulgarian police officers that served the president escaped with their weapons and went into Drama, where they notified the authorities. A Bulgarian military detachment was sent to Koudounia and arrested 45 of its men, locked them up in a warehouse full of straw and then proceeded to set it on fire, burning all of them alive. Anestis escaped both, the Bulgarians and the rage of the villagers, including the numerous widows and orphans that cursed him for his lies.

Bloody Bazaar Day (Monday, 29th of September 1941)

Monday, September 29 was a bazaar day. The bazaar, extending to the south and west of the central square, was a sprawling area next to the banks of the mostly dry gulch that flows through Drama. Every family in Drama sent a person to the bazaar to buy their weekly supplies.

Like all Monday mornings, the tobacco workers woke up early in the morning and started walking to their factories. Near the bakery of Papadopoulos, in the first square of the Central Subdivision, two Bulgarian police officers stopped some of the workers, saying in Bulgarian.

"Go back to your homes. There is no work today."

Some lucky workers came back home. Unfortunately others, either did not understand, or did not believe the sincerity of the police and went to work. Among those that returned was Basil Bostantzoglou, my newly wed neighbor and friend. I was the best man in his wedding.

What these workers did not know was that late on Sunday, after the attack against Bulgarian units by the communists, the Bulgarians put out a marshal law proclamation. The proclamation said that that starting from Monday, September 29 all Greeks must stay indoors. Few posters were placed in parts of the city, but not all police precincts knew of its gravity and most Greeks could not read Bulgarian.

As detailed news started filtering through, the proclamation was interpreted by the police to be very severe. Any man caught outdoors will be shot. This proclamation was in effect until October 20.

Even after the police knew what to do, for the Greeks, the problem still existed: all the posters were written in Bulgarian.

The only ones that could read Bulgarian were Bulgarians and some Greek traitors that knew Slavic, who declared themselves Bulgarians and could not be trusted.

Many Greeks also could not believe the idiocy of any rumors of such a curfew; so, they went to the local bazaar. Others never heard the news and innocently went straight to their death. [29]

In the morning hours of that Monday and until the Bulgarian police and army discovered how serious were their orders, they were kind enough to send people to their homes. In the afternoon, after a top official found out what was happening, things changed. The Bulgarians took an active role of seeking and killing any Greek man in sight. Somehow, their orders were limited in not being allowed the right to break down a door, unless a prisoner ran into a household.

The Innocent Victims

Based on information that I received on Sunday, I decided to stay home that day.

---

29   A. Boinodiris, Book 1, p. 245-247.

Those that violated the curfew in the afternoon hours were arrested. With tied hands they were led to the pine trees of Korylofos, a hill north of Drama, set in a line and machine-gunned. Some of them that tried to run were shot on the spot.

All of those that were caught in the bazaar were innocent people, whose main purpose was simply survival. Some close witnesses saw their friends and relatives, as they were peering through the windows of their homes in Perithalpsi. They were taken in-groups of three, with tied hands over their heads, walking on Chrysostomou Street towards Korylofos. My brother in law Michael Aslanides and his wife Urania were peeking at them through their window curtains, facing that street. A Bulgarian guard, leading the prisoners must have seen a slight movement on the curtains. He turned his submachine gun towards the window and fired a burst. The bullets passed narrowly between their heads and shattered the glass and mirror of their living room credenza. [30] When a woman recognized her husband on the street and rushed out to save him, she was taken with the rest of them and lost her life too.

All of these innocent victims were buried in a mass grave, which has yet to be found, after so many years. Since the relations between Greece and Bulgaria are relatively good these years, the government does not want to bring into light the atrocities committed by the Bulgarians during that period. Yet, I hope that one day the new generation would find this grave among the big caves that abound at Korylofos, with about 10,000 bodies in it and give these innocent victims of this atrocity the proper burial they deserve. [31]

John Charakopoulos

My neighbor across the street was a tobacco warehouse worker, named John Charakopoulos. I had many arguments with John, whom I considered a stubborn and thickheaded blockhead. He was among those gullible victims of the communist propaganda. He was married

---

30   A. Boinodiris, Book 1, p. 247.
31   A. Boinodiris, Book 1, p. 245-249.

to Anastasia, a soft-spoken woman and worked in the Greek-Austrian Tobacco factory.

About 18 of these workers ignored police warnings to return home and went to work that fatal Monday. All 18 were working, when the Bulgarian patrols started rounding up civilians from the streets. They peeked into the factory's windows to see what was going on. After seeing these men working, the Bulgarian patrol tried to come in. The workers managed to barricade the steel factory door.

"This is the police. Open up. We have orders to check for terrorists and weapons."

The workers were scared and refused to open the door. The door was locked and made out of heavy steel.

The police, having their orders not to violate these doors, went and arrested the supervisor Parpenides and ordered him to open the doors. The doors were latched from inside. He started pleading with the workers.

"Come on boys. Please open the doors."

"No way …! They will murder us," said John and others.

"Don't worry John. This officer promised us that nothing would happen to you."

"We don't trust them. We saw what they were doing to a whole lot of people out there."

"If you guys don't open these doors, they will blow this place up with dynamite. You have no choice. You have to trust them."

The men decided to open the doors. John was among the seventeen of the men that were arrested and taken straight to Korylofos where they were shot. Only one man decided to play it safe and hid in a pool of water in the flooded basement of the factory. He was the only survivor.

John's wife Anastasia was taking care of their two babies, the toddler Anastasios and the baby girl Sofia when she received the news. She immediately rushed to Korylofos to retrieve his body, dragging the toddler and holding the baby, as all three were crying their hearts out. They were turned back without success, but miraculously they were not harmed.

In later days, one of the neighbors commented on their survival: "The Bulgarian soldiers did not want to shoot these women and children. They want them to starve to death without their breadwinner's support."

Tuesday, 30ᵗʰ of September 1941

Among those that were killed on Tuesday, were the mentally retarded Thanasis from Monastiraki. In the intersection of Chrysostomou and Ethnomartiron streets, right across from the house of Kyriaki Zoumboulidou, Thanasis attacked a Bulgarian police officer with his staff and a second police officer emptied his revolver onto his head. That same afternoon, I lost my best friend, Basil.

Basil Bostantzoglou

That Tuesday, at noon I had Basil and Katina Bostantzoglou as guests in my house. This young couple lived next door and since I was best man in their wedding, a few months ago we socialized a great deal. Basil was a handsome young man of twenty six. We had spaghetti that day, discussing news about the killings in the market the previous day. After eating, he and I joined in his veranda, where we were smoking. I remembered that I had some cheese in the house, which I craved for and went in to get it for us. As I was trying to find it, one-armed Bulgarian soldier appeared and before Basil could react, he shouted:

"Halt."

Basil went immediately indoors.

The soldier approached and started knocking at the door with his rifle. I found out later, that the soldier was a communications specialist, handling a wireless located in the Bulgarian Army Headquarters, which took over the Drama High School building. He was a bloodthirsty bastard, who was out on a prowl to kill the first Greek man he could lay his hands on, regardless if he was in his house.

Katina's grandfather, Peter was a venerable man. He appeared at the door with Katina and her mother. The communications man responded:

"I don't want you old man. I want the young man that was here."

Katina and her mother started screaming.

"We will give you money, watches, anything you want, but do not take my husband. Please."

"If you don't bring him out, I will have to go in and get him."

As I was getting the cheese, I heard screams of women outside. I dropped the cheese and rushed out to see what was happening. My wife Elisabeth saved my life by tackling me on my way out:

"Go back Anthony, hide. A Bulgarian soldier is taking Basil."

I immediately took a chair and climbed up onto the ceiling, opened up a trap door and hid on top of the rafters of the house. I stayed there silently in the dark, listening to the yells and screams, until I was told that they were gone.

I found out later what happened.

As the women were screaming, Charalambos Kertikoglou, the communist group leader, who registered as Bulgarian appeared. He started talking to the soldier in Bulgarian.

"He is a good man. Do not take him. I can vouch for him."

The soldier got angry and reached for his revolver. Charalambos started running. A shot was fired, but missed. The soldier did not want to chase Charalambos, insisting on getting Basil.

He barged in and grabbed Basil from behind the door.

Katina, his wife and Katina's mother were screaming even louder.

The soldier started dragging Basil towards Korylofos to deliver him to the firing squad. On his way, the soldier took some flyers from his pocket, with communist revolt material and stuffed it in Basil's pocket. Basil took the papers out of his pocket, complaining of being framed. The soldier started beating Basil on the head with the rifle butt, placing even more flyers in the pockets of the fallen Basil. The soldier then raised him and began dragging him again towards Korylofos. By the time he reached Perithalpsi, Basil was dazed from the vicious beating.

Various people witnessed all this through their windows, as Basil was dragged through the streets, all the way to the street in front of Drama High School. There, two Bulgarian police officers approached the soldier. One of them was Savas Petkos.

"Where did you find this Greek?"

"I found him on the road, distributing these flyers."

The two police officers joined the soldier and started beating him with their gun butts. The communications soldier left his prisoner with them.

As they approached my father's home, near the High School and knowing very well his fate, Basil made a run for my father's home. The Bulgarian soldiers fired several shots at him. One of them found its mark, wounding him severely. Wounded, he managed to make it through the barn, busted inside my father's home, and crawled under his bed bleeding all over the floor.

My father was behind the house, with a neighbor, named Mrs. Chrysi.

He heard the commotion and rushed in. There, he hears a whimper under his bed.

"Mr. George, please help me."

My father literally wet his pants, seeing the trail of blood leading under his bed. In his confusion, he brought Basil his pillow.

The police officers started following Basil's blood trail, which led them directly to my father's house. They appeared at his entrance, opened the door and aimed their guns at him.

"Why did you take this dog in?"

"In the name of Cyril and Method, God help me," he uttered in Russian.

The Bulgarians looked at each other. Then one shouted in Bulgarian.

"Who are you? What are you?"

"Russian..."

"If you do not want to join his fate, I want you to pull him out of there."

George was trembling. He looked under the bed and pleaded in Greek:

"Basil my boy; please come out of there."

Basil was crying but could not move. He had lost a great deal of blood.

The Bulgarians pushed my father to the side and dragged him out from under the bed, making more of a blood trail all the way to the sidewalk of Chrysostomou Street.

"Listen old man; if you want to live, stay inside your house," said one to my father.

Basil was left on the sidewalk bleeding. According to my father's estimates, he lost 4 kilos of blood.

He tried to get up and return home, but could not. He started crying and yelling to my father.

"George, call Katina to come and get me. She can fix me up."

My father George closed the door and started praying, not daring go out.

After two hours of an ordeal, with Basil bleeding on the sidewalk and my father crying and praying, two Bulgarian officers appeared. They saw Basil in his last breath, shaking on the sidewalk. One took off his revolver and shot him on his head. Then, they called for a city cart to pick up his body. He was taken to a mass grave, which has yet to be found, after so many years.

Two days after Basil's death, the communications specialist brought two loaves of bread to Katina, his wife. Katina asked him:

"Where is my husband Basil?"

"We sent him to Sofia."

"Sofia" at that time meant the place of no return.[32]

Then the soldier turned his back on her and left.

To all of us who knew the handsome twenty-six-year-old Basil personally, his innocent soul haunts us all these years. Could any one of us do anything different to save him?

Why did this soldier go after Basil? Why did he appear again two days later?

Rumors about the motive of that soldier to go after Basil with such determination went rampant. Some said that the soldier had a crush on Katina and went after her husband from jealousy. Whatever the reason, no solid information was found for such an insane act."[33]

---

32 A. Boinodiris, Book 1, p.268.
33 These are memories of S. Boinodiris from narration of this story by Anthony and George Boinodiris, as well as Elisabeth Boinodiris. S. Boinodiris met Katina in 1961 in Thessaloniki, who also painfully narrated her husband's unwarranted killing. Also, A. Boinodiris, Book 1, p. 245-249.

Figure 6 George Boyun-egri-oglu (Boidaris),
Anthony's Father during the late 1950's

Figure 7 Photo of Drama, Greece, as Viewed from
Korylofos, a Hill, where Many Were Shot in 1941.

Cease-fire Day, Sunday October 19 1941

The cease-fire order was given on October 19. It was time for those Bulgarian-registered civilians to venture outdoors and harm those on their "hate list."

The Koulouri Peddlers

Several immigrants from Asia Minor, living in villages of the prefect of Drama near the Bulgarian border were forced to move to the city of Drama during the War, so that they are safe from the Bulgarian infiltrators. They managed to settle in small lots on the outskirts, even farther out from the center of the city. They started selling a kind of a Greek sesame bagel, named koulouri. The koulouri is crustier than the bagel but bigger in diameter and somewhat slimmer. It was an important breakfast snack for the merchants, peddlers and shoppers, who were in too much in a hurry to have breakfast. It was the "fast-food" of the era. They sold these round breads in wooden trays, or held by a long stick, which passed through the hole of each koulouri.

These people were getting up very early to catch those hungry entrepreneurs, who also ventured out early. One of them was a family of a widow, named Theano, consisting of her daughter, her son-in-law Minas, who was a tinsmith and three young sons. One of the older sons was a police officer in Thessaloniki.

On Sunday the 19thth of September, after the cease-fire was issued, two friends visited Theano's family. One of them was a vineyard worker named Anestis Halatsis, who was guarding his vineyard near by. The other was the next-door neighbor and shoemaker, named Peter.

As they visited the family, John, the Bulgarian-speaking Greek traitor from Monastiraki saw them. He called the police, accusing the family of illegal assembly.

The police commissioner took a troop of police officers and surrounded the house. They grabbed Theano's three sons, her son-in-law, Peter the shoemaker and Anestis Halatsis.

"Are they communists?" asked the commissioner in Bulgarian, facing John.

"How am I supposed to know where their alliances lie?"

"Why are these six men in that house?"

"I have no idea."

"Ask them."

John asked them. They told him that they visited their friends, having some chicory coffee.[34]

John relayed the message, making no effort to defend them.

That same day, the police rounded up Theano's three sons, her son-in-law, Peter the shoemaker and Anestis Halatsis and shot them at Korylofos.

The women were left all alone to fend for themselves.[35]

Gatsoulis

That day of 1941, the already limping old timer Gatsoulis was forced to take some Bulgarian officers fishing to a near-by river; they knew of him, as a handy fisherman. After he caught the fish for them, he was ordered to cook and serve them to the officers. The Bulgarian officers had quite a spread in the river bank and had a good time. They brought plenty of liquor and they were drinking a lot, trying to suppress their conscience for the bloodshed. In his stupor, one of the Bulgarian officers, quite drunk, pulled his revolver out and shot the limping Gatsoulis in the left arm. Although the rest of the soldiers took the revolver away from the drunk and bandaged Gatsoulis, this left him fully handicapped for life. [36] Greek life was considered cheap in those days.

---

34 Chicory coffee was the only coffee that was available, because chicory beans were locally grown. Regular coffee became non-existent during the occupation.
35 A. Boinodiris, Book 1, p. 251. The women later left to Thessaloniki and joined their only surviving male member of the family.
36 A. Boinodiris, Book 1, p. 346-347.

The Results of the 1941 Mayhem

For eighteen days, all civilians were closed indoors. Anyone that dared to go out was shot on sight. Bulgarian civilians had to be accompanied by police, or military escort. The weak, the sick and the elderly who did not have enough to eat, or water to drink were found dead from starvation, or dehydration. [37]

In my small neighborhood of about 10 houses, we lost eight people those days. They were the six members of Theano's house, Basil Bostantzoglou and John Charakopoulos. We were considered fortunate because we were well below average.

Georgia, my 10-year-old sister was Elisabeth's helper with the housework. In those and in subsequent days she became the food link, making sure that my father did not starve. She was also taking food to my mother-in-law Makrina and the family of my brother-in-law Michael Aslanides. Michael had no way of getting food, since he was in the paint and knitting material business. I had the only available supplies, which were now hidden inside a ground pit, under the carpet-hidden door on the floorboards of my bedroom.

Georgia brought us the news about the shooting of Basil Bostantzoglou.

She was a tough little girl and a fast runner. During the curfew of 1941, Elisabeth gave her food to be dispatched to her father. That day she had to dodge a bullet from a Bulgarian patrol, as she was running from house to house. The patrols were shooting indiscriminately at anything that moved. She managed to reach her destination unscathed.

In the occupational period, 17,000 innocent Greeks (out of 35,000) were slaughtered in the region of Drama, but the dark days of September and October of 1941 were the worst. Carts, that carried the dead for burial dripped with blood. In subsequent rainy days, citizens of Drama slipped and hurt themselves on those granite cobblestone streets, because the

---

37   A. Boinodiris, Book 1, p. 250.

human blood had drenched them, making them extremely slippery to walk on."[38]

Many of us started wondering whether we did the right thing by opposing Germany. We knew we had to fight Italy; but why not do what the Rumanians and Bulgarians did? We would not have to suffer so much in the hands of these barbarians. We started blaming the Royal family of King George II, who was pro-British. They knew what happened in East Macedonia during 1915-8 with the Bulgarians. They knew they had a gripe against the Greeks and always wanted to eradicate them so that they occupy the Aegean Macedonia and Thrace. [39] Suffering is often a means by which God improves us for better lives; but many of our neighbors lost their lives, having no chance of doing any improvement. Will our children benefit from this ordeal? Will the people of the future even know that we ever existed, or what we went through?

After October 1941, the number of Greeks fleeing to the mountains, to wage guerilla warfare exploded. At that time, I tried to escape for Thessaloniki, but the door was shut. The Bulgarians closed all routes to Central Macedonia, captured families, shot the men and jailed the women. Edicts were issued which we could not understand; they were in Bulgarian, a language none of us knew. Fear set in, not because of imminent death, but because we did not know what to expect. If we knew what was going on, we could act accordingly. But we did not know. After the massacre of 1941, our ignorance turned into fear. [40]

The Bulgarians also issued a proclamation for volunteers to go and work in Germany. We were starving so much in Drama that we had plenty of incentives to volunteer. Charalambos Kertikoglou, the communist group leader of my neighborhood did exactly that. He ended up in some German factory towns, where he created smoke by burning tar and trash, every time allied bombers appeared. That was one way used by Germans to conceal targets from the allied bombers.

---

38   A. Boinodiris, Book 1, p. 35.
39   A. Boinodiris, Book 1, p. 94.
40   A. Boinodiris, Book 1, p. 89.

I was talked out of fleeing, by my family responsibilities. I had a neighbor, named Nikos V, [41] who was a shepherd at the time. He was born locally, but for self-serving, treasonous reasons he registered as Bulgarian. One day he asked me to teach him arithmetic in exchange for some food. I did exactly that - God save his sinful soul, since he died in 1978 with cancer. This treasonous character, which I will discuss more later on, was one that hurt me, at a time when I needed help the most.

Not all locals registered as Bulgarians. Petrusa is a village, NW of Drama. The old, Bulgarian name of that village was Plevna. Many of these people were soldiers with us at the front, fighting Germans and Bulgarians. Only a handful of them like Nimbus turned traitors. The rest, even though they spoke a mixed dialect of Greek, Bulgarian, Turkish and Slavic, they despised the Bulgarians and whenever possible fought them hard in the underground.

The Carpetbagger Visitor

When the killings were still going on and I was still hiding indoors, one of the local traitors with baggy pants from Xiropotamos walks into our yard. Both his legs were crooked and he limped a lot. He wore a rifle and was decorated with two belts of bullets around his chest and back. He also carried a revolver. He sat under our quince tree, which I had planted before the war.

Elisabeth was outside, doing some laundry.

"Where is Anthony?"

Fortunately, I was inside, in the toilet, a makeshift facility in the back of the house. When I saw him, I decided to stay there. I could hear every word he said.

---

41   Here the author avoids naming this person, for reasons to become obvious, in order to prevent any one from the descendants of his family from being harmed. According to the author's judgment a person's behavior, no matter how abominable, does not merit defamation of anyone in his family, or his descendants. For obvious reasons, Nikos V would change last names over different times. Other aliases would include a Bulgarian ending in "-ov" and a Greek ending in "-is".

I knew the bastard. He was a ruffian, whom I caught stealing from my business before the war. He was always asking for credit, but never paid back anything in his life. In other words, he was a parasite.

"He went to Kavala with his cart."

"All people, like your husband will go to Sofia. He is probably there already. Do you know what that means?"

"No."

"It means that he is dead."

He stayed under the tree for two hours. In the meanwhile, Elisabeth walked in and whispered:

"Stay where you are and don't move."

After two hours, he was bored and walked towards the neighbor's house. It belonged to John and Bethlehem, who had a beautiful teenage daughter, named Charis.

"I want Charis out here," he ordered.

Bethlehem did not like his look.

"Why do you want my daughter?"

"I want her to come out and help us bury those that are killed on the streets."

It was indeed true, that bodies and body parts were all over the streets. Many dogs were seen, dragging arms and other parts of human anatomy in the streets. She did not like the way he grinned. He was thinking of raping her child.

"She is a child, you dirty old man. She will probably faint at the first sight of a body. Please let her be and I will give you two of our blankets."

"Let me see them."

She went indoors, brought out the blankets and gave them to him. He was doing his rounds, blackmailing every other household on his way downtown. By the time he reached the park at the Central Subdivision, he had a bundle of loot on his back.

"Tsakai," said a voice behind him in Bulgarian, meaning "HALT." He turned, to be faced by a Bulgarian officer and two men.

"Who are you? Show me your papers," said the officer in Bulgarian, as his patrol was disarming him.

The ruffian tried to talk his way out, unsuccessfully.

"What do you have here?" They inspected his loot.

"Tie him up," he ordered.

We later found out that he was taken to jail at Komotini, where he died by the hands of other prisoners. We did not find out the details. [42]

The Great Communist "Heroes"

Lately, the communists have praised themselves as the great heroes of that war. Some of the claims were that the main Greek resistance organization, ELAS[43] killed more than 8,000 German soldiers in little over a year. That same organization tied down tens of thousands more Germans and controlled 80% of the country when Hitler withdrew.

To my opinion, the ELAS operation in the Bulgarian sector was a disaster. The Bulgarians lost an insignificant number of soldiers, but they were given the excuse to wreak havoc. Approximately 17,000 civilians died in the immediate region of Drama. The whole operation was poorly planned by cowards, who gained a small advantage by causing the death of many innocent civilians. Their political ambition was without bounds. They wanted to show off so badly, that they were willing to sacrifice the lives of innocent people, to achieve their goal.

---

42   A. Boinodiris, Book 1, p. 268.
43   This claim is true, according to the German army's own records.

They applied the motto: "the end justifies the means," better than the fascists they were trying to destroy.

Their mobilization in Drama was untimely, unplanned and criminally played in the hands of the Bulgarian nationalists, who wanted every excuse to exterminate a population, without being criticized by the international community and they justified it as self defense. [44]

Famine: Most Effective Tool for Ethnic Cleansing (Drama, 1942)

The worst year of occupation was 1942. Until May 1942, we had some amount of rationed food, stored under the house in holes, accessible by trap doors. Non-perishables like cracked wheat, pasta, olive oil and pickled vegetables were stored in sealed glass jars. In May, 1942 the food ran out.

How could I feed six people in my family, half of them children? How do I do that, and manage to escape the Bulgarians who want us dead? They systematically applied hunger as the main weapon in their arsenal for achieving the ethnic cleansing of Greeks in Eastern Macedonia. Their goal was simple: after all Greeks are dead, or gone, the Bulgarians become the predominant population in the area. Bulgaria's eternal dream was to have access to the Aegean Sea. They attempted it several times, but every time they were expelled by the Greeks, with the support of the overwhelming Greek population in that area. Now, they had a means to make that dream a permanent reality, if only they could eliminate the Greeks from that region. The Bulgarians were shooting Greek men, left and right for no reason at all. Every time I ventured to the mountains to collect wood for fuel, my life was in danger. If I did not, my family would start dying from malnutrition, or diseases like typhus that attacked malnourished people. [45] I even received threats by people that tried to blackmail me for few sticks of wood; when I exited with my cart, they threatened me that they would nail me with lies to the Bulgarian bullies, unless I gave them the food they asked for.

---

44   These are discussions of S. Boinodiris with his father.
45   A. Boinodiris, Book 4, p. 84-85.

We got a vineyard for sharecropping at a location of St. Tryphon, beyond the railroad station. The vineyard belonged to an old man, named Aidonopoulos, who died the year before. The vineyard stayed uncultivated, having a great amount of weeds in it. In order to clear the weeds, we had to eat our remaining supplies, because we needed energy to do that work. That vineyard cost us more than we thought possible, because its return was meager. That vineyard took us into the realm of total starvation. We now knew how to conserve our energy, so that we do not consume much food.

Our goats provided some energy to our kids by giving us 2.5 kilos of milk daily, so the kids stayed healthy, in spite of lack of other food.

The kilo of wheat was then 50-60 Leva[46] in the black market. Corn was around 25-30 Leva per kilo. A day's wages for hard labor was only 100 Leva. My father was elderly, in his 60s and had no stamina for hard work. Elisabeth had to take care of an old man and three children, while she worked at the tobacco factory during summer months.

The oldest child, my brother, Paul, was now 14 and his mind was filled with hunger and playing soccer. He could not keep shoes, because he destroyed them faster than we could hope to buy them. So, he played barefooted.

The youngest, my 10-year old son John had the task to feed the two life-saving Maltese goats with the rest of the children of the neighborhood. All these children did the same thing. These goats saved the children's lives. My son was supposed to get help from Paul, but Paul was always dumping goat herding on John, so that he could go and play soccer. Occasionally, Georgia relieved John, because she loved to join other girls of the neighborhood, as they were herding their goats. Upon occasion, so did my father. Other than that, my father was of little help. With his money, he had bought many copper utensils, which he loved. When he ran out of money, he exchanged the utensils for little food, thus wasting his money in the exchange. [47]

---

46   Leva were the Bulgarian currency used.
47   A. Boinodiris, Book 1, p. 106.

Cutting Wood for a Living (July 3-July 5, 1942)

On July 3 1942, I went to Livaderon to cut wood. On a good day, I managed to cut 3000 pieces of wood to feed my family. By going to Livaderon and cutting wood for sale, I had to consume lots of energy. I soon found out that you cannot cut a cart full of wood without some calories. The only intake I had was the sweet melons from Kalos Agros, which were plentiful that year. We had no bread. We managed to seed some wheat in the somewhat barren and low yield acre lot belonging to Costas David, in a sharecropping deal but this crop was not ready yet and in danger of being discovered by the forestry police. When they did, they would confiscate 25% of the crop. This would leave 75% to be split between Costas and us. The 32.5% left would hardly pay for the energy (in food) consumed to cultivate it and the seed used for it.

At Livaderon, I had my portion of 160 grams of cornmeal bread (with its portion of sand) and one cup of non-fat yogurt, made from our goat's milk. I also bought 10 kilos of melon. By the time I reached Livaderon it was evening and I had finished the bread and yogurt. I found the Bulgarian forestry police officers, and showed them my permit. They took me to a mountainside, and showed me where I was allowed to harvest wood. They also told me to turn my forest section into a plowed field, and not to leave any stumps.

"We do not want to see even one thorn on the ground," yelled one of them.

They used these permits to convert forest areas into plowed fields. I can select the big pieces, but I had to make sure that all small branches and leaves are buried in the ground, to be used as mulch by the planters. I complained:

"That kind of work requires food, which I do not have."

"Then why did you come? As far as I am concerned, you can drop dead. Before you leave tonight, we will come and inspect your work. If you fail to do what you are told, you do not leave."

I left my cart on the road, and took the horse over with me, with a load-saddle on.

Since I had no grain for the horse, the poor animal had to be content with grass alone. I carried all the melons down, feeding the peels to my horse. I slept in the forest, saving my energy.

I started in the morning of July 4, cutting trees down and pulling off their roots, separating branches, leaves, roots and wood for burning. Every hour in the hot sun of July, I ate a whole melon. I managed to finish my work by nightfall, having finished all melons except two. I worked into the night, after I passed inspection. Fortunately, I had a full moon for night work. I carried ten loads of wood back to the cart using the horse, loading it heavily. I worked almost all night. My horse worked hard and starved, just like I did.

In the early morning hours of July 5, I hitched it on the cart and proceeded for Drama.

I thanked God that I was young and strong and could stand this punishment. What if I was older, or weaker, like many of my fellow citizens? As I traveled, I remembered a number of starving older people in my neighborhood, roaming the streets aimlessly, with swollen abdomens. I never realized how grotesque a human body becomes under starvation. My mind wandered, dreaming of the good old days, when my mother cooked that mouth watering bulgur …

Suddenly, I saw something that brought me back to reality. I was on a downhill stretch next to a precipice, and I was in danger. I had a ton of wood on a cart, with a starving horse in front. The load could pull my horse and me down to the ravine, killing us both and turning the wood into toothpicks. I stopped the cart and strapped two logs on both sides of the cart, to be used as breaks. It worked. I managed to bring in this fashion my load until the 20th kilometer from Drama. In that position, there is the road fork for Dendrakia (old name Kranista). In that fork, there was a coffee house, run by Costas from Ortakion of Asia Minor, who lived in Kranista. He kept his family there and used that inn-like store in that key location for all cart drivers that passed by the highway towards the Nestos River Bridge. It served as a rest place for a route that accesses a large number of villages. I stopped there, unhitched the horse and took off the brakes that were not needed any more. Then I approach Costas, whom I knew very well:

"Costa, give me any food or bread you have. I am starving."

"He laughed. My friend Anthony, we are starving too. We have no bread and such luxuries. My wife made boiled eggplant and peppers."

"That's OK, Costa. Give me anything."

He served it and I started wolfing it down.

"Naturally we have no access to salt," he said. "My wife saved this for us."

He pulled a crumpled newspaper with about a teaspoon of salt. He took a pitch of it and sprinkled it on my food, as if it was gold dust. As I finished eating from my bowl, I saw two Bulgarian police officers with civilian clothes coming from the direction of Kranista.[48] They entered and started talking to me in Bulgarian. Since I could not understand them, I asked Costas to help me out. [49]

"They are asking you for your identification and license," he said.

I showed them both. Then, they started inspecting my cart. They found my military overcoat and food bag, with the two melons, which they took. They left one of the melons in the cart, because it was beaten up. They also saw my water canteen, which they appropriated. Turning to me, they asked:

"Soldat (soldier) ...?"

I explained to them through Costas:

"They are mine, since I spent six months in the army. The Germans let me keep them. It seems that you are poorer than we are."

48   A Boinodiris, Book 1, p. 98 and Book 4, p. 82-84.
49   A Boinodiris, Book 4, p. 82-85.

One of the police officers, which I did not know then, is going to be well known later on, in our ordeal of occupation. He was president to a village, northwest of Drama, called Xiropotamos. The short-cut road from Drama to Xiropotamos passes directly in front of my home. His name was Vergos. Once he was a Greek soldier and an aid to a general of the Greek army. He responded:

"Bulgaria is not poorer, but since it is military it is confiscated. I do not like your smart mouthing. The next time, if I see you in these mountains, even with a permit, I will break your legs. If you want to live, go to Germany. Germany needs workers."

I hitched back my horse and started my trek to Drama. "These bastards want all the Greeks to go to Germany, so that they can have the place to themselves," I mumbled. When I reached the heavy artillery barracks on the northeastern outskirts of Drama, I stopped by a tree shade, split the discarded melon and ate it, including its seeds and peel. I let my horse graze for a while.

After a short rest, I resumed my trip to my client. I had a client for the wood, named George Hatzopoulos. He was a black marketer, who used to work in the Greek salt monopoly. This person had no conscience, or rather a cold-cash conscience. As I came to Liberty Square, it dawned on me. How do I take it to my client, having to go uphill with a ton of wood up the Venizelos Street? To my good fortune, I meet two good friends, Aristotle and Tryphon. They helped me climb Venizelos Street and Chrysostomou Street to the Justinian Street, where I unloaded the wood at the place that Hatzopoulos told me. After being paid in cash I came home hungry and eager to eat. I had managed to buy 20 kilos of wheat, which I hid at home underneath some melons under a trap door in our bedroom. [50]

The Cracked Wheat (July 5, 1942)

In addition to the 20 kilos, the children had saved 10 kilos of wheat, collected at night, in secret from fields that were already harvested. These leftovers, picked by children, a little at a time amounted to a life-

---

50   A Boinodiris, Book 1, p. 98 and Book 4, p. 82-84

saving amount for a few days. The collected wheat was taken to a hollow stone down the street that was used like mortar and pestle, a little at a time.[51] It was beaten to take off the husks and peels; then it was taken to a neighborhood oven to be dried, using the dried branches from trees to heat it. When it dried, it was placed in a linen sack, which was mine, left over from my army days. It was typically issued to all soldiers to carry their clothes. It also had my name on it.

Earlier that day my wife, Elisabeth, knowing I would be coming home hungry, as was her routine, prepared something to eat. After having cleaned the wheat in the previous days, this time she prepared all 30 kilos to be dried. As she was returning from the neighborhood oven, she took a shortcut from the fields, hiding her precious, rather heavy cargo under her apron. As she was passing behind the house of Kyriakos Peloponides, she had the bad luck to bump onto a vineyard police officer, named Nikos Melachrinos from Kastoria. He wore a uniform, with the Bulgarian crown on it. He was hiding in the shadows, so Elisabeth did not see him.

The Terrorist from Kastoria (July 5, 1942)

Nikos Melachrinos was from Kastoria, but must have had Bulgarian roots, because he spoke Bulgarian very well. Before the war, he lived in Drama. Instead of guarding vineyards from theft, he was on a prowl for contraband food. He became the terror of Xiropotamos, where he confiscated food from everyone, including beggars. We were told about an old man, who managed to feed himself by making vinegar and selling it or bartering with it for food at Xiropotamos. Nikos caught him in front of our home, confiscated everything he had and beat him senseless in front of our eyes. I wanted to go out and kill him. Elisabeth stopped me.

"Where are you going? After you kill him, you would have to go to the mountains and we would be left to starve after they confiscate everything. Do you want us to die too? "

---

51   The author remembers this stone as a child. In later years its hollow was used to water chickens.

I controlled myself. The man barely managed to reach his home and never showed himself outside. He probably died from hunger. People that were too weak, had no stamina to wait in line for their bread, or could not gather greens from the fields died from hunger.

On this day in July, this vile beast saw Elisabeth and told her to show him what she is holding under her apron. When she did, he opened the sack and saw that it is warm cracked wheat (bulgur).

"This shall be confiscated," he declared in Greek.

"Why are you doing this my good man? Do you know that the lives of six souls depend on this sack of food? Please spare them," she pleaded.

Nikos immediately turned to speaking Bulgarian, which Elisabeth could not understand. Elisabeth started asking for help from a native Bulgarian woman, who lived in a near-by house of Philip Philippides. She came out, with a number of neighbors. When she arrived, he turned his language into Greek.

"This contains 30 kilos of grain. My hand estimation is like a scale. I have something to do now and must leave. I am leaving this with you, but I will be coming tomorrow to pick it up. I do not want to see one gram missing from this sack."

He dropped the sack and abruptly left.

When I came home, happy to be finished and eager for some food, I found a depressed Elisabeth, who told me what happened. I felt sick at heart. I started blaming her for taking the shortcut instead of the road where this varmint had no jurisdiction. Finally, I decided:

"Bring over the sack. Let's eat what we can and let them confiscate what is left from it."

We made a good amount of pilaf and had our fill, all of us.

The following morning we anxiously waited for Nikos. I prepared to ply him with cigarettes, to see if I could discover his good side. Elisabeth prepared coffee, made out of chicory with saccharin.

He finally appeared, brandishing a long stick. We tried politely and with a smile to offer him cigarettes and coffee. His face turned harsh and menacingly he shouted in Bulgarian. I responded:

"Niko, we are refugees from Asia Minor. We do not know Bulgarian; and you are not Bulgarian, since before the war I saw you often in Drama. You can speak Greek better than we can, or you can speak in Turkish if you so choose."

"I speak no Turkish," he responded in Greek, "and this filthy Greek language I do not care to use. Anyway, the government prohibits us, government employees from using the Greek language."

"All of the government employees I dealt with for licenses and other affairs were accommodating in either Greek or Turkish."

Next to us, my widowed neighbor, Katina Bostantzoglou was outside, listening and watching us. Her husband, Basil, was brutally shot last fall. Being the best man at their wedding, I was close to that family. Meanwhile, Elisabeth took two cans and started going down the street to fetch water from the neighborhood faucet.

"Regarding the bulgur," I continued, "please let it be Niko. We are six people, three of them children, at their growth period. The government does not give us anything, besides 160 grams of corn bread."

"Why should I feel sorry for you?"

"If you have a gram of humanity, you would feel sorry for us. What we had to eat is gone. Leave us in peace, so that we do not die. The beans that were brought from Bulgaria and sold for 60 Leva per kilo disappeared before we could get any. The beans were full of live worms, but the people ground them up, made bean bread and ate them anyway."

"Wake up my man," he replied. "Do you honestly think that the Bulgarian government has no food? The warehouses are full and busting at their seams. They do not give you anything because they want you to die from starvation. We in Kastoria waited for a day like this, because we are Bulgarians at heart. Our ancestors came down many years ago, but the Greeks took over these lands in 1912 and forced us to accept their government. Then, they brought all of you Turks here, who took over our lands and property. It is time for you to disappear; go back to where you came from, or die. I am not going to feel sorry for you."

"Please my man …"

"Forget it. Bring the sack over right now, or I will bring the police here and you will be in trouble."

We brought the sack.

"What is this? You stole from it."

"We did not steal anything. We just ate one pot's worth."

"Where did you get the wheat?"

"I bought it from farmers and paid dearly for it."

"Which farmers…? What village?"

"I don't know their names. I do not remember what village."

I saw Elisabeth approaching the house, after having filled two large cans full of water.

"You are thieves. I am coming back and you will be punished severely. You …" [52]

As Elisabeth approached with the cans full of water, she interrupted him in an angry manner:

"Niko, what harm did we do to be punished?"

He turns angrily, raising his stick to hit Elisabeth, for her interruption.

My blood pressure went sky high.

"Go ahead," I yelled angrily "hit her, and see what happens." He lowered his stick, facing me angrily.

52   A. Boinodiris, Book 1, p. 103 and Book 4, p. 85-89.

Katina next door was shaking. Melachrinos dropped the sack on the floor, made a turn and left. As he walked away, he turned, pointed the stick on us and angrily uttered something in Bulgarian.

I started thinking. If he brings the police, their standard procedure is to beat men up, until they cannot stand for several days, many times breaking bones or causing internal injuries. They typically do not harm women.

Katina spoke:

"Anthony, take the horse and cart and run to my vineyard. You do not know their language and if you are lucky, they will beat you senseless. I do not want you to get shot, like my husband Basil."

I took Katina's advice and went to her vineyard, where I put my horse to graze. I started pulling off some weeds, to help Katina with her work. As I worked, my mind was at home. What had happened to Melachrinos, so that he needed to be more Bulgarian than the Bulgarians? Were his people among those that fought tooth and nail the local Greeks during the Balkan Wars? How could the Greek government allow these people to live among us, infiltrate our armed services and then become the police dog of the occupiers?

I came back at 4 PM. Not finding my wife at home, I walked to the market and went straight to the store of Michael Aslanides, Elisabeth's brother. He had a tiny store, selling paints and cloth, on a side street next to Venizelos Street. I asked him if he heard anything about his sister. He sat me down and told me.

"You just missed her. She is on her way home." Then he explained that they were three who took Elisabeth to the police station. She carried on her shoulder a bag full of something, like bulgur. She told me later that they took her to the offices of Cypritov, the chief of police. One of them, presumably Nikos started talking Bulgarian, while others were taking notes. They were writing and writing, eight sheets of paper on both sides, sixteen pages. As he was talking, the bureaucrats were shaking their heads. One of them got up, started yelling at her and struck Elisabeth on both sides of her face. Elisabeth could not understand the language to respond in any way against any libels of Nikos. Finally, through Nikos they asked:

"Where is your husband?"

"He went to work."

After talking among them, Nikos ordered:

"Sign here."

She signed all 16 pages of a document she could not understand and after leaving the bulgur at the station she went home, passing by her brother's store and telling him what happened.

I rushed home and saw her trying to control her tears. She did not want me to see her crying, in fear that I might do something crazy. I wanted to leave for Thessaloniki, to a relatively free Greece, under German occupation. However, I could not.

The Bulgarians had closed even more tightly all routes to Central Macedonia, captured families, shot the men and jailed the women. Eighteen men, all from a single village of Drama were shot at the Strymon River earlier. So all hope for escape had disappeared.

Escape to Bulgaria (Upper Nevrokopi, Late Summer, 1942)

I was not blaming the Bulgarian civilians that came from Bulgaria for our plight. I blamed the turncoat Bulgarian minority we had among us in Macedonia. I cursed those dogs, that claimed to be Greeks a few months earlier; they lived and prospered among us, but are now libeling and blackmailing us, in a language we could not understand and we could not defend ourselves against them. [53]

I searched for a way to escape from these dogs and I found it. The Bulgarians were asking Greek laborers to work in their fields in Bulgaria. I signed up.

---

53   A. Boinodiris, Book 1, p. 104 and Book 4, p. 85-89.

The Trip to Upper Nevrokopi (July 10, 1942)

On July 10, 1942, four large trucks pulled up on the Liberty Square. We were loaded 50 men per truck and took off for Bulgaria. [54]

I managed to sit next to the driver and his aid. He was a funny Bulgarian who knew a bit of Greek, enough to communicate.

He started teasing us with a sarcastic smile.

"How come you, the glorious Greeks that all of us learn about you in our history books managed to fall so far down in the gutter? Why is it that you are now our slaves?"

I kept quiet, while he was laughing.

"I guess you must like what you do. Maybe you are not Greeks after all."

He continued.

"You grabbed Thessaloniki from us and made us enemies. You got so many ports. Why don't you let us have one on the Aegean?"

I kept my silence.

"Eastern Macedonia is only 300 kilometers from Sofia and 800 from Athens. Do you think that we do not deserve to own this land? Just because you surprised us once in Lahana, it does not mean that we will stop trying to regain the land that we lost."[55]

He kept on talking politics to me all the way to our destination.

---

54 A. Boinodiris, Book 1, p. 106 and Book 4, p. 89-91.
55 This claim of Aegean Macedonia by the Bulgarians still continues. With the free expression facilitated by the use of the internet, some descendants of these Bulgarians still keep on that theme. See http://www.bulgarmak.org/make-donia.htm

We reached northern Nevrokopi, the Bulgarian Nevrokopi.[56] The southern Nevrokopi is the Greek Nevrokopi, both cities having the same name. Many fields were white from crosses. The driver said:

"You see these?"

"Yes."

"All these are your doing. There are about 10,000 Germans buried here, soldiers that you have killed more than a year ago."

"I saw them when I was facing them at the front. It is not our fault that they are dead. They attacked us, wanting to enslave us and deserved to be killed. Even if we knew that they would win, we would still fight hard and kill them."

Then it was my turn to smile.

"You Bulgarians, how is it that I did not see you fight with them?"

He smiled back.

"What do you think we are, crazy, like you? You won against a very powerful Italy for heaven's sake. We waited until these Germans here spilled first their blood. Then we moved in, after you were destroyed. My man, you have to be smart in this world to survive."

I realized that the man was truthful, bearing no malice against the Greeks. In fact, he may have had some admiration for us, in spite of our condition at that time.[57]

He dropped all fifty of us off at the syndicate and waved good-bye. The rest of the Greeks got upset with me.

---

56 The Bulgarian name now is Gotse Delchev. Near this town there are the remains of a walled city established by the Romans in the 2nd century AD to celebrate victories over the Dacians. The Greek populated town was called Nikopolis ad Nestrum by the Romans and Nikopolis of Nestos by the Byzantines. There has been archaeological work on the site, which ceased due to lack of funds around 1986.

57 A. Boinodiris, Book 1, p. 108 and Book 4, p. 89-92.

"How come you talked to him in that way? He can destroy us. Are you crazy?"

"He is alright," I responded, "don't worry."

The Filling Meal

At the syndicate, we were assigned to an engineer. We placed our clothes at the syndicate housing and asked if there was something to eat. It was afternoon and we were all starving. Someone pointed us to some stores. We started walking towards the indicated direction. I was up in front. There we saw restaurants with loaves of bread, pilaf, potatoes and other food. Bakeries were loaded with cakes, chocolate halvah and other sweets. I entered a shop and greeted the man at the entrance in Greek. He was Albanian and knew some Greek, Bulgarian and Turkish. I then said:

"Friend, we have money. Can we eat what we want, or is the food restricted?"

He froze.

"Eat. Eat whatever you want, as long as you pay."

All fifty of us sat in tables around the restaurant. We first attacked the God blessed bread. We asked for one loaf to a person.

I ordered pilaf with sheep's yogurt, which was my favorite food.

Then I ordered a whole kilo of halvah, half-chocolate and half-plain.

The Albanian could not believe his eyes. He had not seen such starving characters, not only buying the whole store, but also paying for it immediately. He asked us:

"Where do you come from? Where are you going? Why are you so hungry?"

"We are from Drama and came here for work. We have a great hunger there because they are not letting us Greeks have any food."

"How about the Bulgarians there …? Do they have food to eat?"

"They eat everything. Their warehouses are full. They take all the crops from the Greeks, leaving nothing for them. The only place you can buy anything is in the black market. We have no food there, so we are forced to work here, so that we can eat."

"I knew it," he said. "Among those that went to your place from here, most of them were scum. They let all the criminals out of our jails and sent them there. They had a choice, either go to Greece or serve their jail sentence. Most of them went there for the loot. They are starving you, so that they can grab all your goods for a slice of trashy bread. I feel sorry for you."

Then he smiled. "Have a soft drink on the house."

I managed to eat a large bowl of pilaf with yogurt, half a kilo of bread and half of my halvah.

After picking up the leftovers, we exited, while I was crossing myself.

'God be praised,' I said. 'We finally had our fill of food.' "

Work and Lice

We slept at the syndicate that night. Next day, the engineer and his aid took us to the work site, about 30 kilometers away, to the NW, carrying our bags with our clothes. On our way, we passed a village, called Musemista, and followed to the western bank of Nestos River. They showed us at a distance a mountain, called Pirin, where the Nestos River originates. After Nestos comes out of a narrow gully, it runs down the plain of Northern Nevrokopi. There, on both embankments we set up our camp, made out posts, holding a tin roof, to protect us from rain. Otherwise, it was open all around. This was on purpose, because in the summer that tin roof became a hot tin roof. Even a small breeze was welcomed, for cooling us off. I hung my clothes on a line and filled my sack with the leftover bread and halvah on the post. We prepared cots for sleeping.

As I lay down, I started thinking of my family. Before I left for Bulgaria, I told my father and Elisabeth to sell the cart and horse after they picked up the grapes from the vineyard, so that they would not starve.

We started working immediately the next day, opening large drainage canals on the banks of Nestos. The canals communicated with smaller irrigation ditches, equipped with valves, which irrigated each field, whenever it needed watering. The engineer measured the fields and canals, marking their location with wooden posts, each with its own tag attached to it. We excavated all we were told to excavate, based on his instructions. We had no complaints regarding food. After so many months of hunger in Greece, we were now well fed. We ate half a loaf of bread daily, meat, potatoes, peppers (which is the national food of the Bulgarians), tomatoes, rice and even fruit.

We bought food from a local grower, named Ilias Tamboulas from Musemista. [58]

The only complaint was lice infestation. I had never seen lice like that. It seems that the lice infestation was running rampant those years because the Bulgarian-made soap was made out of pork fat, with minimal amount of lye in it. It had no effect at all on that menace. It was bad in Drama, but it was even worse here; when you have fifty workers, sleeping next to each other, lice pass from one to the other. Every time we lay down to sleep at night, lice were eating us up. Our bodies started having sores from scratching our itching skin. The lice on our bodies sucked our blood and soon became as large as a grain of rice. The pastime of many was to pick lice from their bodies and kill it by pressing it with their fingernails. As it was squashed, it made a characteristic bursting sound of "tsak." I was so disgusted that I decided to abandon the tin roof structure and built a cot, under a wild pear tree. I used tools from our workshop to cut some branches, build the cot, and added ferns for softness. After boiling water, I immersed my mattress, blanket and clothes in it, to disinfect them from lice. After drying them, I moved into my new location. It did not work. Very soon, lice were all over me

---

58   A. Boinodiris, Book 1, p. 112 and Book 4, p. 91-94.

again. It seems that they were coming out of the ground, hunting for human bodies where they had a sweet feast.

Supply Duties

I worked there for 5 months. I proved to be good in knowing how to purchase the best quality food from the market. As a result, the engineer assigned me the responsibility for all provisions. Since I did not know Bulgarian, I took a Greek refugee from Russia with me, who acted as a cart driver and translator. He had come in 1939 to Greece. We used the syndicate cart and horse to provision food for all workers. I passed the food to the cooks, who were also Greeks. We were regularly going to the farm of Ilias Tamboulas; we loaded watermelon, melon, grapes, apples, plums, pears and fruits of the season. We placed them in a tent, which served as a storage place. I distributed them to workers, kept a ledger and when we were paid, each gave me the cost of their share and I paid the farmer. Because of my duties, I was assigned half the excavating work, which others were doing during the full working day. [59]

With us was a man from PERITHALPSI of Drama, named Stefanos Ectaroglou. He may have been an alcoholic in the past, but was a very good digger. He was normally drinking 320 grams of ouzo per day, but dried up when alcohol was non-existent in Drama. Now, he found out that he could get some plum ouzo, made by the farmer I was dealing with. As a result, he traded with me. I was bringing him 160 grams of ouzo per day and a pack of cigarettes in exchange of him working my assignment for that half-day. Occasionally I brought him some mastic ouzo, and that made his day. Everything went well, and I was able to save all my money for my family, since I had almost no personal expenses. My expenses were minimal, since I was getting most of my food allowance from the farmer. I negotiated with him to give me some extra food, as part of the deal I made directly with him. With my fringe benefits, I could buy some extras, but the amount was minimal.

---

59   A. Boinodiris, Book 1, p. 114 and Book 4, p. 91-95.

Malaria

I was hoping to finish the War in Bulgaria, but luck was not on my side. I caught malaria, having high fever, and my teeth chattered to the breaking point. I continuously shook in my bed, to a point that they were forced to tie me up and put a towel in my mouth.

The engineer took me to Upper Nevrokopi to a doctor, who was resident within a pharmacy. His diagnosis was that I was very sick because we were drinking polluted water, directly from Nestos River, and contracted malaria from all the mosquitoes that were around us. He gave me quinine. For 15 days, in spite of the quinine, I had the routine of shakes. This happened every noon, like clockwork, for a few hours. The rest of the day I was better. Not being able to continue, I had to return to the hell of Drama. Before doing that, I went to the café in Musemista and found Ilias Tamboulas to tell him the news. He treated me into appetizers with ouzo from plums, so powerful, that my eyes started watering when I drank it. He took me to his house, consisting of a large yard with high walls. The yard was full of fruit trees, including apple, plum and pear trees. I ask him:

"Is this your orchard?"

"No. It is over there, where I have 10 more hectares," he said as he pointed at a distance.

His children walked towards us. They were harvesting tobacco. I had left with him my good, traveling clothes, so I had to give him the news.

"I have to leave. I need to get my clothes back, to travel. It is time for me to clear my debts to you before I leave. How much do I owe you?"

He froze.

"Why are you leaving? Where am I going to find another person to take your place? We need the syndicate because they are my best customers. I am extremely happy with you."

"I am extremely happy too, but my health has failed me. I need to get to my family. "

I paid him what I owed him and his wife gave me my clothes. They also prepared a food package for me. [60] He hitched his horse and buggy and took me to Northern Nevrokopi. On the road, he told me about the Bulgarian komitatzides. The name komitatzides was used to describe the irregular army used by the Bulgarians in the Balkan wars. Most of them were born in the Greek territories and were terrorizing the Greek population. They were always causing problems, walking provocatively in the streets, and they often attacked refugees from Turkey, to discourage them from settling in Macedonia. After their defeat, these komitatzides[61] had to resettle in Bulgaria. The local Bulgarians had a great deal of problems with them and considered them as criminal elements, especially since many of them continued to bully civilians, even if these civilians were now Bulgarians. They were looked down upon, and dreamed that they would return to the Aegean Macedonia, which was now Greek. They had never forgotten that they were part of a Great Bulgaria dream that extended all the way to the Aegean Sea.

"Before the war we had no peace here. Theft and robbery was rampant. After the komitatzides went to your place, we have peace and quiet. After you paid me, I put my money under my mattress. Whatever I get from my crops, I store there. I do not lock my doors. Before, our home was like a fortress and still they managed to rob us. We thank Germany for letting us get rid of these scumbags. Unfortunately, you have to suffer. My advice to you Anthony is, after the War ends to please kill these bastards. It is the only way that both, you and we can live in peace."

He took me to the bus depot and in a very brotherly way, we said our good-byes. A number of workers were there, from various villages of Drama who gave me money for their families, in addressed envelopes.

---

60   A. Boinodiris, Book 1, p. 115 and Book 4, p. 91-94.
61   Ever since then, the term "komitatzides" had been associated with "terrorist Macedonian bands" supporting a Greater Bulgaria, which includes the Aegean Macedonia.

They trusted me. All together, I carried 5,000 Leva with me and I made sure to safely deliver every one of them.

The Return to Hell (Drama, End of 1942)

I returned to Drama around the end of November of 1942. When I arrived, I found out that the Bulgarian leadership had imposed a curfew on all Greeks between the hours of 5 PM and 6 AM.

I discovered that Elisabeth had sold the cart, horse and reins for 50 kilos of flour and 20 kilos of wheat to a family that were registered Bulgarian. He was Dimitrios Papoutsis, who was an exception to the rule. Although a turncoat, he treated us fairly and delivered what he promised. He was the only one that could bring us flour, because Greeks were not allowed to use mills.

Some Greeks used hand mills, which made so much noise that they had to be muffled with blankets so that the Bulgarians do not hear them. They did not have to be police; any Bulgarian, including your nasty next-door neighbor could arrest Greeks. If they did, they would confiscate mill and grain, in addition to dragging you to the station for a good beating. [62]

In the months to come, a number of Greeks left for Thessaloniki, calling the German occupied country "Free Greece, in comparison to Bulgarian occupied Hell."

I could not leave, since I had my aging father in Drama. I also had to take care of my siblings, my brother Paul and my sister Georgia, in addition to my son John. Several times, I pleaded with him to leave, but he stubbornly refused.

"Father, the Bulgarians want to annihilate us. Let us leave to Thessaloniki. I have a horse and a cart. I also have a cart, which I can use to sell fruits and vegetables and make a living there."

He refused.

---

62   A. Boinodiris, Book 1, p. 115 and Book 4, p. 95-97

"I do not know German, but I know Russian. One way or another I can negotiate with the Bulgarians, but not with the Germans. I do not like the Germans."

Because of him, we braced ourselves and suffered for 42 months of brutal Bulgarian occupation. It was a sheer torture.

In the months that followed, wheat bread, oil, olives, butter, cheese, fish, salt, black pepper and meat of any kind disappeared for the Greeks. Only the Bulgarians were entitled to these. The bread was made out of cornmeal with 5% ground sand in it. To survive hunger, people were selling all they had. We sold rugs, clothes and furniture. By the end of the occupation, most Greeks were with rags and sleeping on the bare floor. As for food, we could only eat cabbage, leeks and rotting potatoes, discarded by the Bulgarians. We were somewhat fortunate than most. Since before the war, we had two Maltese goats that helped us immensely. We hid them from outsiders indoors in a fenced area, taking them secretly at night to feed in the fields. From them we received milk for the children. When the Bulgarians discovered what we had, we had to pay 15 Leva for each goat as tax.

In spite of all this pressure of starvation and mistreatment, in the face of death from starvation, only a handful of Asia Minor immigrant Greeks chose to enroll as Bulgarians. Was it stubbornness? Was it nationalistic pride? Was it our way to fight tyranny? Many of the Bulgarians called it stupidity. What they did not realize was that most of the people they were trying to convert into Bulgarians by force went through centuries of such torture by the Turks and refused to change their nationality, even in the face of imminent death.

Live in Hell or Become a Traitor?

I started working as a partner with Dimitrios Petsikoglou, selling squash, grapes and nuts. I heard then of another call, enlisting workers for Germany. [63] I had already enlisted, when my neighbors Lakis Samaras and the miller George Kasapis sat me down and told me news

---

63   A. Boinodiris, Book 1, p. 117 and Book 4, p. 95-96.

that they heard through the grapevine. Lakis lived with his wife Kyriaki and his mother Maria.

"Anthony, Germany is under attack from allied bombers. Do you really want to go there and have your head blown off?"

"What can I do? I have six souls that must be fed here. How am I supposed to do that when the Bulgarians have shut off all avenues for survival?"

"Come with us and let us see. If you still feel that way after this, then you can do what you plan to do."

Not knowing what they intended to show me, I followed them. They took me to a house, behind the Ekpedeftiria elementary school, where a teacher named Heroides lived. After having exiled teachers like Heroides and Georgiades to Thessaloniki, the Bulgarians opened offices in their houses. We walked in the office and the Bulgarian behind the desk looked at my identification. After filling a form, the man asked me to sign.

"What am I signing?" I asked.

"That you are Bulgarian," Lakis said.

I walked outside the door, with them following me.

"I cannot accept this. I was born Greek and Greek I shall die. You, Macedonians may find it easy to register as Bulgarians, knowing their language. However, we, immigrants from Asia Minor survived as Greeks for hundreds of years under various occupiers, much more powerful than Bulgaria. Many of them tried to adopt us, but failed, because they did not understand what we were. For us, keeping our identity is much more important than keeping our lives. Besides the wealth of property in Asia Minor, left to the Turks, we left the bones of many generations of ancestors, who insisted to die as Greeks, rather than save their lives. We came to Greece as starving refugees to be free. Do you really think that you can talk me in registering as Bulgarian now?"

"If we do what you say, we will die and be of use to none."

"Let us die. We will be of greater use dead, in the face of tyranny, than alive under tyranny."

"You act like a patriot, who thinks of his nation as an exclusively special institution. What makes being Greek better than being Bulgarian?"

"To be a Greek is not just by claiming that you belong to a Greek nation. Greek is a set of ideals, followed by our ancestors and their descendants throughout the years. I am ashamed on your behalf for abandoning these ideals. Most of these Bulgarians do not know what it is to be Greek. They do not even know what it means to be Christian, a religion that Greeks helped them adopt. Greeks believe in freedom, a right you must give to all human beings to pursue their dreams equally. Where do you find freedom in this society? Where is democracy, where ordinary people are allowed to perform extra-ordinary feats?"

"It is not worth dying for it," said Lakis laughing slyly. "I say sign and live, so that you can fight them another day."

"We had so many saints, martyred for Christianity and its beliefs. They did not say:

'Let's pray to a statue today, so that I can save my life.' There is no such thing as a secret Christian, or a secret Greek.[64] If I give in today, tomorrow you will blackmail me for the rest of my soul. These occupiers are the blackmailing kind. No! This stops here and now, so that I do not have to explain to my children, why I betrayed my Greek ideals."

"You are an idiot Anthony. Greece does not exist any more. Even Crete is lost. Greece has as much chance of recovering, as having hair grow on my palm. Greece is dead."

I walked away from them. I found out later that they did sign up as Bulgarians, pressured by starvation. Immediately later, the Samaras family was able to get the same food as the Bulgarians. They ate meat, fish, salt, cheese, rice, oil, flour, sugar and pasta. Some of it was sold illegally in the black market to people like us. The price for anything

---

64   A. Boinodiris, Book 1, p. 118.

was all you had. We were forced to pay it. This did not bother me as much as Lakis' irony. One day, Lakis returned from the market with all his groceries and he shouted to me:

"Anthony, you better run to the market. They are allowing Greeks to get meat and other foods."

I ran to the market, only to find out that Lakis was lying. When I asked if I could get some meat, the Bulgarian pushed me out of his store.

"Get out of here filthy Greek, before I call the police. Do you really want to be beaten up today?"

I returned home, quite upset, only to see Lakis eating something and laughing at me.

Another time, Lakis said to me:

"Genov from Varna brought lots of fish. He asked me to tell all Greeks that there is so much that they decided to let Greeks have what is leftover."

I ran again to the fish store, which was located where later was the "Sun" bakery. When I asked for leftover fish, I was told:

"Get out, before you are beaten up."

I stopped believing Lakis any more.

In 1942, it was still unknown who was the winner. Hitler could come up with a secret weapon that we were hearing about and Germany could win, having now Japan on their side. From the Italians the Germans expected very little. After the Italian humiliation by the Greeks, they were placed in a secondary role. [65]

After getting the run-around from Lakis, I had to rethink my options. I was in a difficult situation. I hated to enlist to go to Germany as a worker, but if I did not, what was the possibility of survival in this

65   A. Boinodiris, Book 1, p. 356.

killing field? Yet, wouldn't my going to work in Germany make me a traitor against the allied effort?

In the Jaws of Despair (1943-1944)

The Trap (January, 1943)

Among those people that found out about my visit to the house of Heroides was my neighbor Nikos V, who registered as Bulgarian himself and was renamed with a Slavic name ending in "ov," as in "Popov." As I was trying to decide late in 1942 whether I should go to Germany, he approached me.

"You cannot leave now Anthony," he said. "Face it. You have a five-member family that will starve if you leave. Also, if you go to Germany, you have a chance of dying from the heavy bombardment that is going on there."

He must have heard from someone to whom I was telling my concerns.

"What do you suggest that I do Niko?"

"I have a proposition. There are three Bulgarian merchant friends of mine, who purchased the forestry rights from a public auction for several mountains. They are Mr. Kambourov from Sofia, Papaioanov from Petrousa and Stoitsos from Komotini. These people left in 1926 with the Kafantaris Accord as exchanged populations; they left, while Greeks from southern Bulgaria came to Greece.[66] They hired me as a

---

66   As the exchange of populations was going on between Greece and Turkey, the division of Ottoman Macedonia between Greece and Bulgaria created problems, which did not admit easy resolution. Greeks lived all over Bulgaria, especially Plovdiv (Greek Phillipopolis), while Bulgarians lived in Macedonia. These problems were addressed in September 1924 when during a session of the League of Nations the representatives of Greece and Bulgaria, Politis and Kalfov, signed a protocol in which they defined their obligations towards their minorities. The Treaty of Neuilly-Sur-Seine (1919) and the Kafantaris-Moloff Accord (1926) provided for the voluntary and compensated exchange of Bulgarians from Thessaloniki and for Greeks from Bulgaria. (See: "Foreign Banks in Bulgaria," The William Davidson Institute Working Paper No 537, University of Michigan Business School, Jan. 2003, p. 10.)

guard at Touloumbari during this past summer. They told me that I could set up a retail store in Drama and they would allow me to sell their wood and charcoal for a good profit. I told them that I do not know this business, but I know of someone that does. What we need though is 6000 Leva each, payable to these merchants for security. What do you say?" [67]

Wood and Charcoal Business (Drama, Spring, 1943)

After some debate, I agreed. To find 6000 Leva, I had to sell Elisabeth's venerable Singer sewing machine, which was a precious wedding present. I had the rest of the tools needed: sacks for charcoal, a weighing hand scale, a heavy axe and two large saws.

We went to work and soon we bought a cart to carry wood and charcoal to houses. We also bought a floor weighing scale which was capable of weighing larger weights faster. We rented two neighboring stores, on Chrysostomou Street from a man called Stylides. Each store was 4 meters by 6 meters. We filled the north one with charcoal and the south one with wood. After settling the investment for the equipment and space, we needed to accumulate some working capital. Since Nikos was illiterate, I was the bookkeeper. After selling each order, I logged it properly in the books, and paid for it. I gave Nikos detailed report on our activities, to make sure that I was straight with him.

Everything would turn out all right, except that Nikos had an ulterior motive. After he baited me in, he planned to milk the partnership at a higher percentage than 50-50, because he had the Bulgarian political leverage to do it. He started slowly, when he gave his 5 tons of wood for his family. Nikos' father, named Giantzo, after registering as a Bulgarian, also got a license from the occupiers to harvest lumber. They cut lumber for 15 days. Then, they had an accident and burned five acres of forest with their cigarettes. (If any Greeks did that, they would have been shot on the spot). Then, they bought an ox-cart and two cows to carry the lumber. He came over to ask for help to carry them. Every night we would take them from the pile to a location, named Touloubari.

67   A. Boinodiris, Book 1, p. 253 and Book 4, p. 95-96.

We carried 25 tons, from which 5 tons were taken to his father and 20 tons to the store. We sold the wood at the store at two Leva per kilo. After the sale, he refused to absorb the 5 tons of wood that was taken to his father.

"Nicola, please be reasonable," I said. "How are we to pay for the wood, the rent and the expenses we have, if each one of us takes merchandise without pay? Who is going to pay for my effort in cutting and carrying the lumber? Is this why you kept me from leaving to Germany, so that you can turn me into your slave? "

"If you want to live Greek, you better do exactly what I am saying. You will get only 0.2 Leva per kilo on all you sell to anyone else, but I am taking the rest. Otherwise, I will do you harm and you know I can do it."

He could really harm me, since he was registered Bulgarian and knew the language. All he had to do is go to the authorities with a false accusation and I would be sent to Korylofos to be shot. From that time on, I knew where he stood, but it was too late. He was a deceitful crook and did not openly show his true colors, but only after he entrapped me into this partnership. Now, I was his virtual slave. [68]

From that day on, he started appearing increasingly less and less at work. I alone had to go to Livaderon, cut wood, sell the charcoal and distribute wood to the bakeries, ceramic factories and other industries. When he appeared, he acted like as big shot. While we had to obey a curfew and be locked up at 5 PM, he was coming late at night after getting drunk in taverns with his friends, most of whom were Bulgarian police officers.

After two weeks, he came in, holding his jacket over his shoulder.

"Give me the key to the cash register."

"Wait Nicola, I will open the register and count our cash for distribution."

He smiled.

---

68   A. Boinodiris, Book 1, p. 254-255 and Book 4, p. 99-104.

"No. I want the key. From now on, all of you Greeks are our slaves. Starting tomorrow morning, the Bulgarian army will take over Thessaloniki. Greece is dead. With Crete gone, there is none that can stop the allies of Bulgaria."

My blood started boiling.

"You are a sneaky, thieving bastard! You really stopped me from leaving to Germany with the plan to enslave me. I taught you everything you know, including how to count your money."

I knew that I was taking chances when I talked to him in that manner. Yet, I also knew that he was smart enough to know that he needed me more alive than dead. (If Nicolas was a hothead by nature, I would not be alive now to write this to you, my son).[69] He smiled and walked out.

I kept working, trying to manipulate my sales to my benefit without him knowing it.[70]

One day we had a lot of work. Nikos did not go to the mountain. We had to cut lots of lumber. Due to time shortage, we asked someone to bring to both of us food. The food that we received was based on our status. For me, as a Greek they brought baked winter squash with a few drops of sunflower oil and some boiled hominy. To Nikos they brought a pot full of Bulgarian ham with six eggs, floating in fat and bread. As we were eating, three tobacco workers arrived to order wood, two Greeks and one Bulgarian. The Greeks showed to the Bulgarian what I was eating and what the Bulgarian-registered Nikos ate. I turned to them.

"I have not eaten enough food for several years now. I have been weakened from starvation. Yet, I dare Niko to get up and wrestle with me. What do you say Niko?"

"No way," he responded.

---

69   This notebook of A. Boinodiris was written in the late 1970s. This sentence indicates that he addresses these comments to the author, his son.
70   A. Boinodiris, Book 4, p. 102-105.

The three customers laughed and left.[71]

The Mechanics of Hate
(Dachau Countryside, Germany, Summer, 1943)[72]

Basil walked like an automaton, following a long string of prisoners. They walked in a straight line on a dirt road, leading to farms, where they were taken daily to work. In the front and the rear of the column, there were German guards on motorcycles with side cars. Each side car had mounted on it a machine gun. Besides these men, there were about a dozen more guards on horseback, armed with rifles and pistols.

"Attention!" said one guard. "Anyone that talks gets shot. Anyone that stops gets shot. Anyone that leaves the straight marching line gets shot."

Basil Leonides looked around him and wondered how in hell he ended up here. He was a good student. He had finished Drama High School, in Greece, and by working hard as a photographer, he earned enough money to study and learn four languages. Besides the Greek, he knew Turkish from the language spoken at home by his own family, the Aslanoglou family. He also managed to learn French and German and because he excelled, he was given a scholarship to the School of Journalism at Sorbonne, in Paris, France. It was there, in the spring of 1940 that World War II caught up with him.

He became a newspaper editor during the Battle of France and reported the French defeats to the bewildered citizens of Paris. He did not use his actual name, Aslanides, but his reporter's pseudonym, Leonides, which in fact translates to the same meaning: "Leo's son." Initially, there was some good news. On May 14th, 1940 two French tank battalions and supporting infantry counter-attacked a German bridgehead without success. The attack was partially repulsed by the first German armor. Every available Allied light bomber was employed in an attempt to destroy the German pontoon bridges; but, despite incurring the highest

---

71   A. Boinodiris, Book 4, p. 116-117.
72   This is a relayed story of Basil Leonides by Elisabeth Boinodiris.

single day action losses in the entire history of the British and French air forces, they failed to destroy these targets.

While the French Second Army had been seriously mauled and had rendered itself impotent, the Ninth Army began to disintegrate completely. In Belgium its divisions, not having had the time to fortify, had been pushed back from the river by the unrelenting pressure of German infantry. This allowed the impetuous Erwin Rommel to break free with his 7th Panzer Division. A French armored division was sent to block him but advancing unexpectedly fast he surprised it while refueling on the 15th and dispersed it, despite some losses caused by the heavy French tanks.

On the 16th both Guderian and Rommel moved their divisions many kilometers to the west, as fast as they could push them. On the morning of 15th of May, French Prime Minister Paul Reynaud telephoned newly minted Prime Minister of the United Kingdom Winston Churchill and said "We have been defeated. We are beaten; we have lost the battle." Churchill, attempting to console Reynaud reminded the Prime Minister of the times the Germans had broken through allied lines in World War I only to be stopped. However, Reynaud was inconsolable.

Churchill flew to Paris on May 16. He immediately recognized the gravity of the situation when he observed that the French government was already burning its archives and preparing for an evacuation of the capital. In a somber meeting with the French commanders, Churchill asked General Gamelin, "Where is the strategic reserve?" which had saved Paris in the First World War. "There is none," Gamelin replied. The French decided to create a new reserve, among which a reconstituted 7th Army, under General Touchon, using every unit they could safely pull out of the Maginot Line to block the way to Paris. Colonel Charles de Gaulle, in command of France's hastily formed 4th Armored Division, attempted to launch an attack from the south and achieved a measure of success that would later accord him considerable fame and a promotion to Brigadier General. However, de Gaulle's attacks on the 17th and 19th did not significantly alter the overall situation.

While the Allies did little to either threaten them or escape from the danger they posed, the Panzer Corps used the 17th and 18th to refuel, eat, sleep and get some more tanks in working order. On the 18th Rommel made the French give up Cambrai by a feint armored attack.

On the 20th of May also, French Prime Minister Paul Reynaud dismissed Maurice Gamelin for his failure to contain the German offensive, and replaced him with Maxime Weygand, who immediately attempted to devise new tactics to contain the Germans. More pressing however was his strategic task: he formed the Weygand Plan, ordering to pinch off the German armored spearhead by combined attacks from the north and the south. On the map this seemed a feasible mission: the corridor through which von Kleist's two Panzer Corps had moved to the coast was a mere 40 kilometers wide. On paper Weygand had sufficient forces to execute it. These units had an organic strength of about 1200 tanks and the Panzer divisions were very vulnerable again, the mechanical condition of their tanks rapidly deteriorating. But the condition of the Allied divisions was far worse. Both in the south and the north they could in reality muster but a handful of tanks. Nevertheless Weygand flew to Ypres on the 21st trying to convince the Belgians and the British Expeditionary Force of the soundness of his plan.

That same day, 21st of May, a detachment of the British Expeditionary Force under Major-General Harold Edward Franklyn had already attempted to at least delay the German offensive and, perhaps, to cut the leading edge of the German army off. The resulting Battle of Arras demonstrated the ability of the heavily armored British Matilda tanks (the German 37mm anti-tank guns proved ineffective against them) and the limited raid overran two German regiments. The panic that resulted (the German commander at Arras, Erwin Rommel, reported being attacked by 'hundreds' of tanks, though there were only 58 at the battle) temporarily delayed the German offensive. German reinforcements pressed the British back to Vimy Ridge the following day.

Although this attack wasn't part of any coordinated attempt to destroy the Panzer Corps, the German High Command panicked considerably more than Rommel. For a moment they feared to have been ambushed, that a thousand Allied tanks were about to smash their elite forces. But the next day they had regained confidence and ordered Guderian's XIX Panzer Corps to press north and push on to the Channel ports of Boulogne and Calais, in the back of the British and Allied forces to the north.

That same day, the 22nd, the French tried to attack south to the east of Arras, with some infantry and tanks, but by now the German infantry had begun to catch up and the attack was, with some difficulty, stopped by the 32nd Infantry Division. The British garrison in Boulogne surrendered on the 25th, although 4,368 troops were evacuated. Calais, though strengthened by the arrival of 3rd Royal Tank Regiment equipped with cruiser tanks and 30th Motor Brigade, fell to the Germans on the 27th.

While the 1st Panzer Division was ready to attack Dunkirk on the 25th, Hitler ordered it to halt on the 24th. This remains one of the most controversial decisions of the entire war. Hermann Goring had convinced Hitler the Luftwaffe could prevent an evacuation; von Rundstedt had warned him that any further effort by the armored divisions would lead to a much prolonged refitting period. Attacking cities wasn't part of the normal task for armored units under any operational doctrine.

Encircled, the British, Belgian and French launched Operation Dynamo and Operation Ariel, evacuating Allied forces from the northern pocket in Belgium and Pas-de-Calais, beginning on 26 May. Confusion reigned, as after the evacuation at Dunkirk and while Paris was enduring its short-lived siege, the First Canadian Division and a Scottish division were sent to Normandy (Brest) and penetrated 200 miles inland toward Paris before they heard that Paris had fallen and France had capitulated. They retreated and re-embarked for England.

The German offensive in June sealed the defeat of the French. The best and most modern French armies had been sent north and lost in the resulting encirclement; the French had lost their best heavy weaponry and their best armored formations. As the British were evacuating the Continent, a particularly symbolic event for French morale was intensified by the German propaganda slogan "The British will fight to the last Frenchman".

On 10 June, Italy declared war on France and Britain. On 21 June, Italian troops crossed the border in three places. Roughly thirty-two Italian divisions faced just four French divisions. The Italians suffered casualties of about 5,000 to French losses of only 8 men.

On June 14, the Germans entered Paris. All French newspapers were ordered to become German propaganda machines. It was then, that Basil's language skills were identified by some keen German officers. Knowing German and French, they immediately selected him as a candidate to write flyers and news broadcasts that help the Third Reich. Within a few weeks from the fall of Paris, he was taken as a prisoner to Hamburg. There, he was given a subsistence salary, an apartment and a job with the information ministry.

Everything was working fine for him. Other than the fact that he was a prisoner and could not go anywhere other than his apartment and his job, he had a good life. On top of that, he had a landlady that liked him a lot. She was a young widow, having lost her husband recently in the Battle of France and she looked after Basil and his needs. By Christmas of 1940, they started having some romantic moments together, enjoying each other's company. Who says that prisoners do not have some fringe benefits? Through his girlfriend he was also receiving news of the Greek victories against the Italians in Albania.

Then, George appeared. George was from Kastoria, Greece, and was given a similar job because he knew German, Greek, Slavic and Bulgarian. Basil immediately recognized his character. This was not a person to be trusted, because he was not a prisoner. He was a volunteer. He was one of those Slavic and Bulgarian speaking minorities that were born in Macedonia. When the Germans attacked Greece in 1941 and after they introduced Bulgarian troops as the occupying force in Macedonia, George found an opportunity to assert his doctrine of a Bulgarian Macedonia. Since Basil was a Macedonian, born by a Greek immigrant family from Asia Minor, he represented the enemy.

"We will make sure that you and your Seljuk family get packed and go back to Asia Minor!" he yelled at Basil one time sarcastically.

These Bulgarian-speaking, Bulgarian-thinking residents of Ottoman Macedonia were about to become a majority in Macedonia at the end of the 19th century through continuous attrition against the Greek-speaking, Greek-thinking population. Most of the Greek-thinking population had migrated to Western Europe. Then, during the Balkan Wars, the Greeks managed to defeat the Turks and the Bulgarians. These people were trapped, but had never lost their Bulgarian vision. Then, in a twist of history, with the exchange of Turkish-Greek populations in 1923, millions of Greeks from Asia Minor came and settled in Macedonia.

As far as George, and the rest of the Greek residents with Bulgarian alliances these immigrants had to go, or get eliminated all together. Or, at least, their willingness to stay in Macedonia must be crushed. Within a few months after Bulgaria joined the axis on March 1, 1941, George was on the attack. Under the conditions set by Germany, after the Germans overrun Greece and Yugoslavia, Bulgaria would own all of Eastern Macedonia and Western Thrace, plus the part of Yugoslavia that today is called the FYROM.

George immediately ordered Basil to write certain propaganda articles in several languages about the Bulgarian rights on Greek territories, especially Macedonia. Basil refused to do so. He suggested that if George wanted it written, he should write it himself, but he would not put his name on such an idiocy. To show his allegiance to Germany, George had to report this, while a rather naïve Basil underestimated the underhandedness of his opponent.

It was during those rainy days in the fall of 1941, when Basil, as he was sleeping in bed, felt the metal barrel of a Luger pistol on his head. As he turned, a man in a raincoat, ordered him to get up. He got up and in his pajamas was led to the Gestapo headquarters, his terrorized landlady following him all the way there. As he exited the door, she handed him his heavy coat.

"I am coming with you, to see why you are being arrested," she told him.

George, through the Gestapo prosecutor accused Basil on two counts.

The first and most serious charge was that of being a spy for the allies. He openly told the court that he saw Basil carry secret documents to his home in order to pass them over to allied agents. He also helped the Gestapo find some confidential documents in his office. Basil declared that none of it was true, and that he had never seen those documents (which were probably plants by George himself), but having one "Greek" declare these things on another Greek was deadly. As far as the Germans were concerned, George was a Greek citizen, who was pro-German.

The second charge was that Basil was a reactionary and liberal. George brought other German collaborators, who testified that Basil refused to cooperate in publishing German propaganda in Greece.

In the Gestapo held court, he was declared guilty on both counts and was ordered for execution within a week.

Basil had sat in that Gestapo high security jail for six days, knowing very well that his young life was over before it began. He was only twenty three years old.

As he was sitting in jail, crying and praying for his soul and hoping that his family in Greece would find out about how unjustly he died, his German landlady was going around all over Germany, trying to call on all the good graces of her husband's influence to save this young man from execution. The husband of his landlady was well respected because of his high rank and because he was posthumously decorated with the iron cross. He had friends in high places. These friends brought Basil's case to the attention of Reinhard Heydrich,[73] who was the head of the Gestapo since 1936.

---

73 Heydrich was assassinated in 1942 and Heinrich Muller would assume command of the Gestapo.

On the evening of the sixth day, a set of guards dragged Basil from his cell and brought him in front of a panel of officers. There, he was informed that his life was spared. His charges as a spy were dropped, but his charges as a reactionary and liberal held. He was to be sent to Dachau prison, designated as an enemy of the state to serve in prison for the rest of his natural life. The enemies of the state were categorized as: Communists (A1), Saboteurs (A2), Reactionaries and Liberals (A3) and Assassins (A4). The Gestapo also designated religious categories: Catholics (B1), Protestants (B2), Freemasons (B3), and Jews (B4). He was given the designation A3B1 because he was caught in France, and because the Gestapo had no designation for Greek Orthodox. They were taken to a Dachau sub-camp and placed in separate quarters where most of the prisoners were French and Belgians.

Dachau was a Nazi German concentration camp, and the first one opened in Germany, located on the grounds of an abandoned munitions factory near the medieval town of Dachau, about 16 km (10 miles) northwest of Munich in the state of Bavaria which is located in southern Germany.

Opened in March 1933, it was the first regular concentration camp established by the coalition government of National Socialist (Nazi) party and the Catholic party. Heinrich Himmler, Chief of Police of Munich, officially described the camp as "the first concentration camp for political prisoners."

Dachau served as a prototype and model for the other Nazi concentration camps that followed. Almost every community in Germany had members taken away to these camps, and as early as 1935 there were jingles warning:

"Dear God, make me dumb, that I may not to Dachau come......"

All these thoughts were passing through Basil's mind as he marched in a straight line on the dirt road outside of Dachau. This outing, to work on the fields was a relative pleasure. While caged up, he and his French and Belgian co-prisoners had it really rough. Four of them shared a tiny cell, and no toilet. Their food, which was nothing more than pig slop, was served in one bucket and water in another. They were to feed themselves with these and after that, use the same buckets for toilets. [74] At least now they were allowed to go out.

Suddenly, one of the Frenchmen run off the dirt road and headed for a field of clover. He dove into it and started eating the clover, pulling it from the roots and stuffing it into his mouth.

"Oh, no!" said another Frenchman. "Marcel has gone mad. He is committing suicide..."

He barely finished his sentence. The loud noise of a machine gun burst cut Marcel's clover feast. Marcel rolled on the clover field full of blood.

"Anyone else wants to try this?" yelled a German sergeant. "Keep walking and pick up your pace!"

The line continued towards a field, where a truck was waiting with mowing reapers. The prisoners were to be assigned to harvest clover, so that they can feed the animals of the German Army.

"You are not permitted to eat any of this," yelled the sergeant. "The animals can eat it, but not you."

Resistance (Drama, 1943)

The hellish occupation in our area of Greece caused further increase in guerilla fighting. The Greek fighting force of guerillas in Eastern Macedonia were of different political parties: the Nationalist Party

---

74   In total, over 200,000 prisoners from more than 30 countries were housed in Dachau of whom two-thirds were political prisoners and nearly one-third was Jews. 25,613 prisoners are believed to have died in the camp and almost another 10,000 in its sub-camps, primarily from disease, malnutrition and suicide. In early 1945, there was a typhus epidemic in the camp followed by an evacuation, in which large numbers of the weaker prisoners died. Together with the much larger Auschwitz, Dachau has come to symbolize the Nazi concentration camps to many people. Dachau holds a significant place in public memory because it was the second camp to be liberated by British or American forces. Therefore, it was one of the first places where the West was exposed to the reality of Nazi brutality through firsthand journalist accounts and through newsreels.

(supporting the King), the Democratic Liberal Party (Fileleftheron) set up by Venizelos, the Leftist Communist Party (ELAS: meaning Greek Peoples Liberation Army), and the Independents.

The Communist party was a small, but very active minority. These guerillas started going active, as soon as the Germans, Italians and Bulgarians entered the country. After the Bulgarian massacres, about 6000 Greek guerillas were dispersed throughout the Falakron Mountain.

Most of the guerillas were frustrated people like me; people who lost their families in the massacre, and orphan boys and girls. Some of these children were brainwashed into vicious killers, having very little hope of rehabilitation later on, when the war ended. One of them, named Rodopi, was a teenage girl of barely fifteen. She was brainwashed by some older children, ended up fighting with the communists in the mountains and was jailed for many years in a remote island. By the time she came out of jail, she was close to thirty years old.

The guerilla teams needed food, which they could not get from the burned up villages.[75] A meager source was available in raiding the storage bins of the local population. Most of their supplies were brought in from abroad by parachute drops.

The Button Messages

In order to coordinate their supply deliveries and their attacks, the guerilla teams needed communication with the allied forces in Cairo. Codes and messages were to be transported, verified and changed frequently. A deep underground network of trusted Greeks, who risked their lives, performed daily this task. In one such network operated Michael Aslanides, the brother of Elisabeth.

A message, in microfiche photo was brought by submarine at a specified night and location near Kavala. A fisherman was strategically there to receive it and deliver a response as well. He stuffed the received message in a fish; the fish was sold to a specific woman in Kavala. She went to a

---

75   A. Boinodiris, Book 4, p. 107-108.

local store, took the small film out of a small glass container and placed it inside a button, which matched the buttons of the woman's coat.

The woman then took the bus to Drama, where she went to the store of Michael Aslanides. There, she asked for a replacement button, because hers was falling off. Michael placed a new button, containing a small return message, with acknowledgements to be returned to the submarine via a similar route. The button that Michael kept was then placed on the coat of a peasant, traveling to his village. He took it to the guerillas at a specified location.

This method was used to exchange actual codes and messages. It seems that the guerillas were equipped with a portable device to view and create microfiche film. Each person knew his or her contact, but not the entire operation.

One day, the peasant did not appear. Michael knew the peasant's home and was told to take it there, in case this happened. He put the button on his coat and left in the dusk to deliver it. It was cold, it was getting dark and it started to rain. Unfortunately, as he neared a wooded mountainside he heard a Bulgarian patrol, but not before they heard him too. He hid inside some dense bushes for almost six hours, while the patrol was trying to find out what made the noise. By the time they left, it was daylight and he was half frozen. He headed straight to the peasant's house in the near-by village. He found out that the peasant did not come because he broke his leg. He left the button with him and in spite of pleads from him to stay and thaw out, he returned to his store, so that none would see any change in his pattern.[76]

The guerillas gathered in the mountains, in caves and remote mountain regions planning how to survive and disrupt the operation of the occupying forces. After the massacre of October 1941, the guerillas became a sizable force. They would have been a serious threat, if they were united.

---

76   These are memories of S. Boinodiris, as narrated by Elisabeth Boinodiris and Michael Aslanides in the early 1950's.

Frequently though, instead of fighting the common enemy they fought each other. I was close to joining the guerillas in the mountains two times. I knew the villages in the mountains well and could easily find welcomed support and refuge. Yet, I decided not to join because they soon started killing each other, Greek against Greek. During Christmas of 1942, 25 Greeks were slaughtered, killing each other in the mountains of Drama on the altar of political ideology. Communists and nationalists were killing each other, in spite of the bloody killings by the Bulgarians, the starvation and the suffering imposed on the population by the occupiers.

I did not want to have to kill a fellow Greek for any ideology. When faced with ideological discussions, I stayed neutral throughout all the civil strife among Greeks. I was not alone. Most of my friends did the same. If Greeks were united, the guerilla war in Greece could have made life for the occupiers unbearable.

Miller and Fostirides

During the occupation, a British agent called Miller operated in both Greece and Yugoslavia. He operated in Drama, working with the local guerillas, including the leader of the Nationalist group called Anthony Fostirides (Anton-Cavus) with the Turkish nickname of Anton-Cavus (meaning sergeant Anton, from his former military rank). Miller knew how to survive in those mountains. Men that served as guerillas under Anton-Cavus told me a story about these two men. They met in a barn, but there was a traitor among them, that betrayed them to the Bulgarians.

"You speak English?" Miller asked Fostirides.

Anton Cavus was an immigrant peasant from Pontus (Black Sea of Asia Minor), with very little education. Not only he did not know English, but he barely knew how to read and write. The closest he could understand of what Miller was talking about was "spiti" (meaning house in Greek) and "England." Putting both together, he responded in Greek:

"I don't have a house in England, but in a village close-by."

Laughing, a translator intervened and helped them communicate.

As the translator was helping them communicate, a whole squad of Bulgarian soldiers surrounded the farm, tipped off by the inside traitor on the meeting. After they surrounded the barn, they shouted for the group to give up. Miller went into action, telling them to take positions in front of the bales of hay and when told to shout that they surrender, tossing their weapons in front of them.

Miller took position on the floor, behind them, hidden by bales of hay and armed with a machine-gun on a tripod. As soon as the Bulgarians entered and gathered their weapons, he opened fire, shooting between the feet of one of the partisans, killing all members of the squad inside the barn. The remaining few outside vanished, when the guerillas faced them with their weapons, now a more superior force than they were.

Fostirides' lack of education was compensated by his keen intellect as a military strategist in running guerilla military operations. In one encounter, with a small force, he managed to trap much larger Bulgarian forces. One time he lured such a force in a ravine, after being sighted by a spotter plane, causing Bulgarian artillery to kill hundreds of their own troops in a friendly fire disaster. [77]

Jewish Extermination (Drama, March 1943)

Drama had about 250 Jewish families (about 1000 people), most of them merchants and professionals.[78] Not one was known to be farmer, but few were factory workers in tobacco factories; among these was a character, called Samugias.

Samugias was half bum, and half peddler; he sold cigarettes and matches. What was characteristic about him was that he was a foul-mouthed pest

---

77   A. Boinodiris, Book 4, p.106-107.
78   Based on records quoted from the Jewish Virtual Library, approximately 76,000 Jews lived in Greece: 55,000 in Salonika in the German zone, 6,000 in western Thrace under Bulgaria and 13,000 under Italian control. On March 4, 1943 all Jews under Bulgarian Occupation were arrested and imprisoned. About 200 escaped. The other 4,100 were deported to Treblinka. The extermination of Jews in the German and Bulgarian zones was completed by the summer of 1943.

of a character in the marketplace. He had no home, living like Diogenes in abandoned factories and houses in the winter. His preferred living quarters in the summer were outdoors, under the huge oak trees of Drama, still standing today in the City Gardens. He used to go to the market with his tray hanging on his neck, carrying his wares. The tray was covered by a wire mesh and had a lock, which he opened only to paying customers. Many, especially children seem to have gotten stuff from his tray without pay in the past. In response to such acts, they had to bear his extremely foul language that followed them for years. He had the memory of an elephant.

If someone ignored him, Samugias became very upset, saying that he failed in his job to be noticed. Before the occupation, he liked to have fun, especially in the Greek Mardi Gras, when he donned clothes to look like a Mayor, sporting a tuxedo, a tall hat and a false beard. He looked very important. He hired a coach and ran all around the town, waving at all the people and shouting foul names to those that ignored him. He must have gathered all his money throughout the year just for that one occasion.

One time he went to Thessaloniki to see his brother Moses. He told us that did not like the people there. He could not stay more than a month, in spite of his brother, who begged him to stay. We asked him why he did not stay, and he responded: "In Thessaloniki there are a lot of people, but there are very few human beings there."

"When the Germans came, they marked all Jewish establishments by a stamp, and each person had to wear a Star of David on their lapel. The Bulgarians were given orders to maintain this ruling, shooting anyone who violated this practice, or took the signs out.

Suddenly, at about February 28, 1943, the Bulgarian police and army collected all the Jews and placed them in the tobacco factories. Only one was left out, Samugias.

Since he had no home or establishment, the authorities did not register him. He felt strange, finding all Jewish homes and establishments empty. Without thinking, he said "good-bye" to all his friends and went straight to the police station. There, he used his sharp tongue, chastising the police officer for messing up things and leaving him behind. We never heard from him again.[79]

On the midnight of March 2, 1943, the Jews were loaded on locked train wagons, destined directly for Germany. This was not unusual, because several times Bulgarians rounded certain people up, including me, to be used for forced labor.

As I found out shortly later, this case was quite different; these people had no food, no drink no care for bathrooms, or for the sick and dying, until they reached their destination. It was a very cold March that year, and I doubt that they reached their destination without a good portion of them dying on their way. We did not know this until much later, through people working on the railroads, too late to do anything about it.

What remained was the bitterness of seeing people, ignorant of their destiny and led like animals to their slaughter in such inhumane manner. The only ones that survived were a few young Jewish men, who were drafted in the Greek army; these men followed the Greek troops to Cairo, after the fall of Crete, to fight in Africa and Italy with the Greek army against the Germans. There were close to 13,000 Jewish men in the Greek Army during the War. Those that fled to Cairo, returned with the Greek Army later and inherited all the property of the lost, Jewish community, as they related to the lost for 12 generations. Most of them sold their inheritance and left for Israel. Only a few remained.

Nevertheless, from all Jewish people, none made such an indelible impression on the population of Drama, as Samugias. His memory remains in Drama to this date, by those that experienced his humor. In fact, decades later, the name Samugias became an adjective, describing a person who goes out of his way to get attention from others.[80]

---

79 A. Boinodiris, Book 1; p. 41.
80 I distinctly remember my aunt Georgia chastising me around the mid-1950s for trying to get attention, by the expression: "Re Samugia, stamata tis ataxies," or: "You, Samugia; stop acting up for attention."

In the beginning of March 1943, the Bulgarians confiscated many carts and drivers from farmers for forced labor. As I was going to my makeshift shop where I sold wood and charcoal, a Bulgarian police officer ordered me to join him on forced labor.[81] He asked me what I do and I told him that I sold charcoal, showing him my license. He told me that he is commandeering my cart to get goods from Jewish homes. This included foodstuff, clothing, and furniture, destined for a tobacco factory, where they were all collected. In the meanwhile, I heard of several other officials and local opportunists that looted Jewish establishments and homes. Some did it by slipping a small fee to the police. Others simply walked in and stole it. Many hid their stuff at my store, which was closest to the Jewish houses, so that they can go and get some more.

After I completed the orders of the police officer, he asked me to help myself. I found my father, who knew Russian and after communicating with the Bulgarians, he joined me. People were carrying food and trying out pants, pullovers and shoes, inside an empty factory, where the police collected the stuff. These things were in high demand in that starving and poorly clothed town. When my little brother Paul found out, he went and loaded himself with 10 kilos of pasta and beans. My little son John got a jar of honey, and he was hungrily eating it with his fingers all the way to the store on top of my cart.

There was something strange happening that day. I distinctly remember that as we were helping ourselves to these goods we never asked what happened to their owners. No questions and no remorse; that is, no remorse until much later, when reports started arriving in 1945 about the fate of our neighbors. We did not feel remorse because we were in danger too. That food that we took from the Jewish families unquestionably would help us survive for several months. But after that, guilt befell upon us, which still remains within us.

We were all numb, after witnessing all that we did. We all had a strange look, as if we were continuously staring at something a million miles away. This lasted until we were liberated. Then, every time we gathered

---

81   A. Boinodiris, Book 1, p.39.

in groups and looked at each other, recalled what happened. We had visions of images of bloody bodies piled on carts, of roads slippery from blood, the swollen bodies of the elderly and the very young, lying in front of their homes dead from starvation. We also remembered the faces of our Jewish neighbors before they vanished for ever. As we looked at each other, we broke out in tears.

"Why?" I asked one time, turning towards the icons in the sitting area.

All we could hear was the sound of silence.[82]

A Light at the End of the Tunnel (Drama, Summer, 1943)

Early, in 1943, we realized that the war was turning around. Not because we knew what happening, but because the Bulgarian attitude started changing. I went and bought a Bulgarian world map then. When a Greek turncoat, whom I knew personally, threatened me that he would call the police, I took the map and showed it to him:

"See this map. It has changed already. You probably no longer have what you and the Axis powers had last year. Watch out on how you conduct yourselves. You do no harm to us Greeks, if you want us to allow you to stay here when the war ends. Otherwise, when the Bulgarians leave, you must also leave. And, guess what? They will hate your guts in Bulgaria."

---

82   In July 1942, 9,000 Jews of Salonika were called to forced labor. In October a ransom was set by the German civilian administrator of Salonika, Max Merten, to redeem these men and the 1.9 billion drachmas that the Jews paid drained all of the community's wealth. He collected jewelry, antiques, cash and anything else of value and supposedly loaded the treasure onto a fishing boat that he sank. On December 6, the Jewish cemeteries of Thessaloniki were also confiscated and pillaged. By March 15, deportations began. In the next three months, 45,649 Jews were sent from Thessaloniki to Auschwitz. Only a handful survived.
Merten brazenly returned to Greece after the war to search for his lost loot. In 1958, a survivor spotted him and told the police. He was arrested, tried and sentenced to 25 years in prison. The Greek Prime Minister, however, sent him to Germany after just eight months. He was retried there and acquitted for lack of evidence that he had rounded up Jews and stolen their property. He died in Germany.

Naturally, this was not wise on my part. If any one of those turned me in, I would surely be killed. They did not.

One day, in the summer of 1943 my father took me aside:

"I am interested in marrying again, if I find the right woman. That way, I will take my children back in the house."

"Why didn't you marry in 1938 or 1939? Why did you wait more than five years to take them back, now that they are almost grown up? We fed your children through the worst years of occupation and now you want to claim them as your children?"

"Yes. They are my children."

"Fine; you first find a good wife and then, and if the children have no problem living with her and do not object, they can go and live with you."

Meanwhile, Elisabeth had become pregnant by accident in 1943. She easily kept it a secret from me. She was so concerned that we already had too many mouths to feed, that she considered abortion. She was going to the local dry riverbed to carry sand, hoping that such heavy work would help her to abort the child. The Bulgarians had ordered the local population to barricade houses and public buildings from bombardment with sand that the civilians collected. Her older sister Kyriaki saw her and immediately understood what was going on. I on the other hand, like most men, had no sense to see it coming. Kyriaki confronted Elisabeth.

"How can I keep this child, when everyone around me is starving to death?" Elisabeth said crying.

"Do not worry. I will take care of your baby," said Kyriaki, who was childless.

She and Jordan had been trying unsuccessfully to get a child for years. Kyriaki and Jordan had adopted their niece, named Tasoula, a twin sister of George Zoumboulides, son of Anestis Zoumboulides, Jordan's brother. Unfortunately, Tasoula died from medical complications when she was two years old. Both of the twins had these complications caused by the drug thalidomide, used to cure nausea in pregnant women. These side effects were not discovered until it was too late for many children. On top of that, George Zoumboulides ended up with a degree of mental retardation and numerous other handicaps.

"I will baptize your child, clothe him and feed him with whatever we have, or can get in our possession," asserted Kyriaki.

Elisabeth came home and told me what was going on. I also told her about my conversation with my father. Elisabeth and I thought things out. The following morning, Elisabeth announced that she would keep the baby.[83] She openly told me:

"I have a feeling about this baby. I have seen Holy Mary in my dream, and she advised me to keep it."

As a result, we decided to keep the new child, making sure we were not left with only one child, after my father pulled Paul and Georgia from us. [84]

My work with the turncoat Nikos was a continuous torture. After all we went through we could use some good news. We soon got news that the allies would land in Greece. We heard that Germans mobilized, placing some heavy artillery on rails in the coast of Kavala. They also mined a great piece of land, right next to Nea Karvali. Years after the war, this minefield was fenced, but it claimed many victims, from unsuspecting children, to stray cows.

---

83   This baby turned out to be the author of this book.
84   A. Boinodiris, Book 1, p. 357.

Figure 8 Drama Train Station in 1930 [85]

Run for Your Freedom (Drama, August, 1943)

One August afternoon, in 1943, two large carts of lumber arrived and unloaded big logs of birch and oak in front of our store. I had a few hours to cut this wood and take it inside, before curfew started. If I left them out, the police would be after me. I hired another woodcutter named Charalambos and my neighbor Markos to help me out. Then I saw Nicolas.

"Thank God Nicolas. Please come and help me."

"You take care of it. I have better things to do."

He disappeared with his friends and as usual, went to a tavern to get drunk.

We finished the work ten minutes before five. I locked and started running home. As I was walking in the empty lot in front of the Drama High School, which was full of big marble blocks of stone, I heard an order.

"...Tsakai!" This meant: "Halt!" in Bulgarian.

---

85 This station and many like these were used by the Bulgarians, Italians and Germans to transport Greek Jews to Germany during the infamous roundup.

Two young Bulgarian scouts, in their late teens, stopped me. These scouts were used by the Bulgarians to perform light police duties. They were typically dressed in their uniforms, armed only with knives on their belts. They were recruited at the ages of 16-18, to train as police officers, or army officers.

"Greek, why are you late going home?" they said in Bulgarian.

By now, I knew few words in Bulgarian.

"... Rapota Terveni Vuglitsa." This meant: "I work in the wood and charcoal business."

"You can tell all that to the police superintendent downtown," one said to the best of my understanding in Bulgarian.

I knew that I was in trouble. If I went to the police station, no matter what, they would beat me up and incapacitate me for a minimum of a week, if I was lucky. Then they would send me to a jail, to await a hearing where I would pick up a kilo of lice. Suddenly I noticed my shoes, which had loose laces because I was in a hurry when I changed shoes before going home. I pointed to my shoes, bent down, and started to tie my shoelaces on the sandy field. As they were looking at me, waiting to tie my shoes I made my move. I moved so fast, that they had no reaction time. In a fraction of a second, I grabbed two handfuls of sand and tossed one to the first and the other to the second's face. Fortunately, my aim was good. When they cleared their eyes, I was nowhere to be seen. As I turned around the corner, I saw that they were still struggling to clear their eyes.

I started heading home in the shadows, my heart pounding. Then, I raised my head towards the starry sky, and after raising both of my hands, I yelled.

"...God! Why have you forsaken us? When are we going to see a day of freedom?"

What I did not know was that the allies had already landed in Sicily that day.

For several days, I was very careful, not to be seen during the day. The two scouts could easily recognize me. [86]

The Nasty Customer

During those guarded days, I was startled when an armed Bulgarian walked in. He had a handlebar moustache, a big, two-edge knife in a sheath, and a revolver, looking like a veteran of the Balkan Wars. He handed me a sack and pointed to the charcoal.

I started shoveling the first load, when I felt the gun barrel on my head.

From his Bulgarian words, I could understand that after he dressed my mother with all sorts of obscenities, he wanted me to fill the sack by hand. He did not want any charcoal dust.

My hands started trembling from anger. Then I started thinking. What if I disarm him and kill him on the spot. What would happen to my family and me?

"Topre Vospotin," I said in Bulgarian, meaning "Yes Sir," and started loading the sack by hand. I weighed 8 kilos of charcoal.

"Kolkou Iskas?" he asked, meaning "how much?"

The charcoal was selling for six Leva per kilo. I responded:

"Seisi osem, tsetirisi osem," or "six times eight makes forty eight."

He hands me fifty Leva. I dig in my pocket and hand him two Leva.

"Nisto," he barks at me, which meant: "forget it."

This big spender gave me a tip. Yet, what is left was the dust. He saw me looking at the dust and uttered a sentence, which meant:

"Sell the dust to the Greeks. We came here to guard you and we will eat the best, burn the best and live the best."

I responded as best as I could.

---

86   A. Boinodiris, Book 1, p. 268-269 and Book 4, p. 104-106.

"Sir, we came from Asia Minor into Europe, thinking that we came to a more civilized group of people. I am disappointed to see that we were wrong. How can a person draw a gun on a human being for 8 kilos of charcoal?"

He did not respond. He took the charcoal and left. I thought that he might not have understood my broken Bulgarian. [87]

John the Traitor

John Pais, Katina's husband, an ex-Greek from Monastiraki was among the first to register as Bulgarian and he was given a civil service post in guarding the graveyard of Drama. He was the traitor, who caused the deaths of six in my neighborhood, four of them members of Theano's family.

He came to my store once and grabbed four 20-kilo sacks of grade 'A' charcoal, selling for eight Leva per kilo. He was leaving without paying, when I asked:

"640 Leva please..."

"Tomorrow..."

Six months passed before I saw him again.

"John, why aren't you paying your debt of 640 Leva?"

"Charcoal sells for 6 Leva per kilo."

"That was grade 'A' charcoal. It sells for eight Leva. 6 Leva is the grade B charcoal, which has charcoal dust."

"Sell the dust to the Greeks. "

"Alright John; pay me 480 Leva."

"I don't have money with me now."

---

87   A. Boinodiris, Book 1, p. 270-271.

He left again without paying. This man would eventually pay for his crimes in the near future.[88]

Nikos (1943)

In 1943, Nikos V was becoming rich in the black market. He could buy foodstuff cheap from the Bulgarians during their occupation. Even though he needed one item for himself, he bought eight. Each one of these items he sold to the Greeks for more than what it cost him to buy all eight.

As a result, Nikos' black market dealing provided extra money to burn. In 1947, he bought the vineyard of Palanassos, close to him. His father Giantzos paid 22,000 Leva. The grapes were harvested by our women and I sold them all at my store. At this time, Elisabeth and Efthalia (Nikos' wife) were pregnant. They had good food to eat, since they ate grapes as they picked them. They eventually gave birth to boys, my son Stavros and his son John. After I had sold all the grapes and gathered 22000 Leva, I brought them over to his house. He had gone to Paranesti, a town to the east of Drama.

At that time, the communication center of the Bulgarians moved next to my house, at the house of Mr. Petros. As I was approaching the V house, I saw that most of the soldiers that were staffing that communications center were all out. They broke the fence to the vineyard and were helping themselves to the grapes.

I enter the house and see Giantzos.

"The soldiers are ravaging the vineyard," I said. "If you let them, there will be no grape left. Let us harvest them all and split them among us, before they are all gone. We can make grape juice, retseli and all sorts of other things. I sold all these grapes without any profit for me. This would be our profit."

"Alright, let's do it, "he responded.

---

88   A. Boinodiris, Book 1, p. 252 and Book 4, p. 100-101.

We went and harvested the grapes, weighed them and split them in half. The children were elated, since they had not seen anything sweet for many years.

After a week, Nikos V appeared. He called me to his home where his sister and son-in-law were stringing tobacco leaves.

"What did you do to my vineyard? You are responsible for this and I know it. What happened to the grapes?"

"I sold them before it got ravaged by the soldiers; I did it with the consent of your father and we split the harvest. That pays me for my labor."

"I would rather have the soldiers eat the grapes than you."

"Do you really mean what you are saying?"

"Yes. As far as I am concerned, your children do not deserve to eat grapes."

I left very upset, disturbed at how much evil fanaticism was buried inside this man.[89]

Bulgarian Nazis and Counter-Nazis

Meanwhile, a fanatic nationalist called Georgiev started a campaign of exterminating Greeks in all occupied lands. He started speaking in cinemas and public halls, inciting Bulgarians to rid the land of all Greeks, for the sake of Greater Bulgaria. He urged total extermination of Greeks, from infants to old men, similar to that preached by the Nazis. In spite of his rhetoric, he found strong resistance from the regional Bulgarian Bishop and the General of the Armed Forces. The General suggested that if he wanted to fight, let him fight the Greek guerillas in the mountains, but if one innocent Greek is hurt, he will go after Georgiev himself. At that time the guerilla activity was flourishing. The Bulgarian corpses were brought into the church of St. Nicholas. They were the soldiers' bodies that were sent to Bulgaria for burial.

---

89   A. Boinodiris, Book 4, p. 113-115.

Meanwhile the allies had invaded Italy, and the German troops moved out from Macedonia. News of the Italian campaign trickled through my brother-in-law, to be followed by news from Normandy and the Russian campaign. We soon heard about Italians fighting the Germans. We heard how several Italian officers and men were killed by the Germans in the Ionian Islands. [90]

Having no radio, we depended on Michael Aslanides to tell us what was happening. Anyone found with a radio was shot as a spy. At that time, we did not know how he knew, but he knew. It seems that one of his links (the woman or the peasant) had a hidden radio and was getting news indirectly from them. At that time, the Bulgarians were telling us about German inventions, like unmanned planes that were sent to England, which they bombed and turned back to Germany on their own. I later found out that they were twisting the truth somewhat in describing the V rockets. [91]

A Dream of Hope (October, 1943)

In 1943, the allies invaded Europe in South Italy and Japan had lost a big part of their fleet. We, the tired, starving masses under occupation started seeing light at the end of the tunnel. The happiest time was at the end of each day that we managed to survive, bringing the payment for our sins nearer and nearer every day to the end.

The Germans that we saw in 1943 were not the same arrogant ones we saw in 1941. I had met one in 1941, named Hans, who was in Drama shopping salamis and sausages from us before delivering us to the Bulgarians. He came back through Drama again. When I saw him, I asked him in sign language how he was.

"Africa, Germania kaput," was his answer.

---

90   Reference: Captain Corelli's Mandolin, by Louis de Bernieres was made into a movie by Universal Studios. This is a story, which widely varies from actual events, as noted by Seumas Milne on Saturday July 29, 2000 (see http://books. guardian.co.uk/departments/generalfiction/story/0,6000,348087,00.html)

91   A. Boinodiris, Book 1, p. 125.

His words were music to our ears. We knew now that the Germans could not last a lot longer and we, the starving, suffering masses of occupied people would be free again. We were lucky, because we were still young and could withstand the punishment of starvation and the fear of death.[92]

In October of 1943, while Elisabeth was getting ready to give birth, I had a strange dream. A beautiful baby was born to a couple. The baby had blue eyes and a rainbow was over his head. I woke up and told Elisabeth my dream.

"You will have a son and he will be enlightened, religious and truthful," she told me as she smiled.

"I hope God sees all of our suffering and hunger we went through, and considers them as a full payment for our past sins. Maybe God will provide us with some hope with this child. I only hope it is born healthy."[93]

We were desperate for a good omen, and we grasped on any encouraging sign we could imagine. We hoped that this child would turn out to be God-fearing and a truthful man of society. All the suffering, fears and starvation were all atonements that we had to go through for our past sins and those of our ancestors. This second son, given to us as a gift from God in the worst timing of our life, opened up our future.

After several years, we both looked back and thought what would happen if I had left for Germany. By the time I would come back, Elisabeth's birth cycles would be over and the second son would not exist. As the Greeks say, every obstacle in life may turn out to be for the better; anyway, for us it did. Nikos' trap that I fell into worked both ways. It made me suffer as a slave, but gave me a son that later would grow and become a scientist in America.[94]

---

92   A. Boinodiris, Book 1, p. 356-357.
93   A. Boinodiris, Book 1, p. 361-362.
94   A. Boinodiris, Book 4, p.131.

Meanwhile, in the later part of 1943 our food and bread started becoming more plentiful. The occupiers were broken down and in six months they would start leaving.

A Son is Born ... (1943)

In October of 1943, I went to get a permit for childbirth from the Bulgarian authorities, so that I could have the needed papers to run in the middle of the night (after curfew starts) to get a doctor. Instead of a doctor, I was assigned a Bulgarian midwife, who lived near the Kelekis Clinic, a five-story building on Venizelos Street. She was a kind-hearted woman that served us well.

On the Monday morning of November 15 1943, my wife Elisabeth gave birth to a son. The Bulgarian midwife helped the baby to life and took care of Elisabeth.

After she had finished the delivery, she came to me at the store.

"Anthony, you have a strong son. When he grows up he would go and bam-boom ... would kill many Bulgarians."

I laughed.

"Thank you for your services. Why should we kill Bulgarians? We are all human beings and Christians as well."

She often came by my store, after visiting Elisabeth, as I was cutting wood outdoors. She examined Elisabeth and the baby and gave baths to the infant. She did all that for 40 days. I started getting worried. "What is she going to ask me for a fee?" I thought. I gathered 4,000 Leva and asked Jordan to loan me another 4,000 Leva, so that I have the money to pay her. I knew very well that they might not be enough.

Around December 20, 1943 the midwife came to my store.

"Vospotin Antonief," she announced herself. "I am finishing up my duties with you. I will let you know when I will come for the final visit. Both mother and son are doing great in health."

Then she joked, smiling. "It must be all this diet that you Greeks are imposing on yourselves."

She appeared on 24 December, Christmas Eve, on her way to the house.

"This is my last visit. After this visit, the two will be in your hands."

She went and did her final examination, washed and played with the baby. She came back with Paul, Georgia and John trailing her.

"Why are they all coming with her?" I asked myself.[95]

I set a chair for her to sit.

"Everything is fine," she said. "They are now in your hands. Let me know if anything out of the ordinary happens and I will be at your disposal."

"I don't know how to thank you for 40 days of watching over my family," I said. "How much do I owe you?" My heart started pumping fast, expecting the sky to fall on me.

"Wait a minute," she said. "Let me find out your category. Oh, here you are. You are part of the poor class. You owe me exactly 980 Leva."

I gave her 1000 Leva and she gave me back 20 Leva! I was shocked. So shocked that she had to ask me what was bothering me.

"Aren't you asking too little for your efforts?"

"This is what the statute says and that is what I get paid."

"I must give you something as a gift," I said. "A goat...?" I was thinking of the baby goat we had just acquired from our hidden treasure. I also had two lambs and five rabbits.

95   A. Boinodiris, Book 1, p. 358-361.

"No, I want nothing," she responded. She pointed to the children. "You have all these children to feed. Now you have a fourth. They will be fighting each other for food, because you have so little. It is not right.

"How about a rabbit …?" The mother was ready to give birth again, so we would soon have a new crop of bunnies."

She hesitated, but since I persisted, she nodded.

"Fine, one rabbit..."

I sent the children to fetch the rabbit, which they brought in a burlap sack, while she waited in her chair.

"Can you spare three more sacks?" she asked.

"Of course," I said, handing her three sacks. She took the children with her, carrying the rabbit to her home. They placed the rabbit in a cage she had at her house and she took them indoors. She pointed them to the floor of a room, where there were piles of wheat, corn and beans. The midwife gathered these grains as gifts from visiting patients in various villages, from Nevrokopi to Philippi.

"Fill these sacks with grain and take them home."

The eyes of the children lit. They had never seen this much of food for years.

"How much can we take?"

"…As much as you can carry."

"Gee, thank you," said the children with giggles.

They went immediately to work, loading their sacks to the fullest. When they could not lift it any more, they had to empty some on the floor. Straining under the weight of the sacks, they went out, thanking the midwife Santa Claus. By the time they arrived at the store, they were dragging the sacks on the ground and were exhausted. They must have carried double their weight in grain.

From that day on, I felt that things were about to change.

Starting in 1944, I applied for a ration coupon for the newborn. They refused to do so, unless the baby was baptized.

I refused to let my son get baptized by a Bulgarian priest. Fortunately, for us, the child was in good health and there was no fear of its death before baptism. As a result, we waited.[96]

Early in 1944, I discovered that my father was remarried to his third wife, Helen. His best man and woman were Prodromos and Barbara Katranzis, who proceeded to tell me about the event before he did.

Tzoras

When things started turning badly for Germany in Russia, Hitler started requesting help from his allies. He called King Boris of Bulgaria to Berlin, requesting the Bulgarians to send soldiers to fight against Russia. Boris refused, since Russia helped Bulgaria against the Turks. Boris did not make it back to Bulgaria alive. The Bulgarian mission for the King's burial brought his body to Sofia, his capital. Someone had shot him with a pistol. Rumor had it that Hitler ordered his assassination. A rebellion against the Germans began in the late months of 1943 led by a Bulgarian communist.

In Drama, the Bulgarian spirit was broken. The funeral of King Boris was attended by a number of Macedonian komitatzides, the ex-policemen with baggy pants that harassed us all these years. Among those that attended, the funeral was my nemesis Tzoras. Although he had no Bulgarian connection, Tzoras, who was a Russian immigrant was among the first to register as Bulgarian and was involved in numerous treasonous acts which seemed normal to his distorted nature.[97]

---

96   A. Boinodiris, Book 1, p. 358-361.
97   A. Boinodiris, Book 1, p. 207 and Book 4, p.106-109.

Soon after the war, Tzoras was among the few traitors that were brought to justice. He was given a year's jail term for his collaboration with the enemy.[98]

My Partner Nikos ... (1944)

The times have changed in 1944. I was busy working just to avoid starvation. I transported a great deal of wood and charcoal in the winter of 1943-44. Many wagons were unloaded, wood split and I went home with little or no pay for it.

By springtime of 1944, the mountains were blossoming, not only with flowers but also with armed guerillas. By fall of 1944, traveling to the mountains for lumber and charcoal became so dangerous, that all fuel commerce stopped. Around September, the peak month for fuel sales the store was totally closed. The Bulgarians were feverishly discussing what to do. Do they stay, or do they leave? We needed food, even though there was no fuel selling business. As a last resort, I went to the market and started selling grapes, chestnuts and walnuts with Lazarus Charalambides. We managed to get some grapes from the vineyards of Mikrohori and a region, called St. Tryphon.

While I was near the hand pump, here came the wood merchant, Stoitsos.

"Hi Anthony...! We cleared the account with Nikos. The deposit of 12,000 Leva has been repaid to him. You can get your share of 6000 Leva from him and we have cleared our accounts. Now, we do not owe each other anything.

That same night I went to my partner's home and asked him outside.

"I like to have my deposit money back of 6000 Leva."

He did not respond to me. Instead, he turned his back and was ready to re-enter his home.

"Wait a minute. Who am I talking to? ...A wall?"

---

98   A. Boinodiris, Book 1, p. 207.

He shut the door behind him and locked it.

I thought for one whole minute outside the door. If I made a scene, he could shout for his Bulgarian friends at the communication center and I would be taken in instantly. I waited until January of 1945, when I grabbed him and forced him to dissolve our partnership. [99]

Filov (1944)

The Bulgarian President Filov visited Drama, to find out how to patch things up with the Greeks, now that the Bulgarians were loosing the war. Bulgaria started suffering the results of allied bombing, starting from November of 1943 to April of 1944. The capital of Bulgaria, Sofia was now destroyed. Filov called several Greeks that knew Bulgarian for a meeting. Among them was my neighbor, old man Vagenas, a woodcutter.

He told Filov:

"The Greek element is decimated from starvation and any of your words would go to deaf ears. Black market is rampant. Wheat is 50 Leva per kilo and corn is 30 Leva per kilo. The daily wages are between 50-100 Leva, no matter what you do. If you made available bread to the Greeks like the Bulgarians, that would alleviate the situation. That has to be at least 500 grams of good quality bread per person per day. The 160 grams of bread, most of it full of sand is not enough for someone to survive. How do you want us to be merciful to you now that you are fallen if you continue to kill us through starvation?"

Filov accepted the proposal. The Bulgarians started selling us more bread at the set price. The black market on bread died instantly. Stavros was lucky. He would not suffer the hunger that the other three children had to suffer.[100] At the same time, they relaxed regulations regarding baptisms by Bulgarian priests.

---

99   A. Boinodiris, Book 4, p. 114-115.
100   A. Boinodiris, Book 1, p. 358-361.

We soon brought Father Basil, the old priest of St. Panteleimon to baptize the baby and gave him the name Stavros. Stavros was also one of Elisabeth's uncles, who lived around the turn of the century and died young (in his 20s) from cholera in Constantinople.

Figure 9 A Recent Photo of a Typical Street of Drama, Greece

Raphael Lemkin: Genocide, a Modern Crime[101]

"ONE of the great mistakes of 1918 was to spare the civil life of the enemy countries, for it is necessary for us Germans to be always at least double the numbers of the peoples of the contiguous countries. We are

---

101   Published in the "Free World," Vol. 4 (April, 1945), p. 39- 43, by Raphael Lemkin , April 1945

therefore obliged to destroy at least a third of their inhabitants. The only means is organized underfeeding which in this case is better than machine guns."

The speaker was Marshal von Rundstedt addressing the Reich War Academy in Berlin in 1943. He was only aping the Fuhrer who had said, "Natural instincts bid all living human beings not to merely conquer their enemies but also to destroy them. In former days it was the victor's prerogative to destroy tribes, and entire peoples."

Hitler was right. The crime of the Reich in wantonly and deliberately wiping out whole peoples is not utterly new in the world. It is only new in the civilized world as we have come to think of it. It is so new in the traditions of civilized man that there is no name for it.

It is for this reason that I took the liberty of inventing the word, 'genocide.' The term is from the Greek word genes meaning tribe or race and the Latin cide meaning killing. Genocide tragically enough must take its place in the dictionary of the future beside other tragic words like homicide and infanticide. As Von Rundstedt has suggested, the term does not necessarily signify mass killings, although it may mean that.

More often it refers to a coordinated plan, aimed at destruction of the essential foundations of the life of national groups so that these groups wither and die like plants that have suffered blight. The end may be accomplished by the forced disintegration of political and social institutions, of the culture of the people, of their language, their national feelings and their religion. It may be accomplished by wiping out all the basis of personal security, liberty, health and dignity. When these means fail the machine gun can always be utilized as a last resort. Genocide is directed against a national group as an entity and the attack on individuals is only secondary to the annihilation of the national group to which they belong.

Such terms as 'denationalization' or 'Germanization' which have been used till now do not adequately convey the full force of the new phenomenon of genocide. They signify only the substitution of the national pattern of the oppressor for the original national pattern but not the destruction of the biological and physical structure of the oppressed group."

Philosophy of Genocide

"Germany has transformed an ancient barbarity into a principle of government by dignifying genocide as a sacred purpose of the German people. National Socialism is the doctrine of the biological superiority of the German people. Long before the Nazi leaders were unblushingly announcing to the world and propagandizing to the Germans themselves the program of genocide, they had elaborated. Like Hitler and Von Rundstedt, the official Nazi philosopher Alfred Rosenberg declared 'History and the mission of the future no longer mean the struggle of class against class, the struggle of church dogma against dogma, but the clash between blood and blood, race and race, people and people.' As the German war machine placed more and more defeated nations under the full control of Nazi authorities, their civilian populations found themselves exposed to the bloodthirsty and methodical application of the German program of genocide.

A hierarchy of racial values determined the ultimate fate of the many peoples that fell under German domination. Jews were to be completely annihilated. The Poles, the Slovenes, the Czechs, the Russians, and all other inferior Slav peoples were to be kept on the lowest social levels. Those felt to be related by blood, the Dutch, the Norwegian, the Alsatians, etc., were to have the alternatives of entering the German community by espousing "Germanism" or of sharing the fate of the inferior peoples."

Techniques of Genocide

"All aspects of nationhood were exposed to the attacks of the genocidal policy.

POLITICAL: The political cohesion of the conquered countries was intended to be weakened by dividing them into more or less self-contained and hermetically enclosed zones, as in the four zones of

France, the ten zones of Yugoslavia, the five zones of Greece; by partitioning their territories to create puppet states, like Croatia and Slovakia; by detaching territory for incorporation in the Greater Reich, as was done with western Poland, Alsace-Lorraine, Luxembourg, Slovenia. Artificial boundaries were created to prevent communication and mutual assistance by the national groups involved. In the incorporated areas of western land, Luxembourg, Alsace-Lorraine, Eupen, Malmedy, Moresnet, local administrations were replaced by German administrative organization. The legal system was recast on the German model. Special Commissioners for the strengthening of Germanism, attached to each administration, coordinated the activities designed to foster and promote Germanism. They were assisted by local inhabitants of German origin. These, duly registered and accredited, served as a nucleus of Germanism and enjoyed special privileges in respect to food rations, employment and position. National allegiances were impaired by creating puppet governments, as in Greece, Norway and France, and by supporting national Nazi parties. Where the people, such as the Poles, could not achieve the dignity of embracing Germanism, they were expelled from the area and their territory (western Poland) was to be Germanized by colonization.

SOCIAL: The social structure of a nation is vital to its national development. Therefore the German occupant endeavored to bring about changes that weakened national spiritual resources. The focal point of this attack has been the intelligentsia, because this group largely provides leadership. In Poland and Slovenia the intellectuals and the clergy were to a large extent either murdered or removed for forced labor in Germany. Intellectuals and resisting population of all occupied countries were marked for execution. Even among the blood-related Dutch, some 23,000 were killed, the greater number of them being leading members of their communities.

CULTURAL: The Germans sought to obliterate every reminder of former cultural patterns. In the incorporated areas the local language, place names, personal names, public signs and inscriptions were supplanted by German inscriptions. German was to be the language of the courts, of the schools, of the government and of the street. In Alsace-Lorraine and Luxembourg, French was not even permitted as a language to be studied in primary schools. The function of the schools was to preserve and strengthen Nazism. Attendance at a German school was compulsory through the primary grades and three years of secondary school. In Poland, although Poles could receive vocational training, they were denied any liberal arts training since that might stimulate independent national thinking. To prohibit artistic expression of a national culture, rigid controls were established. Not only were the radio, the press, and the cities closely supervised, but every painter, musician, architect, sculptor, writer, actor and theatrical producer required a license to continue his artistic activities.

RELIGIOUS: Wherever religion represented a vital influence in the national life, the spiritual power of the Church was undermined by various means. In Luxembourg children over 14 were protected by law against criticism if they should renounce their religious affiliations for membership in Nazi youth organizations. In the puppet state of Croatia an independent, but German-dominated Orthodox Church was created for Serbs, in order to destroy forever the spiritual ties with the Patriarch at Belgrade. With the special violence and thoroughness reserved for Poles and Jews, Polish church property was pillaged and despoiled and the clergy subjected to constant persecution.

MORAL: Hand in hand with the undermining of religious influence went devices for the moral debasement of national groups. Pornographic publications and movies were foisted upon the Poles. Alcohol was kept cheap although food became increasingly dear, and peasants were legally bound to accept spirits for agricultural produce. Although under Polish law gambling houses had been prohibited, German authorities not only permitted them to come into existence, but relaxed the otherwise severe curfew law.

ECONOMIC: The genocidal purpose of destroying or degrading the economic foundations of national groups was to lower the standards of living and to sharpen the struggle for existence, so that no energies might remain for a cultural or national life. Jews were immediately deprived of the elemental means of existence by expropriation and by forbidding them the right to work. Polish property in western incorporated Poland was confiscated and Poles denied licenses to practice trades or handicrafts, thus reserving trade to the Germans. The Post Office Savings Bank in western Poland, taken over by the occupying authorities, assured the financial superiority of Germans by repaying deposits only to certificated Germans. In Slovenia the financial cooperatives and agricultural associations were liquidated. Among the blood-related peoples (people of Luxembourg, Alsatians) the acceptance of Germanism was the criterion by which participation in the economic life was determined.

BIOLOGICAL: The genocidal policy was far-sighted as well as immediate in its objectives. On the one hand an increase in the birth rate, legitimate or illegitimate, was encouraged within Germany and among Volksdeutsche in the occupied countries. Subsidies were offered for children begotten by German military men by women of related blood such as Dutch and Norwegian. On the other hand, every means to decrease the birth rate among "racial inferiors" was used. Millions of war prisoners and forced laborers from all the conquered countries of Europe were kept from contact with their wives. Poles in incorporated Poland met obstacles in trying to marry among themselves. Chronic undernourishment, deliberately created by the occupant, tended not only to discourage the birth rate but also to an increase in infant mortality. Coming generations in Europe were thus planned to be predominantly of German blood, capable of overwhelming all other races by sheer numbers.

PHYSICAL: The most direct and drastic of the techniques of genocide is simply murder. It may be the slow and scientific murder by mass starvation or the swift but no less scientific murder by mass extermination in gas chambers, wholesale executions or exposure to disease and exhaustion. Food rations of all territory under German domination were established on racial principles, ranging in 1943 from 93 per cent of its pre-war diet for the German inhabitants to

20 per cent of its pre-war diet for the Jewish population. A carefully graduated scale allowed protein rations of 97 per cent to Germans, 95 per cent to the Dutch, 71 per cent to the French, 38 per cent to the Greeks and 20 per cent to the Jews. For fats, where there was the greatest shortage, the rations were 77 per cent to the Germans, 65 per cent to the Dutch, 40 per cent to the French and 0.32 per cent to the Jews. Specific vitamin deficiencies were created on a scientific basis. The rise in the death rate among the various groups reflects this feeding program. The death rate in the Netherlands was 10 per thousand; Belgium 14 per thousand; Bohemia and Moravia 13.4 per thousand. The mortality in Warsaw was 2.160 Aryans in September 1941 as compared to 800 in September 1938, and for the Jews in Warsaw 7,000 in September 1941 as against 306 in September 1938. Such elementary necessities of life as warm clothing, blankets and firewood in winter were either withheld or requisitioned from Poles and Jews. Beginning with the winter of 1940-1941 the Jews in the Warsaw Ghetto received no fuel at all. Even God's clean air was denied - the Jews in the overcrowded ghettos were forbidden the use of public parks. The authoritative report of the War Refugee Board published in November 1944, and the overwhelming new evidence that appears daily of the brutal mass killings that have taken place in such notorious "death camps" as Maidanek and Oswiecim are sufficient indication of the scope of the German program. In Birkenau alone between April 1942 and April 1944 approximately 1,765,000 Jews were gassed. Some 5,600,000 Jews and around 2,000,000 Poles have been murdered or died as a result of the extermination policies. Whole communities have been exterminated. It is estimated, for instance, that of the 140,000 Dutch Jews who lived in the Netherlands before occupation, only some 7,000 now survive, the rest being transferred to Poland for slaughter."

International Implications

"Why should genocide be recognized as an international problem? Why not treat it as an internal problem of every country, if committed in time of peace, or as a problem between belligerents, if committed in time of war?

The practices of genocide anywhere affect the vital interests of all civilized people. Its consequences can neither be isolated nor localized. Tolerating genocide is an admission of the principle that one national group has the right to attack another because of its supposed racial superiority. This principle invites an expansion of such practices beyond the borders of the offending state, and that means wars of aggression.

The disease of criminality if left unchecked is contagious. Minorities of one sort or another exist in all countries, protected by the constitutional order of the state. If persecution of any minority by any country is tolerated anywhere, the very moral and legal foundations of constitutional government may be shaken.

International trade depends on the confidence in the ability of individuals participating in the interchange of goods to fulfill their obligations. Arbitrary and wholesale confiscations of the properties and economic rights of a whole group of citizens of one state, deprives these people of the possibilities of discharging their obligations to citizens of other states, who thereby are penalized.

A source of international friction is created by unilateral withdrawal of citizen rights and even by expulsion of whole minority groups to other countries. The expulsion of law-abiding residents from Germany before this war has created friction with the neighboring countries to which these people were expelled. Moreover mass persecutions force mass flight. Thus the normal migration between countries assumes pathological dimensions.

Our whole cultural heritage is a product of the contributions of all peoples. We can best understand this if we realize how impoverished our culture would be if the so-called inferior peoples doomed by Germany, such as the Jews, had not been permitted to create the Bible or to give birth to an Einstein, a Spinoza; if the Poles had not had the opportunity to give to the world a Copernicus, a Chopin, a Curie; the Czechs a Huss, and a Dvorak; the Greeks a Plato and a Socrates; the Russians, a Tolstoy and a Shostakovich."

Safeguards and Remedies

"The significance of a policy of genocide to the world order and to human culture is so great as to make it imperative that a system of safeguards be devised. The principle of the international protection of minorities was proclaimed by post-Versailles minority treaties.

These treaties, however, were inadequate because they were limited to a few newly created countries. They were established mainly with the aim of protecting political and civil rights, rather than the biological structure of the groups involved; the machinery of enforcement of such political rights was as incomplete as that of the League of Nations.

Under such conditions the genocide policy begun by Germany on its own Jewish citizens in 1933 was considered as an internal problem which the German state, as a sovereign power, should handle without interference by other states.

Although the Hague Regulations were concerned with the protection of civilians under control of military occupants, they did not foresee all the ingenious and scientific methods developed by Germany in this war.

Genocide is too disastrous a phenomenon to be left to fragmentary regulation. There must be an adequate mechanism for international cooperation in the punishment of the offenders.

The crime of genocide includes the following elements:

- The intent of the offenders is to destroy or degrade an entire national, religious or racial group by attacking the individual members of that group. This attack is a serious threat either to life, liberty, health, economic existence, or to all of them. The offenders may be representatives of the state or of organized political or social groups.

- Liability should be fixed upon individuals both as to those who give the orders and to those who execute the orders.

- The offender should be precluded from invoking as his defense the plea that he had been acting under the law of his country, since acts of genocide should be declared contrary to international law and morality.

- Since the consequences of genocide are international in their implications, the repression of genocide should be internationalized. The culprit should be liable not only in the country in which the crime was committed, but in the country where he might be apprehended. The country where he is found may itself try him or extradite him.

- Since a country which makes a policy of genocide cannot be trusted to try its own offenders, such offenders should be subject to trial by an international court. Eventually, there should be established a special chamber within the framework of the International Court of Justice.

- The crime of genocide should be incorporated into the penal codes of all states by international treaty, giving them a legal basis upon which they could act.

- It is also proposed that the Hague Regulations be modified to extend to captive nations the controls provided for the treatment of war prisoners by the Convention of July 1929. Attempts to rescue or alleviate the suffering of captive nations have been hampered by lack of accurate information.

Germany has reminded us that our science and our civilization have not expunged barbarism from the human animal. They have merely armed it with more efficient instruments. We must call upon the resources of all our social and legal institutions to protect our civilization against the onslaught of this wanton barbarism in generations to come."

The Full Circle of Raphael Lemkin

Raphael Lemkin had gone a full circle from 1933, when he was making a presentation to the Legal Council of the League of Nations conference on international criminal law in Madrid.

Then, the concept of crime against humanity was about others. Now, it was about him, his friends and family. In those days, the concept of the crime - which later evolved into the idea of genocide - was based mostly on the experience of Assyrians massacred in Iraq during the 1933 Simele massacre and the Armenian Genocide during World War I by the Turks.[102] In 1934, Lemkin, under pressure from the Polish Foreign Minister for comments made at the Madrid conference, resigned his position and became a private attorney in Warsaw. While in Warsaw, Lemkin attended numerous lectures organized by the Free Polish University, including the classes of Stanislaw Rappaport and Waclaw Makowski.

In 1937, Lemkin was appointed a member of the Polish mission to the 4th Congress on Criminal Law in Paris, where he also introduced the possibility of defending peace through criminal law. Among the most important of his works of that period are a compendium of Polish criminal and taxation law, Prawo karne skarbowe (1938) and a French language work, La réglementation des paiements internationaux, regarding international trade law (1939).

During the Polish Defensive War of 1939, Lemkin joined the Polish Army and defended Warsaw during the siege of that city, where he was injured by a bullet to the hip. He later evaded capture by the Germans and in 1940 he traveled through Lithuania to Sweden, where he lectured at the University of Stockholm. With the help of Malcolm McDermott, Lemkin received permission to enter the United States, arriving on the East Coast of the United States in 1941.

---

102   For political reasons, the Armenian Genocide issue has yet to be declared as an actual event by the U.S. Government. In fact, most Americans are not aware of these events. In a recent poll by MSNBC, when asked: **"Should the United States formally recognize the World War I-era killing of Armenians as genocide?"** only 22% said: YES. The rest said: NO. Close to 2 million people participated in the survey. (See http://www.msnbc.msn.com/id/21253084). Also, in October 2007, by a 27-21 vote, the U.S. House Foreign Affairs Committee adopted the resolution, which formally identified killings of Armenians during World War I as genocide. Turkish officials acknowledged the killings, but vehemently objected to the designation "genocide." (See http://edition.cnn. com/2007/POLITICS/10/17/house.armenian/index.html#cnnSTCVideo).

Although he managed to save his life, he lost 49 relatives in the Holocaust; they were among over 3 million Polish Jews who were annihilated during the Nazi occupation. Some members of his family died in Polish areas annexed by the Soviet Union. The only European members of Lemkin's family who survived the Holocaust were his brother, Elias, and his wife and two sons, who had been sent to a Soviet forced labor camp. Lemkin did however successfully aid his brother and family to immigrate to Montreal, Canada in 1948.

After arriving in the United States, Lemkin joined the law faculty at Duke University in North Carolina in 1941. During the summer of 1942, Lemkin lectured at the School of Military Government at the University of Virginia. He also wrote Military Government in Europe, which was a preliminary version of his more fully developed publication Axis Rule in Occupied Europe. In 1943 Lemkin was appointed consultant to the U.S. Board of Economic Warfare and Foreign Economic Administration and later became a special adviser on foreign affairs to the War Department, largely due to his expertise in international law.

In 1944, the Carnegie Endowment for International Peace published Lemkin's most important work, entitled Axis Rule in Occupied Europe, in the United States. This book included an extensive legal analysis of German rule in countries occupied by Nazi Germany during the course of World War II, along with the definition of the term genocide. Lemkin's idea of genocide as an offense against international law was widely accepted by the international community and was one of the legal bases of the Nuremberg Trials. In 1945 to 1946, Lemkin became an advisor to Supreme Court of the United States Justice and the chief counsel Robert H. Jackson of these trials.

From 1948 onward he gave lectures on criminal law at Yale University. Lemkin also continued his campaign for international laws defining and forbidding genocide, which he had championed ever since the Madrid conference of 1933. He proposed a similar ban on crimes against humanity during the Paris Peace Conference of 1945, but his proposal was turned down.

Lemkin presented a draft resolution for a Genocide Convention treaty to a number of countries in an effort to persuade them to sponsor the resolution. With the support of the United States, the resolution was placed before the General Assembly for consideration. The Convention on the Prevention and Punishment of the Crime of Genocide was formally presented and adopted on December 9, 1948. In 1951, Lemkin only partially achieved his goal when the Convention on the Prevention and Punishment of the Crime of Genocide came into force, after the 20th nation had ratified the treaty.

Lemkin's broader concerns over genocide, as set out in his "Axis Rule in Occupied Europe", also embraced what may be considered as non-physical, namely, psychological acts of genocide:

"Genocide has two phases: one, destruction of the national pattern of the oppressed group; the other, the imposition of the national pattern of the oppressor. This imposition, in turn, may be made upon the oppressed population which is allowed to remain or upon the territory alone, after removal of the population and the colonization by the oppressor's own nationals." [103]

---

[103] Lemkin also outlined his various observed "techniques" on achieving genocide. For his work on international law and the prevention of war crimes, Lemkin received a number of awards, including the Cuban Grand Cross of the Order of Carlos Manuel de Cespedes in 1950, the Stephen Wise Award of the American Jewish Congress in 1951, and the Cross of Merit of the Federal Republic of Germany in 1955. On the 50th anniversary of the Convention entering into force, Dr. Lemkin was also honored by the UN Secretary-General as "an inspiring example of moral engagement." Lemkin is the subject of the 2005 play "Lemkin's House" by Catherine Filloux. Lemkin died of a heart attack at the public relations office of Milton H. Blow in New York City in 1959, at the age of 59. In an ironic final twist for a great man whose life was dedicated to the remembrance of millions of victims of genocide, only seven people attended his funeral.

Civil War Years

Departure of Occupiers and Traitors (Anthony's Memoirs)

The Germans left in October of 1944, after Bulgaria broke relationships with Germany, a few months earlier. It was during that period that the Germans were restricted to their barracks behind barbed wires. The Bulgarian leadership fell from fascist hands into the communist hands of Dimitrov. All insignia, from royalty to swastikas were replaced by the hammer and sickle. Their soldiers started wearing a red band on their lapels. The officers and soldiers that were slaughtering the Greeks out in the streets and at Korylofos were turned into civilians and new ones took their place. The new ones are now fanatically pro-allied. How fast did these people change their tactics? We knew then that the occupation was close to the end. We managed to survive it, thank God, not losing a single soul out of our family. [104]

When the Germans were leaving, they shelled the Bulgarian headquarters that was the old Tzimas mansion, on the road to Nea Amissos. The mansion still stands because the shells missed the target, but several innocent people were killed on the street in front of it, where the shells landed.[105]

The Bulgarians left in October and November of 1944, forty-two months after their invasion. A Bulgarian minister, called Musanov went to Cairo, where he met with Papandreou and Kanelopoulos, then in exile. They agreed to come to Drama by plane. They came to the city hall of Drama in December of 1944 with Musanov, a Greek Member of the Parliament from Serres, and two Greek army officers. One was company commander Choriambus and the other was major Prokos. On his sides, he had two Greek guerilla fighters. After kissing them, he gave a speech, summing it as follows:

---

104   A. Boinodiris, Book 1, p. 119 and Book 4, p. 109-110.
105   A. Boinodiris, Book 4, p. 109.

"Up to now, Greece and Bulgaria had their history written in bitter blood. No more blood."

Flags were raised of all the allied forces, next to the Bulgarian, from the stock of flags that they kept in the city hall. The Russian, English, American and French flags went up slowly; too slowly for us, who waited long time to see our flag. When the Greek flag came up, we were just as surprised as the Bulgarians around us.

The Bulgarians found a gold-trimmed, huge flag from the time of Metaxas. We all asked ourselves: where did they find it?

That moment was one of the three happiest days in my life. The first was when we were liberated, after leaving Turkey. The third was yet to come, when the communist government was kicked out of Greece, after they had committed so many murders against our innocent civilians. Two Bulgarian public servants (cinovniks) around me did not know the Greek flag. They asked amidst a thunderous hand clapping: "Whose flag is this?" Then, I, coming out of my cocoon hit my chest with my fist and said with pride in Bulgarian: "Assam Girski," or "Ours, Greek."

The moment was so emotional, that I was crying and laughing at the same time. The Bulgarians were dumbfounded with the emotional outburst from the Greeks that surrounded them. I heard one of them say to the other:

"Kolia, I came here because in Bulgaria they fed us propaganda that the Greeks were all gone and that the place was populated by Bulgarians. I have a tough time finding a Bulgarian here, among all these Greeks."

The dumbfounded Kolia replied:

"I do not want any of my children to fall for such a sneaky trick again."[106]

In spite of the 17,000 dead, there were 18,000 Greeks in Drama. These numbers were well known to the bakers, who had to furnish exact loaves of bread for daily rations. They knew it because they had to produce the exact number of loaves of bread for the Greeks and the Bulgarians.

---

106   A. Boinodiris, Book 4, p. 109-112.

The Greeks got a slice of low quality, black bread per day. This bread was heavier, because of a copious amount of sand in it. If it did not have the sand, it would have been healthier, because it contained bran, whose healthy qualities were not so well known then.

The Bulgarians got as much white bread as they wanted, averaging half a kilo per day. The Bulgarians that entered the region, together with those that converted were about 5,000. The flour and bread production was well counted every day, down to the slice.

The complaint of most bakers was that the rest of the starving Greeks looked at them with envy, because of their proximity to bread. What they did not know was that they were under serious scrutiny and some bakers were shot, for daring to take a slice off the left-over bread they made.

Late in 1944 and early in 1945 the Bulgarians were departing. First among the departing people were the Greek traitors.[107] Some of them stayed, under the protection of either the Nationalist or Communist guerilla armies, which they joined to save their hides. Others joined both sides, acting as double agents, because they did not know which side would win.

There were a few Bulgarians, who were good people and helped us. Unfortunately, most of the ones who came with their troops were scum, who found an opportunity to pillage Greek towns. They ravaged houses, businesses and especially the countryside. By the time they left, most of the forested areas were bare. Among the good ones was my neighbor, who was a midwife and delivered Stavros. She came to each of our houses and she bade us a farewell. They had nothing to be afraid of. In fact, we were sad to see them leave.

---

107   These traitors and their descendants would later raise the "Macedonian Issue" by claiming that they have property and heritage rights as "Macedonians." Many of them found life in Bulgaria very tough, simply because the local Bulgarian population could not stand having them back and discriminated against them. Many were forced to leave and immigrate abroad, to Canada, Australia and other places, from where they organized the "Macedonian Movement." (See http://www.makedonija.info/aegean3.html)

As the Bulgarians were leaving with their carts and families on the main highway, I happened to be there with my neighbor Charalambos Gagatsis. One of the Bulgarian farmers was given a Greek's farm, where he lived at Nea Amissos, where he grew wheat, corn and grass for animal feed. He also had chickens. I recognized him among the departing families, because he had sold us his grain and chickens at low price, after he found out that he was leaving. We bought his products together with someone called Theodosiades. This helped us some, but not nearly enough to compensate the loss of income to the farmer that owned that land. [108]

As he was departing, the Bulgarian farmer approached me:

"We came to this land of Macedonia three times and we left three times. The next time, even if they kill me I am not coming back."

Early in 1945, as I was trying to build a grocery store in the building of Stylides, on Chrysostomou Street, I saw Lakis Samaras and George Kasapis, the two turncoat friends that tried to enlist me as Bulgarian walking on the street. I called them into my store.

"I want you to see," I said "that I am not dead, even if I did not register as Bulgarian. I am ashamed for you, not only because you were turncoats, but because of your ironic toying with our hunger." I turned to Samaras. "I don't know about George, but you were from a good Greek family, and finished the Greek High School of Alistrati. I am ashamed of you, who buckled in the face of these dogs."

It so happened that at that time our priest was passing by. His name was Father Theodoros, a priest in the church of St. Panteleimon. He heard me yelling and asked for details. I discovered later that Father Theodoros expelled Lakis from the church one day. Lakis Samaras was part of the chanting group in his church.

"Go and sing in a choir in Bulgaria," the priest told him in the middle of the liturgy, when he discovered what Lakis had done.

---

108   A. Boinodiris, Book 1, p. 271-272.

Both of these traitors were withdrawn, feeling contempt and shame for their actions. The people of Drama were peaceful and did not harm these people. [109] Sometimes the past is something you just can't let go of. And sometimes the past is something we'll do anything to forget. And sometimes we learn something new about the past that changes everything we know about the present.

When the people of Drama looked at these traitors, they saw pitiful wretches of their own friends and neighbors, too weak to withstand the pressures of hunger and misery and who were willing to sell their honor and dignity for survival. These few had not harmed personally anyone.

Those that did harm people though, could not be forgotten. Many escaped to Bulgaria, but even there they were persecuted and an unknown number of them fled to southern Yugoslavia, later to become the Former Yugoslav Republic of Macedonia. There these "Greece-born" traitors converted to communism and intermixed with the other resident traitors that turned against their Serb allies in 1941, and joining the Germans when they occupied Greece. All these people that lost their dignity and honor wanted to forget what happened.

All survivors learned a lot about themselves, about their strengths and weaknesses. Those lucky ones that managed to survive with their honor intact felt as if they were much stronger than they thought before the war. Even though they had lost friends and relatives and had their properties destroyed, they knew that can look for better days ahead.

---

109   A. Boinodiris, Book 1, p. 120.

**Figure 10 Anthony Boinodiris right after
the Occupation (from a photo ID)**

Nikos in Trouble - Repaying Evil with Good[110]
(Drama, January, 1945)

Around the first days of January of 1945, when the Bulgarians left and ELAS was ruling the city of Drama, I called Nikos to come and clear our partnership.

He walked into the store looking depressed and white. The tables were turned around and he was concerned that I might do him harm this time. His friends, the Bulgarians that were in the communications center were all gone and he had none to back him up.

We both knew that I could do it. During that period, if anyone went to ELAS and fingered a person as registered Bulgarian who did, or even said something unjust to them, that person could be shot. All it

---

110   A. Boinodiris, Book 1, p. 256-258 and Book 4, p. 117-120.

took was a short military "court," ran by a handful of guerillas. The communists dealt with their ex-enemies in a fast, harsh and many times unjust manner. All they needed was a couple of witnesses to verify an allegation and the accused was doomed.

I brought in Lazarus Charalambides and the elderly Lukas, both of which knew first-hand my history with Nikos V, to be witnesses as I went through the books. He agreed that he owed me 50000 Leva plus my 6000 Leva of security money, promising to pay me next day.

Nikos disappeared the next day. He was nowhere to be found to fulfill his payment.

I heard a few days later that he joined the guerillas of Vathilakos under Kotza (Turkish, meaning "big") Basil, a Nationalist army group of Anthony Fostirides. Nikos was now an accomplished double agent, betraying one side to the other for profit. Some of his tasks included to transport money and messages for the nationalist guerillas. Aircraft from Egypt were frequently making drops of money, messages and material behind the Falakron Mountain as part of the effort to link up operations with the Greek guerillas.

I felt like a fool, for sticking with what I believed in. I suffered all these years, only to see others make money from my suffering and now become national heroes by switching sides the last minute. The only redemption I saw was that even after all this work and suffering, we ended up being stronger than those who had all that rich food while we were starving. The vegetable diet that was available to us made us healthier. It is true that whatever does not kill you makes you stronger.[111]

I knew that I was not going to be paid by him. I kept all the tools of the trade plus some kindling wood, which paid for the security money he owed me. I wrote off my losses as a payment towards my survival out of this hell we went through.

To recover my business, I joined with Lazarus Charalambides; I kept one of the Stylides stores for charcoal, but also moved into an empty

---

111   A. Boinodiris, Book 4, p. 115-117.

store near the market and made it a grocery store. A Jewish man who had disappeared owned that store. [112]

On Friday morning, January 12, 1945 I was tending my onions in the garden of my house, when I saw two armed men of ELAS in their military uniforms approaching me. Each had a rifle, and a pistol butt showed on their waist, as their open overcoats opened up as they walked.

One of them had a notebook in his hands, which I recognized. It was an official search warrant, which had a number of entries, regarding findings of the search.

"Good day comrade," said the short one with a dark complexion.

"Good morning," I replied.

"Come with us," ordered the taller one. I washed my hands in the bucket of water and followed them.

"What is your name comrade?" said the short one.

"Anthony Boinodiris."

"Anthony, I am from Nigrita of Serres and now a member of the ELAS security. My partner is from Kornofolia of Evros. We want you as our witness."

"Where are we going comrade?" I asked.

"We are going to search that tall house," he said by pointing to Nikos' house. Do you know them?" I nodded affirmatively.

"We had a blind man, led by a 12-year old boy who visited our division headquarters this morning," he continued. "He accused Nikos V of supplying material to the Nationalist Army at Monastiraki."

That was true. Although ELAS was ruling Drama, the Nationalist Army had its headquarters only 5 kilometers away, at Monastiraki that was visible from where we were. The communist army of ELAS

---

112   A. Boinodiris, Book 4, p. 103-105.

could not have a spy mole in their jurisdiction passing supplies to their enemies. Such an accusation was a shooting offense, to say the least.

By the description of the blind man, I knew instantly who accused Nikos. It was old man Kouroukafas, with his 12-year old grandson Dimitris. They suffered a lot from the Bulgarians and Nikos had a good deal to do with it.

"Comrade, I must ask you to be excused from this task," I said. "We were partners during the war and these people would think that I came and accused them. I have a family which must live with these people in the same neighborhood."

"Don't worry comrade. We have families too. We will explain who accused Nikos and the fact that we brought you here by force. You must be a witness of what we find and a witness that we did not steal anything or harm anyone without just cause."

Then, he took off a notebook from his pocket and showed it to me.

"After the search, you must witness this book with your signature giving a report on the search"

We started walking north, towards Nikos' house. A strong, cold, January wind was blowing from Falakron (Baldheaded) Mountain, visible directly to the north of us. On our way, we saw Thanasis Hatzioanides, sitting on his sheltered porch, smoking. The short one, who seemed to be the brains, sent the taller to fetch him.

All four of us headed for the house of Nikos.

The house was a two-story brick building with a barn at the rear. It was standing all by itself, with open fields all around it. The closest houses to it were that of Charalambos Kertikoglou to the East and Thanasis Hatzioanides to the NE, both at a distance of more than 30 meters. The fields to the North were stretching all the way to the mountains. The fields to the West stretched also for many kilometers into the plain of Drama.

As we approached the house, Nicola's wife Efthalia came out of the door. Next to her comes Nicola's father, old man Giantzo. She held a baby boy in her arms (named Chris) and her sister Chrysanthi was holding a young toddler of two (John) and a boy of about six (named Lakis).

"Good day comrade lady," said the short soldier from Nigrita, while the other took off his rifle and took a defensive position in front of the door.

The short soldier went and talked to Efthalia.

"Where is your husband, Nicolas V?"

"He is at our village home, trying to do some repairs."

"We have orders to search your house. We forced two neighbors of yours to act as witnesses. Your accusers are at our headquarters and have no connection to these two. Do you understand? "

Efthalia nodded her head.

The short one went into the house and searched both floors and the ceiling rafters, which were full of drying tobacco. House lofts were ideal in drying tobacco leaves. He found nothing, except some photographs of Nicola. He took two of them, one military and one civilian and came out.

"Is this your husband?"

"Yes."

"Old man," said the soldier from Nigrita. "Take your animals out of the barn."

Old man Giantzo went and took several cows out of the barn, leading them to the fields to the west to feed. In a few minutes, he was out of sight and out of harm's way.

The short man went inside the barn.

As he did that, Efthalia passed the baby to her sister Chrysanthi and moved closer to us, the witnesses. I noticed then that her face started to become white and her hands were shaking.

"Something must be inside that barn..." I thought to myself.

I moved towards the barn, to watch the short man. Efthalia followed me, shaking like a leaf.

The barn was partitioned with reeds. Deep inside the barn was packed with straw for the animals.

"Do you have a hoe?"

"No!" responded Efthalia.

The soldier found a pick with which he easily made an opening on the reed barrier.

Efthalia started shaking even more.

The short soldier went into that straw like a mole. He went left, reached the left corner and then all the way to the opposite corner. He came out, his face covered with straw to breathe some air.

Efthalia breathed with relief.

"He did not find anything," I thought.

Both of us were wrong. The soldier took a deep breath and dove in again, plowing his way at the center of the packed straw. As he dove in, Efthalia buckled limp in my arms and almost fell down from fear. The baby, in the hands of Chrysanthi started crying.

As I was trying to support her, I heard the mole.

"I found me a treasure."

I turned to see the soldier from Nigrita, covered with straw, pulling something out of the opening of the reed barrier. It was a huge bundle, made out of silk.

When the bundle was brought out in the open, we saw that it was a parachute. The man from Nigrita started opening it up and revealing its contents. They consisted of wool sweaters, jackets and military clothing from underwear, socks, pants, tops, hats and belts. The baby continued to cry.

"Comrade-lady, you have some explaining to do," he said after turning to Efthalia. Then he turned to Thanasis and me.

"You two must come and sign this notebook, after you write first your name and address in capital letters."

After we did that, he ordered.

"Comrade-lady, I want you to come with us to division headquarters and carry this bundle with you. The witnesses must come too."

Efthalia was dazed and she had watery eyes. Her motherly instinct took over and she uttered:

"Please, can you excuse me comrade a few minutes? I must feed my baby before I go."

"Of course, go ahead."

Efthalia and Chrysanthi took the baby Chris indoors to be breast-fed.

The armed men took Nicola's photos and were studying them in front of the entrance on the south side of the house, sheltered from the cold, northerly wind. Then, the man from Nigrita started writing his report on his notebook. Thanasis offered them tobacco and paper. They accepted it and started rolling their cigarettes on a wooden bench, attached to the house, next to the entrance.

I decided to walk a bit. As I was walking along the house's east wall, I saw at a distance the shape of Nicolas walking towards his house. Unaware of our presence, he was coming from the plowed fields of the north.

My heart started pumping hard. If I did nothing, I could get my revenge on this bastard, this traitor and crook. When he clears the house, he will face the ELAS men with two of his photos in their hands. But, if I was to do something, I only had a few seconds to do it.

"Excuse me comrades, I need to go and relieve myself. I have not done so since this morning."

"Go ahead comrade," said the man from Nigrita.

I walked fast on the north side, making sure that the armed men do not see me. Nicolas was at quite a distance, but there was a little boy, named Costas Kigmatoglou playing and watching the whole scene. I nodded him to come. While I was pretending to pee, I talked to the boy in a low voice:

"Costa, go to Nicolas and tell him to disappear. Two soldiers from ELAS are waiting in front of his house to shoot him and they found a stash of stuff in his barn. Go silently and tell him, without being noticed. Tell him to hide at Thanasis' home and save his life. "

The surprised boy took off.

I turned back after unbuttoning my fly first and then started re-buttoning it, to show that I did what I was supposed to do.

Costas caught Nicolas just in time. Nicolas ran to the north, made a big loop and hid at the house of Thanasis Hatzioanides. I returned to the south side of the house.

Efthalia got ready to leave. Then I asked:

"Comrades, do you really need me at headquarters? I have a charcoal store to open today and if I do not, several customers will have no fuel. I already witnessed the notebook."

The man from Nigrita looked at me:

"Probably not... We need one witness at headquarters and Thanasis can be the one. You are excused comrade."

As I was leaving, the soldiers took Efthalia with her bundle and Thanasis and followed me all the way home. As I entered, I saw them going south, towards the ELAS headquarters.

As I was changing to my work clothes, I told Elisabeth the events.

"I could not do it Elisabeth, in spite of how much of a fiendish thief and traitor this sneaky bastard is. I could not face his children later on in life and tell them that I could have saved their father's life, but did not. Once, I went through the route of the Law of Moses but did not like it a bit. I served twenty two months in jail, when I sought revenge. At the tiny church of St. Eleutherios of the jail, I vowed not to seek revenge on anyone, no matter what they did to me. I simply could not go back. None could make me go back, even if they threaten to kill us, or starve us to death."

"I did not think that you could Anthony," said Elisabeth. "That is why I love you. Keeping our conscience clear is much more important than having food on the table and roof over our heads. Anyway, how much more can they harm us?"

"Not much Elisabeth."

I departed for the store, to push my handcart around the neighborhood full of charcoal and survive an extra day. That day, as I was pushing my cart, I felt a lot stronger and more confident than previous days.

"Are we going to make it Anthony?" I asked myself.

"You bet we are," I responded. "God willing..."

That same night, Thanasis told me the news. In the ELAS headquarters, the communists interrogated Efthalia for several hours. They told her that if her husband does not surrender in 10 days at headquarters, their house will be torched and all contents will be confiscated.

Being a double agent, Nikos rushed and found some connections in ELAS, who enlisted him in their group; he took an old rifle and his friends with him and appeared at ELAS headquarters. He pretended that he got confused and got in contact with the Nationalist group by mistake, justifying how he received all the supplies in the parachute. The skeptical ELAS held him in prison for 20 days, to see if anyone else had anything against this man. Then they let him free. In that fashion, Nicolas escaped, simply by joining both sides of the Civil War.[113]

It was around the end of February, when Nicolas walked into my house one night.

"Anthony. I know you think that I am not much of a human being, but for whatever it is worth, I must tell you that you did a good deed. Not because you saved my life, but because you saved the life of many other people."

"What are you talking about Nicola?"

"If I was caught, many others would have been killed besides me. With me, I had dozens of letters and payment money in gold, to be delivered to the families of members of the National Army. So, they are the ones that should thank you."

He turned his back and left me with my mouth open. I was shocked. The priest in the jail was right. By applying Moses' Law of an "eye for an eye," you may unknowingly hurt yourself and your friends more than the intended target.[114]

Recovery of 1945-1950 (Anthony's Memoirs)

Around May 1, 1945 the Greek army appeared, supported by British troops. The convoy was long, reaching all the way from Thessaloniki to the Evros River at the Turkish border. This gave us quite a relief.

During this time, since the days that the Bulgarian troops left, we were under pressure from the communist guerillas to join their groups. If we refused and had no good reason for it, we could be shot for counter-revolutionaries. These acts followed, right after the defeat of the communists in Athens in December of 1944. We also heard the

---

113   To avoid further detection from those he mistreated in the past, at around 1950 Nikos V-ov changed his name to V-is.

114   A. Boinodiris Book 4, p. 117-120.

news of a massacre at Kornofolia of Evros, where they killed many of its inhabitants. We were extremely scared of our own brothers, more than we ever were of the Bulgarians. [115]

Nicolas did not pay me my 50,000 Leva that he owed me. He delayed payment until the Greek Government was formed and the Ministry of Economics and Government Coordination under Svolos abolished any debts owed by anyone during the period of War. So, all of his debts were legally wiped clean. What an irony?

A few months after liberation, the Jewish man whose store we occupied up to now appeared. He was lucky, because several Greek families from Drama hid him and his family from holocaust. Lazarus Charalambides and I had to relinquish our store after a relatively short deadline.

I went back to running a grocery store and a charcoal outlet, but I had no money. I sold the scale, cart and 1000 kilos of fire starting wood and got 6,000 Leva. With this money, I partnered with someone named Eustathius Stratis from Kalos Agros and started again selling wood and some basic grocery items at a store owned by Stylides at Chrysostomou Street.

We went into business with almost equal assets. He put some capital, but mostly corn, wheat, flour, lentils, chickpeas and 110 Oka of powdered fenugreek, or "tsemeni powder" used for making tsemeni paste. This paste is used to seal pastourma, the Greek version of beef jerky. We used both stores, one next to the other. We did fine during that winter by improvising. Food variety was still scarce in 1945, but certain basics were now getting into the market.

Instead of rice, we had cracked wheat. Instead of wheat flour, we used corn flour. Instead of sugar, we had petmezi and retseli, made out of grape juice. We made our own dough and dried it for pasta. For ouzo, we used home made tsipuro, which also doubled as rubbing alcohol. Wine was plentiful. For soap, we either used a black Bulgarian soap that was left over, or did not bathe. Lice were plentiful in people. Milk products started to become increasingly plentiful, from animals that the households now started to breed. Drama became a town of herders,

---

115   A. Boinodiris Book 4, p.112.

having goats in their back yards. Fruits and vegetables started to become plentiful, because people started planting onions on the street sidewalks. In spite of the relief, by today's standards our diet was limited and monotonous.[116]

What was non-existent was clothing and shoes. Most of our clothes were in rags. We made shoes out of old wooden planks and discarded tires or belts. Most kids were barefooted.

Finally, around late spring of 1945 we started getting some outside help. [117]

At that time, my partner went back to his village to work on his fields and I was left alone to take care of the store. We made a deal, that I take over for him and in return, he will plant four hectares of melons on my behalf.[118]

The Melon Bombardment (Drama, Summer of 1945)

When time came for my melons to be sold, my partner changed his mind. As he was coming to the store with them, he sold them to stores in Drama and kept the money. He came to the store with five or six beaten melons. After realizing that, I told him that he owed me and he should bring me the melons the next time, so that we can sell them to the tobacco factory workers. [119] He promised to do so.

The next day he again came with the leftovers of his own sale. This business lasted five days. The fifth day, when he brought the bruised melons to me, my blood started boiling. I took the sack of the melons, put it on my back and started chasing him in front of my store, aiming each melon straight to his head.

"You are a filthy peasant," I yelled. "What made you think that you can toy with me? I worked my hands off to gather capital for our operation. Why are you are trying to steal away from it?"

116 A. Boinodiris Book 4, p.120-122.
117 A. Boinodiris, Book 1, p. 261.
118 A. Boinodiris Book 4, p.112-114.
119 A. Boinodiris, Book 1, p. 263.

Each word I uttered, a new soft melon hit his head and back. The melon bombardment lasted until all melons were depleted.

"Today, I am splitting up with you, with or without the melons."

We planned to partition everything. The store stayed closed for a week. After one week, he brought a referee, someone named Dimitris Zemoglou. I also brought a person named Agapios Akojun, an Armenian refugee. I told my partner and his partner the events that transpired.

They both took my side.

"Why didn't you bring the melons you promised to Anthony? He was working at your partnership while you were cultivating your fields," said Dimitris.

"He is lying. He does not have any papers to prove any promises on my part to give him part of my crop."

I blew up again.

"You are a villain. In a partnership, if our word is not enough, trust is non-existent. I doubled our capital in a few months here and could very well have taken it out and bought things for my family. You are lying now for a few carts of melons. You are an untrustworthy scum of the earth."

As I came close to him, the other two held me back. In spite of them, in my anger I managed to spit on him.

The referees inventoried all property and assessed its market value. His portion was worth 10,000 Drachmas. He asked me if I wanted to buy him off. [120]

---

120   A. Boinodiris Book 4, p.120-123.

God Loves the Thief, but He Loves the Owner More [121]
(Drama, Summer 1945)

I had no money to do so. I looked around and found Mr. Zoides, a customer who was willing to loan me the money to pay Stratis off. I was prepared to leave with him as security the second venerable Singer sawing machine that Elisabeth had as a wedding gift. The first one was sold in 1943, to help me get started in the charcoal business. However, before I could go to Zoides, Jordan Zoumboulides bailed me out. He offered to loan me the money of 12,000 drachmas, without security.

I felt awkward, so I wrote him a note, equivalent to an IOU. Meanwhile, I sold the donkey, goats and the pig I had to pay him off.[122] I offered my ex-partner Stathis to buy back the unsold tsemeni powder[123] for 3,000 Drs, at 30 Drs per Oka but he refused. After I got a release form from him, I paid him 10,000 Drs and he left. After dissolving that partnership, Stathis went back to his village to be a farmer and I kept the grocery store at Stylides'.

Days later, when busses started traveling to Thessaloniki, Stratis from Kalos Agros went there, only to find out that they had a shortage of tsemeni powder. The tsemeni powder was selling for over 200 Drs per Oka. He took the next bus to Drama and walked into my store. He lifted the two sacks of tsemeni powder and placed them on the scale.

I approach him politely.

"Hello Mr. Stratis. What are you doing with my tsemeni powder on the scale?"

"I am afraid that the worms are going to eat it and you will have to throw it away. My conscience could not stand it. I came to buy it from you. How much did you sell? I doubt that you sold half an Oka of it."

---

121   This is from a popular Greek proverb.
122   A. Boinodiris, Book 1, p. 264.
123   Another word for the tsemeni powder is "fenugreek," a spice commonly used in the Middle East.

"No, I did not," I said, and then continued with a grin in my face; "... and I am not going to sell it to you either."

"Why? I was planning to give you an additional 5 Drs per Oka."

"I want that tsemeni powder to stay here for the worms. We signed our papers, I paid you off and I want you out of here, before I throw you out."

"I will pay you 50 Drs per kilo."

"...Out!"

"OK. I will pay you 100 Drs per kilo."

"You dirty bastard. I also know how much tsemeni powder sells for. It goes for 200 Drs per Oka. If you want it you must pay me 200 Drs per Oka."

"Blast you, you smart Karamanli. [124] How did you find out? I just came back from Thessaloniki with the first busses that went there."

"I did not have to go to Thessaloniki, you pathetic peasant. Your body language and behavior told me exactly what the price of tsemeni powder sells for. Just because I am honest and truthful it does not mean that I am stupid."

"I will offer you a fair price. If you do not take it, I will depart with a heavy heart against you. I will offer you 175 Drs per Oka. I must have some margin that pays for my transportation expenses."

In the end, I decided to sell his tsemeni powder for 17,500 Drs, the same one which he refused to buy for 3000 Drs. [125] With this money I paid Jordan outright 10000 drachmas and 2000 drachmas in purchases and put more merchandise in my grocery store.

---

124 Karamanli was called a person from the region of Cappadocia, coming from the ancient Karaman region.
125 A. Boinodiris, Book 1, p. 266 and A. Boinodiris Book 4, p.120-124.

The Balkan Mess (1945-1950)

Even before the total defeat of the Germans, Greek guerillas fought each other. One day we heard that at a mountain, called Tsal Tag there were 25 dead Greeks in a fight between leftists and rightists. This was one of the reasons why many more Greeks did not join the guerilla groups. They knew that the Civil War was imminent and such a war would aid traitors and criminals in their escape to Bulgaria.[126]

After the defeat of the Germans, Greece and the Dodecanese fell to the Greek-English forces from Cairo. In one of the meetings that the allied leaders had in Yalta, Roosevelt, Churchill, Stalin, and their foreign ministers agreed how to partition the lands occupied by the Germans. Greece fell in the sphere of influence of the English and Americans. The Dodecanese, previously under Italy, but populated by Greeks were ceded to Greece, with only one objection from Pevin, the English foreign minister. He suggested that Turkey be consulted on this matter. Fortunately, Stalin objected vehemently, repaying Greece for what they did during the war.

"What rights does Turkey have for consultation? They chose not to join our alliance and wait it out to join the winning side, regardless of who wins. You have no choice in this matter but give those islands to Greece, who sacrificed a great deal and took the brunt of German attack to delay them in attacking us, giving us enough time to get ready."

This delay had moved the German offensive to the winter of 1941, which crippled them. Stalin was a bloodthirsty, wicked fellow, but this time he stood up for what was right, primarily because he hated the Turks more than any other neighboring country, including Germany. He knew of the 600,000 soldiers that Turkey had amassed at the Russian border, ready to attack, and capture his oil fields at Caucasus if Hitler managed to win at Stalingrad. When he asked Turkey, why they kept 600,000 troops at Caucasus, their response was: "for our security."

---

126   A. Boinodiris, Book 4, p.106-107.

Stalin's intelligence knew better. The Turks were ready to join the Germans in attacking Russia, as soon as they knew that Hitler had beaten the allies.

The Americans agreed with Stalin, leaving the English objection inoperative. The Dodecanese went into Greek hands without consultation of Turkey. Anyway, the Turks living in the Dodecanese were very few. The English did what they did for one reason only: standard colonialist policy. They must set up precedence for Cyprus, whose independence they promised prior to the War, in order to get support from the Cypriots in their struggle against Hitler.

Churchill repeatedly mentioned Cypriot independence, when the Greeks fought Italy and Germany and Cypriot volunteers were fighting with them at various parts of the globe. If the Dodecanese involved Turkey, Cyprus, that had more Turks as minority would too. This would certainly delay independence of that island for a long time. The Greeks had only one description for this English a policy: "characteristic English political prostitution."

The Russian propaganda made a big bang with the Stalin statement, arming many communist Greeks with a moral cause against the "colonial English imperialism." Pevin's objection could not have been chosen at a worst time. It was a big factor in turning many Greeks into communists.

Another dirty trick that the English played on the Greeks was that of weapons drops. They dropped weapons to opposing sides, communists and nationalists alike. This "mistake" caused a great deal of death on both sides, weakening Greece to the point that it took much longer for them to recover from the war, in spite of the Marshall plan.

The final blow was their strong support of the King, who returned without any national referendum. [127]

---

127   A. Boinodiris, Book 4, p. 25-29.

The only support we had after the war was from America. Greeks must be grateful for that help. The Marshall plan was exactly what Greece needed at that time to recover. Truman's statue in Athens is a reminder of that. The young hoodlums that defaced it in later years, for later American mistakes had no idea what good it did, to a hungry, tired nation. They were too young to remember our plight under the Bulgarian occupation.[128]

There was an agreement màde in Cairo that at the end of December 1944, no Bulgarian force would be left in Greece. The internal, guerilla strife among Greeks helped a lot the Bulgarians and traitor Greeks to depart without having to face justice for crimes against humanity. Instead of being properly judged for their deeds, in slaughtering 17,000 innocent Greeks, they joined with the communists to fight the opposing guerillas. In return, they were given safe conduct back to Bulgaria and other Eastern Block countries, sometimes after burning villages that belonged to Greeks of the opposition party.

In Drama, the strongest parties were the Leftist (EAM-ELAS) and Communist Parties (EPON). As you walked for two hours from the city, you encountered the Nationalist Party, who frequently fought amongst their own warlords. This lasted for 6 months. Many of them, accused as double agents, were shot using firing squads. To supplement the defense of the city against the communists, civilians were drafted as National Guardsmen (MAI).

The Royal family arrived in Greece early in 1946, after the war ended. This angered many of the Democratic factions and they took off to the mountains, joining the communists, who led them. The leader of the band in our area, someone named Markos Vafiades was fighting against the leader of the National Royal Army, General Dimitrios Tsakaliotis. These battles lasted 3.5 years. The communists, led by Zahariades, who was taking direct orders from Stalin in Russia, managed to kill more Greeks in those few years, than all the war and occupation by Germans,

---

128   A. Boinodiris, Book 4, p. 30.

Italians and Bulgarians combined. Cursed be their souls, both Stalin and Zahariades who destroyed Greece. [129]

The infiltration made fighting boundaries non-existent. One day, one of the villagers I knew was going to the next village from Drama to see his goddaughter. He met some armed men who asked him of his political Party. Being close to Drama, he responded that he was Nationalist, only to be beaten up by these men. They were communists on a scouting patrol.

He managed to pick himself up and proceed. As he approached the village of his destination, he met another armed group. They ask him of his political affiliation. Having been beaten up, he responded that he was communist, only to be beaten up again. They happened to be Nationalists, on a similar patrol towards the village.

He picked himself up and went to the house of his relatives, where he recovered from his wounds. On his return to Drama, he met again with another armed group. Before they could ask him of his affiliations, he blows up:

"Don't ask me what my political affiliations are. I am what you want me to be. I was beaten twice, because I could not guess the right answer. So I am not guessing any more. I am a peace loving civilian who wants to be left alone."

Children (Drama, 1945)

My little son Stavros, now about two got sick with diarrhea. I was searching all over the place for rice, without success. I finally found 160 grams of rice from a black marketer, named Dimitris Zahariades. I had to pay 160 Drs for it, an outrageous price, since raisins were seven Drachmas per kilo. We used rice like medicine at that time. We boiled it carefully and fed the baby, a spoonful at a time. [130]

---

129   A. Boinodiris, Book 4, p. 23.
130   A. Boinodiris, Book 1, p. 262.

Schools opened by fall of 1945. My son John, who was now 14, started going to school again. The child had gone to the first grade and part of the second grade when in 1941 schools were closed. Now, he and other older children had to join 8-year olds in school, to complete the second grade.

It was soon realized that schools had to segregate older kids, to avoid problems created by the large age difference. Education also was accelerated with night schooling. In two years, John was forced to be educated for four elementary school grades. By the time he entered high school in 1947, he had problems with reading and writing, although his math was relatively good.

Help from America – UNRA (Drama, 1945)

Sunflower oil started appearing in the summer of 1945 from Komotini and Alexandroupolis. That was the first cooking oil we saw for many years.

Since the Germans blew up all bridges and railroads were not operating, none of the products from the lower Greece could reach us.

Olive oil was not yet available.

Few olives started coming from Thasos, a welcome sight after five years of deprivation. [131]

The American Marshal Plan was becoming in effect and arriving by the summer of 1945. Rice started appearing, in white cotton sacks with the initials of the United Nations Relief Association (UNRA) and MADE IN THE USA.

The rice was used for cooking and the sack became our underwear. Most of my families had UNRA underwear, with the stamp: MADE IN THE USA.

Sugar was in similar sacks, paid by the USA but saying UNRA and MADE IN CUBA.

---

131   A. Boinodiris, Book 1, p. 262.

Traitor Retribution

Among those criminals that managed to escape to Bulgaria after the war was John Pais from Monastiraki. The Greek Civil War made his hurried escape possible. He took advantage of the fighting, by joining both sides as a policy of convenience. John was the traitor that killed all the male members of Theano's family, except one of her sons who was now a police officer in Thessaloniki.

When John made his escape, he took with him his daughter and son-in-law. In his escape, his daughter loaded their goods onto the cart, but there was no room for John's wife, or the goods of his own household. Therefore, his wife Katina was left back in Greece.

Katina kept on sending messages to her husband to come and pick her up. One day, in 1945, Theano sees this same person, leading his wife to a bus station, trying to retrieve her. She immediately fingers him to one of the ELAS leaders, who sent several of his soldiers to arrest him on the bus.

John Pais was dead after a great deal of torture. Katina was left a widow in Greece and died later on from natural causes. [132] Her daughter and her family settled in Bulgaria.

The animal dealers from Pontus named Constantine Vamvakidis, together with his partner George Baltoghlu continued to be bullies during the war. I had the bitter experience in dealing with them since 1938. During the war, they escaped the draft and went to Thessaloniki, were declared deserters, and sought by the police. When the Germans arrived, we found out that they collaborated with the Germans. They terrorized villages, by confiscating the field animals that people hid from the occupiers, and slaughtered them, so that they can be frozen and shipped to the German army. Several of the villagers told the guerilla leaders of their activity. They were given a warning, but these bullies did not stop, thinking that they had protection. Soon, they were ambushed, taken somewhere in the country and shot on the spot. In

---

132   A. Boinodiris, Book 4, p. 100-101.

this fashion, the mafia ring of the bullies from Pontus was harshly eliminated. [133]

George Spanos

I was working hard, selling charcoal in the neighborhoods, when I heard a familiar voice behind me:

"How much for the bag of charcoal ...?"

I turned, only to face a raggedy man with torn pants, looking a lot worse than I did. I recognized him as my old acquaintance from jail, George Spanos, my arrogant jail guard. This was the person who had married the only daughter of a local priest, was dipping into the priest's salary and thought of himself as a big shot, and treating all inmates like mosquitoes. It was my turn to pay him back for demeaning me and calling me a mongrel in the market in 1937.

"What are you doing here George, running around like a mongrel?"

"Forgive me Anthony for not recognizing you. I could not leave for the Peloponnesos and had to stay here through the ordeal of Bulgarian occupation. I have children to raise, my father-in-law passed away and I am really broke."

Then, my question sank in. He looked at me and with his face down, approached me.

"I really deserve the tongue-lashing Anthony. I have spoken to you exactly the same way, a lifetime ago. You really remembered what I said to you; right? I must have really hurt you with my arrogant attitude."

"As a guard in jail George, you had my respect, but greeting me in the market in that manner, you caused me to lose any respect about you as a human being. I hope that you have learned something out of this George. "

"I sure did."

---

133   A. Boinodiris, Book 4, p. 78-79.

I sold him the charcoal at cost, feeling sorry for him. [134]

As I watched him leave, I learned my own lessons too. You never know whom you might need in the future. It reminded me of a story that my neighbor told me:

The Story of the King's Joker

Once upon a time, there was a King, who had a joker in his court to entertain him. In those days, jokers were the entertainment as TV and movies are today. After many years of service, the King got tired of the joker's jokes and kicked him out of the court.

"Your majesty; I spent a lifetime here and have no other trade. What should I do now?"

"I don't care. Start cleaning our streets. Go and start dragging all the dead varmints from the streets. I pay a piece of gold for every 200 animals."

The joker was devastated. Finally, he found a job as a coastal lifesaver, since he was a good swimmer. In fact, it did not take too long for him to excel in his job. His salary was reasonable and he found out how much he loved swimming.

One stormy day, his crew was ordered to save the King's ship, which was caught in a storm, as it was coming home from a royal visit to his domain. As they approached the ship, it struck a reef and the ship started sinking. The crew managed to save the Royal Family. The ex-joker was the one who dragged the King to safety.

"I know you," said the King. "What are you doing here?"

"I followed your advice, Your Highness," said the lifesaver. "I have learned how to drag varmints. How much is going to be my reward for dragging a King?" [135]

134   A. Boinodiris, Book 1, p. 225 and Book 4, p. 66-67.
135   A. Boinodiris, Book 1, p. 227.

The King and the Civil War

After the war, we were desperate for good leadership. In my opinion, the Royal Family became the major obstacle in finding such leadership. If the King did not return to Greece, we could have avoided a deadly civil war, by choosing the right leader.

With the Civil War at hand, all the money from the Marshall plan that was generously provided by the Americans to Europe was wasted in Greece, on defense. While the rest of Europe was building their destroyed infrastructure, Greece was building city fortifications in thousands of pillboxes, buying weapons and ammunition and losing more lives than during the whole World War II.

The Royals failed to see the interest of the country, because they had their own interests and alliances to protect, rather than those of the people.

In the First World War, they aligned themselves with Germany, causing a near disaster, which Venizelos managed to stop. If it were not for him, Macedonia would be in the hands of the Bulgarians. Since then, the friendship with the Serbs continued.

In the Second World War, the King took the side of the British. I consider the Royals arrogant, corrupted by power, and extremely inflexible in thwarting the Civil War with the communists.

Panagiotis Papadopoulos

Our acquaintance from the village of Vathilakos, Panagiotis Papadopoulos was active during those months of 1944. You may recall him, when his greed led him to ambush and stone my father, only to be beaten up instead. Panagiotis was greedy and stupid enough to belong to the communist and the nationalist side at the same time. In fact, he was being paid by both and passing vital information from one side to the other for a price. His allegiance was only to his bottom line. He was coming in Drama and shopping supplies for the communists, unhindered, because he had registered as Bulgarian first, and as a nationalist later. He flaunted his wealth, by capping all his 32 teeth with gold. [136] Soon, the communists put a warrant for his arrest, because of some suspicious information that he sold to them.

When the communist guerillas attacked the nationalist garrison at Monastiraki, they were a lot more organized than their opponents were. They managed to rout them, killing several soldiers outside the village. Their victory took them all the way to Vathilakos. Vathilakos consisted of a village that was mostly burned by the Bulgarians in the past few years. All of the villagers took off and ran to the high mountains, to escape the battle. Panagiotis left with them, but he forgot to pick up a sack of gold sovereigns, hidden in his house. Afterwards, when the battle subsided, he decided to go back to get them, not knowing about his arrest warrant, in spite of advise from villagers and relatives. His greed was too strong.

He managed to get his gold, but the communists grabbed him on his way out. They took him in a ravine, between Vathilakos and Monastiraki for interrogation. After continuous investigation with torture about the gold in his bag and his mouth (golden teeth), they pulled all his teeth out. Then they proceeded to burn his eyes out, cut off his hands, feet, and ears and finally cut off his genitals, which they placed in his mouth. He was still alive, bleeding to death slowly when they left. The next day, after the communists were gone, the villagers came back to their homes.

Panagiotis' relatives started searching for him, and found his mutilated body in the ravine. They picked up the pieces and brought him in the village where they buried him as a "national hero."

This "national hero" was nothing more than a "hero of greed."

I found out about this event from his relatives and villagers who knew what he did to us.

---

136   A. Boinodiris, Book 1, p. 198.

Nobody deserved such a horrible death, not even Panagiotis. God Rest his soul. I felt sorry for his wife, his two boys and the rest of his relatives, who had to go through the pains of seeing this cruel aftermath. [137]

Starting from mid-1947, I served in the National Guard until 1950. During these last years, my youngest son Stavros, a mere toddler, brought me lunch in the pillbox, only a few hundred yards from my home, which was at the outskirts of the town.

A whole string of such pillboxes, made out of stone and concrete were built around every city, about 500 meters from each other and visible to its neighboring ones. Each pillbox had a single door, protected by a protruding wall from direct fire. It also had six firing windows, with wide interior opening and a small external opening. The walls were about one meter thick and the roof was made out of steel-reinforced concrete, half a meter thick, to withstand mortar attacks. The interior was about 3 meters in diameter, adequate for sleeping accommodations of six cramped men.

My son was very entertaining to the rest of the men in my pillbox. He had a toy rifle, with which he marched along the dirt road, bringing me such lunch as beans and bread in an army aluminum container that someone sold us after the war. In spite of the fact that part of my bean soup was spilled most of the time, the sight of my son with his toy rifle made the men around me appreciate the situation of why we were standing guard there. We were not there to achieve any political or military objectives; we were there to protect our own families from harm by the communist guerillas.

Traitors and Communists

During the Civil War, most Bulgarian collaborators turned into either Communists, or double agents. Among these, the most populous group consisted of people who spoke a mixed Greco-Turkish-Bulgarian-Slavic dialect. This native dialect, which they called "Macedonian," was the result of the multiple years of Slavic, Turkish, and Bulgarian presence

---

137   A. Boinodiris, Book 1, p. 199-200.

in the region. In actuality, the real Macedonian language, from before Philip, throughout the Roman times and into the Byzantine Period was Greek. Slavic language appeared after the 6th century AD, [138]Bulgarian in the 7th century,[139] and the Turkish after the 15th century AD.

Many of these local people were not collaborators and did not participate in the communist atrocities against the civilian population of Greek Macedonia. But a good portion of them did. After collaborating with the Bulgarians and seeing that they lost their ground of being in power, they became fanatic communists, hoping that the Greek Macedonia is ceded to the Communist Block, so that they are allowed to remain in their homes for good.

In order to increase their chances of converting the local population into communism, they started a methodical forced abduction of children into Albania, Yugoslavia, Bulgaria, Rumania and other communist regions.[140] A great number of these children were taken with their parents, separated from them and sent into Communist indoctrination school camps. This process, called "PAEDOMAZOMA," created terror in the minds of all Greek parents.[141] Children (like the author of this book) witnessed parents instructing their toddler to know who they are, and occasionally branding them at birth with a hot iron, to recognize them in case of abduction. A great number of these children and their parents ended up in the Yugoslav part of Macedonia, later to be named FYROM.

After the Civil War ended in 1950, many of these children and their parents returned to Greece with the help of the International Red Cross. To avoid a communist infiltration, all those that participated in

---

138   This introduction into Slavic happened after the Slavs overran the Balkans in 548-550 AD during Justinian's reign.
139   The Bulgarian presence in the Balkans began to be seriously felt in Macedonia at around 680 AD, during Constantine IV's era.
140   "Eleni," the book by Nicholas Gage, made into a movie (starring John Malcovich and Kate Nelligan), is a very representative, and true story of that era.
141   The 1957 movie "Action of the Tiger," with Van Johnson and Martin Carol depicts some of these abducted children and the world anger against "paedomazoma," during the early fifties.

atrocities of the Civil War against the public were banned from entry until 1985.[142] Even then, the repatriated Greeks had to take an oath of allegiance to the Greek constitution. The hate of the Civil War was so intense and divisive, that many collaborators or ex-communist fighters refused such oath. Many of these people with their children chose to remain in the communist block countries, hoping that one of these days communism would prevail and they would come home as heroes. Some of them (like the daughter of John Pais) stayed back, even after they had decided that communism was a lost cause, simply because they did not trust the Greek government and were afraid of public anger and legal prosecution for the crimes that they or their parents committed during the Civil War.

Based in Skopje, of the former Yugoslav Republic of Macedonia (FYROM), and many places abroad (including some close contacts of President Bush in the United States), they continued to claim their rights of property in Greece. Behind the scenes, they diligently and covertly work politically, with a specific purpose in mind: the splitting of Greek Macedonia from Greece.

The people of FYROM call themselves Aegean Macedonians and their language "Macedonian." This mixture of Bulgarian, Turkish, Slavic and Greek is an evolutionary linguistic soup that is the result of four centuries of Ottoman rule in that region. Although these people were a small minority prior to the Civil War, they were seen to represent a cultural threat. The threat is directed not only to the native Macedonian Greek population, but also to the relatively new Greek immigrants from Asia Minor that never spoke such language. The Macedonian Greeks had a lengthy historical heritage, many centuries before the Bulgarian, Slavic, or Turkish invaders arrived. Some of these Greeks fled to Western Europe, after the repeated attacks by Slavs, Bulgars, Normans and Turks, but their culture and heritage did not change, even as their numbers diminished. Slavs can take the Macedonian land, the people's homes, but they cannot take away the people's name, culture, historical past

---

142   At that time, everyone who brought proof of being born in Greece, and sign an affidavit of Greek citizenship was permitted to enter and live in the country. Among those that came back in 1983 was Markos Vafiadis.

and way of thinking. Any invaders that do so must have a problem with their culture and identity. If so, they should try to enrich them both, by adapting, but not stealing the culture of a neighbor. If they think as Greeks do, let them join Greece, like most of the Venetian transplants in Greece, called Arvanites[143] did. Greeks would welcome any such cultural enrichment of their neighbors. Anyway, that is how Greek culture became richer; by blending with other cultures through millennia of Greek immigration abroad. As those immigrants returned to their native lands they brought back some new knowledge. Some of it (like Aristotelian logic and epistemology) was theirs from the start, but most of it had been further enriched by the post-Renaissance European thinking.

Results and Lessons of the Civil War

I served two and one half years soldier, three and one half years as National Guardsman and nearly half a year of forced labor in Bulgaria. Four years of my life was wasted because of war and two and one half years in preparation for the war.

It took a great deal of struggle by General Papagos and a lot of money from the United States to subdue the rebels on 29 August of 1948. By then, the cemetery in Drama was full of graves of our young men, who died for nothing.[144]

---

143   Arvanites were named in general all the people brought in by the Venetians from the Dalmatian coast to populate Greece between the 15th and 17th centuries. As Greeks were fleeing to the West by millions, Venetians had to import labor from their conquered colonial trade posts. Many were from Albania, but some were from what today consists of Slovenia, Croatia, and Montenegro. These Christian immigrants still hold some of their native customs and language. They blended with the remaining native Greek population and fought alongside of them in the revolutionary war of 1821. The strange thing about these people is that they speak an Illyrian dialect, which relates to ancient Greek. The Carian and Pelasgic family was known to have lived in the Balkans even before the Greeks and are common ancestors to both, Illyrians and Greeks. The Illyrian offshoot that resided on the Dalmatian coast during Roman and Byzantine times was tapped by the Venetians as a very likely candidate to blend with their cousins, the Greeks.
144   A. Boinodiris, Book 4, p. 24. More people died in Greece from the Civil War, than the whole World War II.

The youngest son of Father Kalinikos, named George, who was a Marathon runner in the army in 1928, was one of the victims of that war. He was working with his knife on a pair of shoes, in his shoemaker's shop when a machine gun burst cut him down.[145]

People built during peace. War causes heavy destruction. When war comes, death, misery, hunger and shortages prevail. Humans simply destroy with their own hands what they or others have created in peace. They destroy lives, businesses, factories and all means of communication, which is necessary for humans to evolve through the process of creation.

With all my regrets, I dare say that Drama had no able leaders in those difficult times. The Marshall Plan that took effect after the war was not taken full advantage. Other neighboring regions, like Kavala, Xanthi and Serres were somewhat better. We spent a lot more on defense, for the construction of pillboxes and fortifications, than we should. [146]

The Civil War reconstruction started immediately, from 1948 until 1955 when Greece had some peaceful years. The Papagos government followed the Plastiras government.[147]

Lessons in Human Behavior

My life's experience taught me that among all nations, there are good and bad people. In every country, there are good and bad people and every type in between the two categories. The question is always: what do you do with the bad ones?

You can find this spread of good and bad behavior in all other beings including the animal kingdom. For example, I have observed my chickens. I have had many chickens in the past, as house animals and sold chicken feed in my grocery store to people that raised them. Most families in Asia Minor and in Greece were accustomed to having at least half a dozen chickens in their yards for fresh eggs and meat.

---

145   A. Boinodiris, Book 1, p. 285.
146   A. Boinodiris, Book 4, p. 23.
147   A. Boinodiris, Book 4, p. 24.

I had a black hen, which I fed plenty of feed and was rewarded with frequent delivery of eggs. She delivered me at least six eggs per week, while all the five other chickens added up to less than ten eggs per week. Yet, this black hen was very greedy and did not let the other chickens eat. After eating her food, she stood guard and attacked by pecking the other chickens with her bill and preventing them from feeding. Even after I chased her, she insisted upon returning to the feeding grounds and guarded the food that she could not eat, turning the other hens into a bleeding mess. The beneficial black hen suddenly became a problem. She would starve the rest of my chickens, not allowing them to become productive. One day, without thinking properly I became upset and chopped off the black hen's head. In retrospect, I should have spent some effort to isolate her. By isolating her, I may have gotten five eggs from the black hen and maybe fifteen from the other five.

Are we humans an extension of this animal kingdom? I know of dogs that fight other dogs to become an alpha dog. We must have resolved this issue through our logical ability, when we decided to sacrifice some of our own independence and join a family, a clan, a city and a country, but many of us still have that "animal" instinct to look after our own self interest in a very narrow sense of animal survival that deals only with our own self-preservation, rather than our preservation through the survival of our community. We become so greedy, that we prevent others from becoming successful. Isn't that what is happening every day in the world, especially in the poorest countries of the world? You can find corruption, starting from the highest dictators and politicians, all the way down to the smallest bureaucrat. The higher someone is allowed to climb in the ladder of bureaucracy, the higher the possible degree of corruption. How much of that corruption can a society sustain before it collapses? What is frightening is that in my life I have seen several examples of people that acted like the black hen.

One of them was Tzoras, for whom I went to jail in the 1930's. "Humans may loose their lives, but their habits live for ever," says an old adage. We are by nature greedy beings. Are Israelis and Palestinians acting like the black hen? Are the Greeks and Turks? Are we all destined to act like that at one time or another? Humanity has to know this weakness and deal with it. If we are to succeed, we must learn to share wealth and opportunity with other people and people different than ourselves. [148]

On the other spectrum, there are people like my father who assume no responsibility for supporting themselves, or their families. They expect everything to fall in their lap, without any planning, or effort on their part. They are free spirits and the people around them pay for their callous behavior.

It took some time for me to realize that we are born in an environment which we have no control of. Not one of us has a choice on whose offspring they are. Their parents could be saints, or demons. We can only be judged on what we do with our lives. Because of that, the historical events can be stated without any bias, or fear that we may damage the reputation of a person, by disclosing what their father, or mother did in the past. In fact, any person that comes out of a dysfunctional family and achieves happiness deserves a higher praise than those that came from a "normal" family. Historians must tell the truth, even if it does not shed the best light on the historian's friends, family, country, or even themselves. That is the only way that our future generations can learn from our past mistakes, or the mistakes of our forefathers. That is why I am not intimidated in disclosing names and events that others would not have done so openly.[149]

---

148   A. Boinodiris, Book 4, p. 32-33.

149   This entry affirms the ancient tenet of historians, like Herodotus (484BC-425BC), the father of history. Herodotus believed that nothing is stable in human affairs. Moral choice is still important, however, since arrogance brings down upon itself retribution. Herodotus' effective attempt to draw moral lessons from the study of great events formed the basis of the Greek and Roman history tradition which still applies.

The Aftermath

Between 1940 and 1948 Greece suffered a great deal. The poorly equipped Greeks fought four enemies at once: Albania, Italy, Bulgaria and Germany. Their resistance to the Axis lasted 219 days, more than any other occupied country. In comparison, France lasted only 43 days. 50,000 Germans and 25,000 Bulgarians lost their lives in that war with Greece. Proportionally, the Greeks also sacrificed 10% of their population, more than Russia (2.8%). When Adolph Hitler spoke at the Reichstag on the 4th of May 1941, he admitted that "... the historical facts indicate that among our enemies only the Greeks fought us with great courage, ignoring death."

Mussolini also commented on the 10th of May, 1941: "In the case of the War with Greece, it indicates that nothing is certain in military affairs and surprises can come at any time."

Winston Churchill had a way with words, as he said on BBC during the Greek-Italian campaign: "Up to now, we said that the Greeks fought like heroes; from now on we will say that heroes fight like Greeks."

After the Greek surrender, a German Air Force General came and wanted to see the Greek General. He expressed with utter surprise to him stating: "your men were unique, because when we attacked them with the Stukas planes, instead of hiding, or running, like the Poles or the French, they stood their ground and fired straight at us from their positions with their rifles."

In his memoirs, General Georgy Zhukov of the Soviet Army wrote: "... the fact that the Russians were able to muster their strength to stop the Germans in front of Moscow we owe it to the Greeks who delayed the German attack and gave us crucial time to build our defense."

On top of World War II we had the Civil War, which lasted until August of 1948, when General Alexander Papagos wiped the remains of communist guerillas in the mountains of Grammos and Vitsi of Epirus. A few groups operated after that defeat, until 1950.

Finally, the slaughter was subsiding. Most of the deaths that followed were as a result of mines and unexploded munitions, laid around the countryside. Innocent villagers, traveling in caravans to sell their wares to the market were blown to bits, some losing arms and legs. If they were lucky, they may lose only an animal in front of the caravan.

On April 1 1950, King George died and King Paul, his son took over. To my opinion, he was as dumb as he was tall. His wife, Queen Frederica ran most of his affairs. [150]

Liberation (Lyon, France, Summer, 1948)[151]

Basil sat in his office, editing an article for one of the French magazines he started working for, trying to depict how the allies won this war. He was meticulously adding photographs of allied soldiers fighting in Africa and in France after the D-Day.

It was more than three year ago, on April 29, 1945, that his Dachau sub-camp was liberated by the American Army. When the German guards saw them, they abandoned the sub-camp and took off towards the main camp. At the beginning, when Basil saw them, he could not believe his eyes. These troops had American uniforms, but did not look American. They were oriental.

The prisoners soon found out one of the most ironic coincidences in the liberation of the sub-camps surrounding Dachau. These oriental men were the advance scouts of the US Army's 522nd Field Artillery Battalion, a Nisei-manned segregated Japanese-American Allied military unit. These troops liberated the 3,000 prisoners of slave labor camp. This was an especially ironic coincidence because all their relatives were also interned in the US during the war.

That same day, the main Dachau camp was surrendered to the American Army.[152]

---

150   A. Boinodiris, Book 1, p. 274.
151   Story relayed by E. Boinodiris.
152   A vivid description of the surrender appears in Brig. Gen. Henning Linden's official "Report on Surrender of Dachau Concentration Camp":

American interrogators and medical personnel sorted through them in a speedy way. They found the prisoners in real bad shape. Basil was diagnosed with advanced stages of tuberculosis, and was ushered immediately to a medical facility in Geneva. He spent almost a year there, in the care of some of the best physicians of the world. They managed to save his life. Some of his cell-mates were not so fortunate. Then, he was given a choice to relocate. The doctors suggested that he goes to hot, dry climates, avoiding Paris because of its humidity. He chose Lyon, where he had some contacts.

In Lyon, he had to regularly visit the hospital to get his shots, so that his tuberculosis symptoms do not recur. His contacts secured him a post with a magazine and he started making some money as an editor and as a photographer to bring his life back in order.

Then, one day one of his doctors came with the suggestion:

"Basil! You are from Greece. Athens happens to have some of the best climate for making sure that your disease does not recur. Lyon is better than Paris, but it still falls short when compared with Athens. What if we set you up with a very good hospital in Athens? Yes, Greece has gone through a civil war, but from what I hear, the increased American aid, and all indications point to a communist defeat. If you are interested, we can help you relocate back to your own country."

As we moved down along the west side of the concentration camp and approached the southwest corner, three people approached down the road under a flag of truce. We met these people about 75 yards north of the southwest entrance to the camp. These three people were a Swiss Red Cross representative and two SS troopers who said they were the camp commander and assistant camp commander and that they had come into the camp on the night of the 28th to take over from the regular camp personnel for the purpose of turning the camp over to the advancing Americans. The Swiss Red Cross representative acted as interpreter and stated that there were about 100 SS guards in the camp who had their arms stacked except for the people in the tower. He said he had given instructions that there would be no shots fired and it would take about 50 men to relieve the guards, as there were 42,000 half-crazed prisoners of war in the camp, many of them typhus infected. He asked if I were an officer of the American army, to which I replied, "Yes, I am Assistant Division Commander of the 42d Division and will accept the surrender of the camp in the name of the Rainbow Division for the American army."

He thought about his family and the fact that he had not seen them for eight years.[153]

First Memories (Stavros' Memoirs, 1948)

I was told that I was born on Monday, November 15, 1943. I was an "accident," that occurred in the early cold months of 1943. My family was not in any condition to raise another child. A Bulgarian midwife delivered me at home. When she emerged from the room, she told my father that he had a son, who would soon fight Bulgarians, "boom-boom." He laughed.

During the early months of 1943, when curfews were imposed to curb guerilla action, my father was in hiding, while my mother coordinated our survival. He spent his time babysitting. They told me that when I was few months old, I contracted smallpox. The family had to scramble to get some sugar for me, so that they could dilute it in water and feed me, as a neighbor doctor suggested. My father's initial attempts to get sugar failed. He finally got some from the Bulgarian midwife, in spite of orders from police, not to feed the Greeks.

Markos Vafiadis

Markos Vafiadis was born in Theodosiopolis (today's Erzurum of Turkey) in 1906.

After the Asia Minor Catastrophe of 1922, like many other Greek refugees, Vafiadis went to Thessaloniki and then to Kavala. From 1928, he worked in Thessaloniki as a member of the Federation of Greek Communist Youths (OKNE). In 1932, he was imprisoned and sent to internal exile for his communist political actions. After his release in October 1933, he worked as communist party instructor in many areas of Greece.

---

153 Basil Leonides relocated to Athens, Greece in 1949. He was attended by doctors at "Evangelismos Hospital," and lived in Amarousi for many years. He opened up a photographer shop, named "Foto Bill," at a central location of Amarousi. He married very late in his life and he often visited the German widow in Hamburg, the lady that saved his life.

At the beginning of Metaxas' dictatorship (the "4th of August Regime") he was exiled again to the island of Ai Stratis, but managed to escape in less than a month. Subsequently he worked in the party's underground organization in Crete and was one of the leaders of the Chania communist uprising against the dictatorial regime (28 July 1938). After the suppression of the uprising, he went to Athens, where he was arrested. He was jailed in Akronafplia and then was exiled to the island of Gavdos.

In May 1941, during the German invasion in Greece, he escaped from Gavdos and began underground work against the German occupation, initially in Crete, later in Athens and Thessaloniki. In 1942, he was elected into the Central Committee of the Communist Party of Greece and was named supervisor of the Macedonia wing of the Greek People's Liberation Army (ELAS).

In November 1944, he disagreed with Aris Velouchiotis, another communist warlord, who wanted ELAS to prepare to fight the British. During the December fighting in Athens, the Macedonian wing of the ELAS didn't fight against the British troops. In February 1946, Vafiades again disagreed with Nikolaos Zachariadis, the general secretary of KKE, who wanted to resume fighting.

However, in July 1946, Zachariadis appointed Markos as leader of the communist guerrilla formations. In October 1946, when the General Command of the Democratic Army of Greece (DSE) was founded, Vafiadis assumed its leadership, and in December 1947 he was appointed Prime Minister and War Minister of the Provisional Democratic Government.

During the last stages of the Civil War, Vafiadis disagreed with Zachariadis on issues of military doctrine. This time, this disagreement led to his removal from DSE leadership (August 1948). In spite of that, Vafiadis continued to lead his guerilla formations throughout Macedonia.

Figure 11 Markos Vafiades, Leader of ELAS
(Communist-supported Army)

Figure 12 Communist Partisans during Mortar Training

The Vafiadis Attack (Stavros' Memories, Drama, Fall 1948)

One night in 1948 a group of communist guerillas, under the leadership of Markos Vafiades attacked Drama through the Dablatza ravine. This was a ravine, which is formed by a river passing through Drama. Although mostly dry, when it rains, it collects into a fierce swell and often takes with it all it finds on its way: animals, people, vendor stands, etc. This ravine forms to the North of the city into a deep gulch. The gulch continues through the center of the city of Drama and joins with the waters from the spring of St. Barbara to fall to the river Angitis, a branch of Strymon River. In later years, the northern gulch was a favorite picnic area for the children and a place where young couples chose for a romantic outing.[154]

The communist guerillas managed to penetrate around a weakened pillbox next to the ravine, infiltrating the pillbox crew. After cutting the telephone wires, they disappeared in the night, leaving a sole, faithful guardsman alone. The guardsman (a known shoemaker) stood his ground with a machine gun but knowing that he could not stop the attackers, which he thought were over one hundred, he decided to stay quietly at his post and observe, without revealing his position in the dark.

After the first shots were heard, the Boinodiris family exited the house and hid from view, quietly spending the night prone in the yard, together with some neighbors. The guerilla group attacked some of the houses at the city's suburbs and, supported by mortars, they withdrew to the north. Some of those mortars fell no more than 50 meters from my home, located also in the suburbs of Drama. This created a deafening noise.

My earliest memories start that night in 1948, when I (the author) was only 4.5 years old. I remember waking up in my crib from a very loud noise in the pitch black night. Surprised, I yelled for my mother.

---

154   Today, the gulch through the city has been covered by concrete, into a continuous pavement, but a large tunnel allows the water to flow under it.

No response, other than another explosion, louder than the first, which silenced my scream. The crib was next to the open bedroom window and the sky was temporarily lit. Scared, I yelled even louder and kept yelling. I remember having a dry mouth. I yelled until a shadow appeared in the window. It was my sixteen-year old brother. He grabbed me and put his hands in my mouth. I stopped yelling. He told me:

"Hush! The guerillas are attacking. We have to be quiet, or they will come and kill us."

We lay flat on the dry, freshly excavated dirt of our yard. From whispers around me, I soon found out that we had guests. The family of John and Bethlehem from across the street was also lying flat next to us. They had a daughter in her late teens and a much younger son. My mother was there with my brother, but not my father, or anyone else. I saw fires towards the northeast. I heard faint whispers, asking whose house was on fire. No one knew. I remember the smell of that night. It was a uniquely distinct smell, which was imprinted in my memory ever since. I experienced that smell only a few times in my life, every time human flesh was burning.[155]

The loud explosions close to us stopped, but a different sound of outgoing shells was being fired from the east. The distant rumbling of tanks was also audible. Everything else was dark and quiet. A few minutes went by. Then we heard footsteps. My brother put his hands over my mouth again. The steps were of multiple men, walking on the street next to the retaining wall of our yard. They could not be more than 10-15 feet away from us, but we could not see them at all in the dark. They walked silently, their shoes stepping on the gravel road. We could even hear the rubbing of their clothes as they moved. After they left, my brother's hand fell down from my mouth.

---

155 I recalled this smell again in Pascagoula, Mississippi, after a house fire. Everyone claimed that the residents were out, but I knew that someone was burned there. It was later discovered that a couple, friends of the family used the house that night for a love affair. The fire department found their charred bodies the morning after.

"They must have been a patrol," my brother said. "Who knows from which side?"

We lay down in the dark, until all shelling stopped. The rumbling of the tanks continued.

"I want to see whose house is on fire," he added and started crawling on the yard towards the northeast."

"No!" my mother whispered in an almost shrieking voice.

"Don't worry Mom," John said. "I will go only until Michael's house, from where you have a clear view."

"That kid," she whispered "never listens."

John disappeared in the darkness. A few minutes later, he came back.

"It seems that it is the house next to one of my friend's north of the High School Gymnasium. I believe that the barn is now burning."

The rumbling of the tanks was getting louder. We lay down in the dark for almost another hour. The rumbling was still going on, when my mother said:

"John, take the baby to his crib and go to bed. I am coming too."

"OK," John responded yawning.

Most of the neighbor's family was falling asleep on our yard. The ground was freshly hand plowed in furrows and we lay down in them, trying to reduce our possible visibility from the occasional flares fired by the nationalists.

Bethlehem said to her daughter:

"We will sleep here for awhile. Can you go and get some rugs and pillows from the house, so that we can get comfortable? Make sure you do not light any lamps or candles."

As we were leaving, the daughter was crossing the street to fetch the rugs and pillows. I was placed in my crib, where after a while I resumed my sleep.

I remember the morning after. All the children were out and talked about what happened. They curiously looked at the road in front of our house, next to our plowed front yard, where we spent the night. The large stones of the pavement were smashed by the tracks of tanks.[156] None saw these tanks in the darkness, but we had all heard them.

I distinctly remember going inside the house and preparing my cloth pampers and my goatskin waterproof bed cover, pajamas and underwear.

"Where are you going young man?" my mom asked.

"To my nouna's," I responded. Nouna is godmother in Greek.

"Why?"

"...Because her home is in the city. Our home is in the edge of town, next to guerillas."

My mother smiled and started talking about me with the neighbor woman.

I started walking to my nouna's house, which was some distance away for a five-year old.

"Wait! You will get lost. I will take you there after lunch," she said.

I returned, placing my bag on my crib.

That night I was sleeping at my godmother's home. I remember being visited by my parents every night, asking me to come home. I refused to leave my nouna's house for almost six months.

---

156   The tanks used by the nationalists at that time were the British Centaur (A27L) tanks. These were Cromwell tanks of World War II, with the earlier Liberty engines. They were 28 ton, lumbering machines. These were ceded to the Greek nationalist government by England after the war to defend the country against the communists.

Even when I returned, the trauma from that incident was etched into my conscience as fear. I was afraid of the dark and of sudden loud noises. I was also afraid of any tube pointed towards my direction, including a camera, thinking it was about to harm me. Not having electricity, but burning kerosene lamps or candles did allow for some limited convenience of lighting a few hours in the dark night. Yet, when a child needed to go to the toilet, there was no light. The toilet was outdoors and in the dark. As result, I ended up wetting my crib and later on my bed more often than not, until I went to elementary school. Wetting a bed required protection of the mattress. At that time, a goatskin was used to waterproof a child's bed. Nylon sheets were unknown to us for some years to come.

One night, I was playing on the floor in a dimly lit room of about 2 meters by 3 meters, where my mother was busy, darning socks under a petroleum lamp on a metal divan. Suddenly, we heard a big bang. It may have been an animal that tried to grab some food from a pantry, and dropped a heavy pot on the floor. Or, it could have been the neighbor woman, whose tin tub loosened the nail on the wall and fell. My mother jumped up to see what was going on and I ran straight to the bed where she sat, to seek comfort with her under the blankets. In my hurry, I hit the corner of the divan. I was little, the divan was tall and instead of landing on it, I hit my abdomen on the steel corner of the divan. I remember crying a lot that night from pain.

My mother took me to a doctor, who diagnosed a forced hernia, caused by the injury. He did not recommend surgery. Instead, he suggested that I do not lift any heavy weights and a strap was placed on the swollen part of the abdomen. My mother had never seen a hernia strap. She made me one around 1949 and I still wonder if her invention came first, before companies started making them for mass consumption. It did its job. I wore it for almost 7 years. When I was checked out, before removing it they found that the lining with hernia had self-sealed.[157]

---

157 Almost sixty years later, my chiropractor diagnosed that because of some early injury the disks of my lower spinal cord were weakened and were the cause of hernia of the spine. Another chiropractor managed to also set a dislocated sacrum-iliac joint, which he believes was weakened at some early event in my life.

As my mother's hernia straps cured my hernia, her tender love and affection cured my fear.

I still remember that cure, more than fifty years later. Every time she saw me afraid, she hugged me.

I distinctly remember walking home in dark, wet nights from my father's store where we all worked. She used to wrap me inside her coat. I walked next to her, while I was hugging her knee and peering out of a tiny opening of her coat onto the dark, wet road in front of us. At that moment, I felt safer than any time before, or after.

Looking back in my youth, being partly crippled through my hernia was not as big of a problem as my fear. Admittedly, having hernia at the pelvis caused me some problems. All the children at that time gave each other a very descriptive, sometimes derogatory nickname. My brother's nickname was "kazamias," or "weather almanac," because he unsuccessfully predicted everything, including tomorrow's weather. My nickname was "broken chair," probably because of the way I walked, or because the kids discovered that I had hernia. As a child, I was told not to lift heavy objects, but as an active boy, I rarely obeyed that advice. Yet, this physical handicap was secondary to the mental scars the Vafiades attack had left me with. As a child, I vividly remember being continuously scared.

After the Vafiades attack, the guerilla group withdrew and the bands continued to harass the cities and villages. They made their bases in the mountains of Macedonia. Vafiades soon lost all his authority from all offices of command (January 1949). In October 1950, he was ousted from the Communist Party, while he was in exile in the Soviet Union, where he had fled after the breakup of the DSE.[158]

The trauma of my fear as a child had shown its face many decades later.

158   After the end of Stalin's era, Markos Vafiadis was restored into KKE and was elected as a member of the Political Bureau of the Central Committee of the party. However, new disagreement with the party leadership led to his removal from office in January 1958 and to his second ousting from the KKE in June 1964. After the party split in 1968, the so called "interior" faction of KKE restored him. In March 1983, ending his 23 years long exile in the Soviet Union, he returned to Greece. Later on, he published his Memoirs. In November 1989,

172 I Stavros Boinodirs PhD

Being continuously scared was like being in a never ending nightmare. In that state, the human mind is incapable of using logic. Every part of all senses is alert and on the defense. Darkness always hid lurking danger. Anyone pointing anything at you- a toy, a camera, a piece of food- is registered as someone who is about to harm you by shooting you or maiming you.

I recall a visit to the Drama Municipal Park with my mother when she tried to get me to pose for a picture in front of a photographer. I must have been around five-years old. I was so scared of the cylindrical lens pointing at me -thinking that I was about to be shot- that my mother had a tough time keeping me from running away (see Figure 13).

A similar situation arose when my uncle Basil, after his long ordeal at Dachau and his recovery in Geneva and Lyon came to Greece. One of his first missions after eight years was to come and see his family in Drama. As an accomplished photographer, he always carried his camera with him. While visiting his sister Elisabeth, he tried to take a picture of his nephew. He could not. It took a long time before my uncle Basil managed to persuade me that his camera was not a pointed weapon that kills. Finally, he took my photo in the yard of our home. As shown in Figure 14, my mother Elisabeth, the neighbor Sophia Peloponides and a neighborhood child are trying to calm my fears.

Nothing is more insidious than the uncontrollable fear of a child with the notion of being continuously in harms way. This mindset came to me initially through the Vafiades attack, but it was concurrently reinforced by the stories passed on to the children around me. People talked about who and how someone that they knew was murdered and the children picked it up and used their imagination to resonate it amongst them, propagating the fear into elementary school and even in the early teen years. Such fear caused many problems in all children that later grew up to be adults. Many of these children ended up with extremely aggressive behavior.

---

and in April 1990, he was honorably elected into the Greek parliament through the nationwide list of PASOK.

One of the greatest myths is that the young are angels. It may be so when people do not try to kill each other. I can personally attest that under war circumstances, scared youth are the most dangerous. I have personally seen seven and eight-year olds torture a drunken person without pity. When I was five, I was personally attacked and buried in the snow by two seven-year olds just for fun. Many youngsters adapted their inherent reptilian instinct for survival as the only important thing in life. For many years after the war they continued to believe that being aggressively defensive is the only means to their own survival in life. To them, life was similar to that of a pack of wolves; you must be aggressive enough to grab and keep what you can get before someone else gets it from you and you are left in the cold defenseless. The lucky ones managed to find someone in their life to teach them more promising concepts as love, teamwork, compassion, understanding, personal sacrifice and volunteerism.

It was soon realized by some brilliant educators of Drama that the only way to fight fear was by providing information on rational thought. Such information came through the schools and churches, but it became believable only through the kind and caring personalities of certain selected, inspiring men. Some of these men were young, educated volunteers who gave their time through the Orthodox Christian Church and the Boy Scouts of Greece, bringing some peaceful relief to youngsters, like me. Others were teachers, with keen sense of observation, educating and training children to act through reason, rather than through the deep rooted instinct of self-preservation, or habit.

Wars are devastating to all people. The victims are the dead, the crippled and their families who suffered afterwards. They are also the people with long term scars, which I personally experienced to last for at least three generations. More than sixty years later, I know of grandchildren, who still suffer because of the war trauma of their grandfathers. That thought alone should be enough to give sense to anyone, who even remotely thinks that a war can be a solution to a problem of humanity as a whole. You may fix a specific problem that few ego-driven people have, but you create a much bigger problem to a much larger population that lasts at least a century.

Figure 13 Stavros' First Photo in 1948: Taken After the
Vafiades Attack in Spite of Tearful Protestations

Figure 14 Stavros' Second Photo in 1949, taken by Basil Leonides

Remnant Greek Civil War Baggage: Communism,
FYROM and "MACEDONIA"

The Greek Civil war left long lasting scars. During the Cold War years, the Greeks were very guarded against those communists and collaborators that created havoc and destruction during that war.

Those that collaborated with the enemies of Greece during World War II and escaped to the Communist Block countries were viewed as traitors and were declared as criminals. When finally the Berlin Wall fell in November of 1989, the Greek communists became disillusioned with USSR and sought new direction. When Yugoslavia was disbanded in 1993, the Macedonian part of it, less than a fourth of the region that is commonly addressed as MACEDONIA, was named the Former Yugoslav Republic of Macedonia.

As was provided for by UN Security Council Resolution 817 (1993), Greece and the Former Yugoslav Republic of Macedonia started carrying out negotiations under the auspices of the UN Secretary General, with the objective of finding a mutually acceptable solution to the name issue of that – now independent - country .

Since 1995, the development of Greek-FYROM relations was impressive. Greece is one of FYROM's main trade partners and is first among foreign investors. Bolstering development and helping to combat unemployment, Greece's economic presence in FYROM is a stabilizing factor. Although a number of efforts have been made in recent years to settle the name issue on a bilateral level, FYROM's domestic political state of affairs has hindered the settlement of the issue in a manner harmful for both sides.

The political state affairs were driven by a movement of those who were descendants of those who participated in either the Balkan Wars or World War II as traitors to Greece, working for Bulgarian interests, or committed atrocities in Greece during the Civil War. Most of those, fearing imprisonment, left Greece on voluntary exile. This becomes evident from the publications and propaganda coming out of FYROM.

In one such publication,[159] the word Macedonian replaces the word Communist Guerilla and/or Bulgarian collaborator.

Many of these people, or their ancestors were born indeed in Greece, but chose to change sides during the war and committed severe atrocities. They avoided punishment by fleeing into countries where they would find asylum and when later were asked to state that they would be law abiding Greek citizens, they refused, thus forfeiting any rights or claims in the Greek society. They created a fictitious country, by stealing the name Macedonia, which belongs to the whole region, populated by Greeks many centuries before Alexander. It is true that often the Greek states that fought each other declared opposing states as non-Greek, in order to mock them, yet, they all had common language, culture and philosophy. Finally, it was Alexander of Macedonia that united them against the Persians, a union that endured Roman and Byzantine times. The Bulgarian and Slavic occupation of the area after the 6th and 7th centuries AD, attempted unsuccessfully to bring a rift between Macedonia and southern Greece. These attempts failed, even during the Ottoman rule. Now, after many failures during the Balkan Wars and World War II, the descendants of the traitors and the communist guerillas that ravaged Macedonia, raise claims on the land and the property that their forefathers abandoned, in order to avoid persecution from justice.

The Skopje government submitted on March 22, 2005, an application for accession to the European Union. At the first meeting of the EU-FYROM Stability and Association Council (Brussels, September 12, 2004), the European Union noted that the difference over the name of the former Yugoslav Republic of Macedonia still persists and encouraged the finding of a mutually acceptable solution within the framework of UNSCR 817/93 and 845/93 by Greece and the former Yugoslav Republic of Macedonia.

On November 4, 2004, the Bush US administration shifted its policy and unilaterally recognized FYROM under its own constitutional name,

---

159 "Oppressive Measures Following World War II," Macedonia for the Macedonians, http://www.makedonija.info/aegean3.html

as "Republic of Macedonia." This unilateral decision undermined the efforts to reach a mutually acceptable settlement, because it reinforced FYROM's inflexibility.

There is no chance of FYROM acceding to the EU and NATO under the name "Republic of Macedonia." FYROM itself has agreed to this stipulation: according to Article 11, Paragraph 1 of the Interim Accord, Greece agrees not to object to the application; however, Greece reserves the right to object to any membership if FYROM is to be referred to in such organization or institution differently than in paragraph 2 of the United Nations Security Council resolution 817 (1993).

The choice of the name "Macedonia" by FYROM directly raises the issue of usurpation of the cultural heritage of a neighboring country. The name constitutes the basis for staking an exclusive rights claim over the entire geographical area of Macedonia. More specifically, to call only the Slavo-Macedonians, Macedonians monopolizes the name for the Slavo-Macedonians and creates sociological confusion, whilst violating the human rights and the right to self-determination of Greek Macedonians. The use of the name by FYROM alone may also create problems in the trade area, and subsequently become a potential springboard for distorting reality, and a basis for activities far removed from the standards set by the European Union and more specifically the clause on good neighborly relations. The best example of this is to be seen in the content of school textbooks in the Former Yugoslav Republic of Macedonia, where history is flagrantly distorted.

In 1992 the Former Yugoslav Republic of Macedonia tabled an application to join the United Nations under the name of Republic of Macedonia. On 7th April 1993 the Security Council noted that although the country fulfilled the criteria for accession to the UN, there was nonetheless a dispute over its name, which needed to be resolved in the interests of maintaining peace and good neighborliness in the region. The country was consequently accepted under the temporary name of Former Yugoslav Republic of Macedonia.

Security Council Resolution 817/7.4.1993 officially states that the difference over the name of the State needs to be resolved in the interest of the maintenance of peaceful and good-neighborly relations in the region and calls upon the parties to work together for a speedy solution to their dispute. The process for solving this dispute is indicated in Security Council Resolution 817/7.4.1993 and Resolution 845/18.6.1993, which calls upon the parties to continue their bilateral talks under the auspices of the UN Secretary-General with the objective of solving outstanding bilateral issues as soon as possible. Also, on 8th April 1993, the General Assembly unanimously accepted the accession of the Former Yugoslav Republic of Macedonia to the United Nations with this name. Consequently, both the Security Council and the General Assembly recognized the validity of the Greek arguments on the name issue.

On 13th September 1995, Greece and FYROM signed an Interim Agreement which constituted the point of departure for normalization of their relations, with the only pending issue being that of the name. According to the Interim Agreement, the Former Yugoslav Republic of Macedonia has officially accepted that the name of the State is a subject of bilateral negotiations with Greece, as provided for by the two Security Council Resolutions, in other words 817/93 and 845/93, and Article 5.1 of the Interim Agreement. It is therefore clear that the object of the exercise is to replace the temporary international name of Former Yugoslav Republic of Macedonia with a permanent name acceptable to both parties.

The issue has not been settled so far because FYROM's intransigence was based on the influential number of the descendants of the Greek Civil War exiles. The present government has not enabled the two parties to reach a mutually acceptable solution, especially after the Bush administration, misdirected by special interests within his administration chose to unilaterally recognize FYROM as "Macedonia." Ever since then, the United States stated that they recognize the need for a mutually acceptable solution within the United Nations framework, irrespective of the reasoning that led to their unilateral recognition, but they have not retracted such name recognition. As they have repeated on many occasions, the United States supports Mr. Nimitz's efforts.

There is no question of a military threat to Greece by the Former Yugoslav Republic of Macedonia. On the contrary, cooperation between the two neighboring countries is developing in many sectors. The fact, however, that the Former Yugoslav Republic of Macedonia insists on achieving exclusive use of the name "Macedonia" or "Democracy of Macedonia" is directed against the cultural heritage and historical identity of the Greeks. The visible risk of future destabilization in the region should therefore not be ignored. Moreover, since the Ohrid Agreement, FYROM has changed its constitutional form and no longer sees itself, as foreseen in the 1991 Constitution, as the state of the Macedonians.

The best way for the residents of FYROM to "return" from the "Odyssey" that their forefathers took them is to work with Greece and the rest of Europe. The road to reconciliation may require them to truly identify who they were and who they want to be. Most of us have some forefathers in the past that made mistakes. If they aspire to join the European ideals, they must try to forget the ideological mistakes of their forefathers (just like the Germans try to forget World War II) and look into the future.

Anthony's Confession
(Based on his Diary, Drama, 1950-1970)

Anthony Boinodiris had to deal with many human predators in his life, in countries and periods where competition was a necessity but also a dirty word. A great deal of unethical people took advantage of him. So, some of his writings in his last years confessed his frustration with the injustice in the system, which allowed things like these to happen. It shows how frustrated this person was with certain human beings.

"Before 1950, competition was both fierce and unfair. The environment worked under the premise of: "my livelihood depended on your death." In addition, routes to go abroad were limited and expensive. This environment created some monstrous behavior in certain people. Every time I felt that I created any property, the environment presented me with people or wars that made me lose everything. Three times, I had to start from zero, to rebuild my life. If we had the opportunity to seek work anywhere, we would not be in such a mess and we could have created a great deal more. [160]

Human greed is one of the most unexplainable things. From all the animals of the universe, man is the greediest. When a tiger or shark hunts, it eats its prey, gets satisfied and stops hunting. This is not the case with man. Man's greed does not stop. Always on the move, always to get ahead, regardless of whom they hurt in the process. Their motto is: you die, so that I can live. They steal, lie, take bribes, libel, perjure themselves and they become traitors to get ahead. I had to deal with so many of the people that I thought that I was in the sewer of humanity. Why did they do these things? How big was their stomach, so that they could not be satisfied? Why could they not allow us to survive with them? [161]

A person called George from Kalos Agros in 1943 brought a four-year-old horse in the market to be sold. He was asking 20,000 Bulgarian Leva. The buyer had to pay 500 Leva in taxes. He sold it for 18,000 Leva to a farmer who had sold his tobacco for 24,000 Leva. He was left with 5,500 Leva. [162]

In 1945, after the occupation came the nationalists with some British Colonial troops, including Indians.

With these troops came the Greek Government, including civil servants. George waits with us in a church at the gate to the town for the parade of troops and dignitaries.

After they arrived, the governor of our county issued an order saying that: "Whoever was unjustly treated by traitors, should sign a complaint against these people for reparation."

In spite of the fact that I was treated brutally by some of these people, I did not sign any complaint.

---

160   A. Boinodiris, Book 1, p. 228.

161   A. Boinodiris, Book 1, p.347-348.

162   A. Boinodiris, Book 1, p.349-350.

Yet, this person George comes to me asking me to come as a witness against the farmer, to sign a complaint of embezzlement. When I asked why, he said: "You will get 2,000 drachmas (then $1000 of today's money). We will claim that he was a farmer traitor, who declared himself Bulgarian and threatened us with our lives to get the horse."

I refused. I told him that he should be ashamed of himself for swearing under oath on lies, which sold his horse for 18,000 Leva and now wants more money for the same horse. Even worse, he should be more ashamed for attempting to drag me into perjury. I told him that I did not want to see him again. He left.

A month later, he comes parading, riding on the horse he had sold two years earlier. I heard that he found another patsy to perjure himself.

It was then that I caught myself with ill will against this greedy man.

Six months later, I heard that the horse ate bad grass and died.[163]

Injustice is not a blessed act, by God or by man. I may have been a poor man all my life, but I never starved, except during the Bulgarian occupation. God provided for us good children and grandchildren to whom we tried to instill a sense of honesty, pursuit of justice and hard work. I sincerely hope that they take that as our primary heritage."[164]

The Rich, the Poor and the Greedy

Anthony's philosophy was similar to that expressed by Socrates, based on simple logic:

"The richest person is the one who is content with the least wealth. Contentment is the wealth given to people by nature. If you think about it, humans do not need much to survive. There are people on this earth that manage to survive on very little money. Even if our population increases tenfold, we could survive, if each one of us were content with fewer resources.

163 A. Boinodiris, Book 1, p.347-348.
164 A. Boinodiris, Book 1, p.351.

Some fundamental needs of human evolution are: daily survival, raising a family and helping the people in our reach to survive as well. Most people though want a lot more, because we are driven to improve our lives, by comparing our improvement to the lives of our neighbors. As we do that, we become greedy. Greedy people are now poor, discontented people, needing a lot more. Unfortunately, they work hard and create ideas and wealth that helps only their own needs. In that, they do not serve humanity in the struggle for survival.

A cynic like Diogenes was a rich person, needing little to survive, but did not care about creating ideas and wealth to help the people around him. In that, he was an egomaniac, serving none. Cynics may be the worst of all humans. Many of these people have what it takes to create ideas and wealth to help others, but refuse to exercise that capability to their full potential. It is a shame, that humanity, after striving for millennia to survive, by painfully creating such capable human beings, such beings waste their skills to self-indulgence.

A rich person, that is content with little to survive, works hard to create ideas and wealth. In that, a rich person is an exceptional human being.

The rest (greedy and cynics) are simply sick parasites of humanity, gathering material wealth only to give it up when they die.

One business that has the tendency to turn rich people into paupers is advertising. Advertising is simply a business of making someone who did not know that he needed something, to need it, thinking that they cannot live without certain goods and services. It is a contradiction in logic to worry about human poverty in the world, and at the same time to spend billions of dollars to advertise products that most of them did not know that they needed in the first place.

Invention and new ideas are the creation of individuals, based on a variety of motivations. Many are exceptional people, addressing badly needed tools for human advancement. Others that create inventions and ideas and help only their own pockets are greedy egomaniacs.

Those that address "mental needs" like religion, politics, fashion, art, exploration and entertainment are also ranging from exceptional to greedy. If those needs are constructive in the human evolution, they generate progress through the creation of opportunities. Our ancestors, for better or for worse discovered these needs, making us progressively poorer. Ancient Greeks, Romans and Jews were some of the worse culprits in pushing such "mental needs."

The "mental needs" are what makes life expensive these days. It feels as if we are moving farther and farther from the ignorance that the Garden of Eden gave us. These needs are our "forbidden fruit of knowledge," which we continue to feed on. Blast those ancestors of ours. Why did they push us in that direction? Maybe they thought that we needed to enhance our mental capacity to survive from partial or total annihilation.

Mass destruction was thought to be eventually inevitable. It is statistically inevitable that over a long period, humanity would not survive if we all became egomaniacs and cynics. Destruction can come at any time, from our sun blowing up, from total annihilation of a war, from being late in developing a cure of killer decease and numerous other possibilities, which humans have not thought of yet.

Not all humans are capable of contributing equally in their lives. Instead, the young, the old, the sick and the mentally and physically impaired need our help. To survive as species and not just as persons, we must help our young, our old, our sick and those that are mentally and physically impaired. We must "balance our ingenuity with our humanity," as Thomas Edison said. Personal survival means nothing, if the whole humanity goes down the drain in the end.

Some "rich" people combine ingenuity with humanity. Only these people think of humanity as a whole, rather than themselves alone. There is no virtue in Ayn Rand's[165] selfishness, unless "self" is seen in the context of

---

165   Ayn Rand (1905 –1982) was born Alisa Rosenbaum. She was a Russian-born American novelist, philosopher, playwright and screenwriter. She is widely known for her best-selling novels "The Fountainhead," "The Virtue of Selfishness," and "Atlas Shrugged," and for developing a philosophical system called

a member of humanity. What good does it do to have improved the life of a single human being or even a small group, if the rest of humanity is at the brink of destruction? How long can that group survive alone? You cannot have a good quality of life for a group of people, unless you create opportunity for all members of that group to contribute their outmost."

Post War Greece (Anthony's Diary, 1950-1960)

In 1950, the Democratic Party of Plastiras took over, bringing together the Left and the Right Parties. After their defeat, the communists left for the neighboring countries of Albania, and the Yugoslavia region of Macedonia. When in 1944 the Socialist Federal Republic of Yugoslavia, under Tito formed a federal state from scratch, Tito gave it the name of Yugoslav Republic of Macedonia (YROM).

The Cyprus independence issue began at that time too. Britain promised the independence of the island, which was in the British Commonwealth after the war, but they reneged on their promise. Cyprus consisted of 500,000 Greeks and 60,000 Turks living in harmony on that island. Cyprus sent 30,000 troops in World War I and 40,000 troops in World War II to fight on the side of British Commonwealth. In their demand for independence, Winston Churchill promised the Cypriots independence in many of his speeches and asserted them that they will eventually be united with Greece. After the War, England did not want to relinquish the island, because of its key location for operations in the Middle East, the Suez Canal and their colonies, many of which were still in their possession.

To prolong the date of independence, England urged the minor Turkish element and Turkey to take a position on a possible independence. Therefore, Turkey started objecting to the independence issue, requesting partition of the island in two parts, the Turkish and Greek

Objectivism. Rand advocated rational individualism and laissez-faire capitalism, categorically rejecting socialism, altruism, and religion. Her ideas remain both influential and controversial.

sector. Seeing the delaying tactics for what they were, the Greek sector rebelled against England, using guerilla warfare tactics.

In 1952, Plastiras got sick and Papagos took over. His presidency had Markenzinis as a minister of Economics. He devalued the drachma in half from 15 drachmas per dollar to 30 drachmas per dollar. Among his ministers, a young lawyer appeared in the ministry of public works, called Constantine Karamanlis, from a village close to Drama.

Before his term ended, Papagos died in October of 1955. Then, King Paul assigned the presidency to Karamanlis. [166] This young lawyer turned out to be a good politician, even though I was not in his Party. I have always supported the Democratic Party of Venizelos and Plastiras and was downright against the Royalists, who caused the Asia Minor disaster.[167]

In 1955, the Turks were encouraged to bring up strong demands on Cyprus and the Aegean. They did so because the United States supported them against the communists and armed them with the latest weapons, which now they turned and threatened to use against Greece. England was not too happy to relinquish Cyprus, where they had continuous fighting and lost a great deal of troops, so they did encourage Turkey to take up their own demands against Greece. Greece armed herself, thus escalating the arms race. Turkey demanded part of the Aegean, the rights to oil drilling and Western Thrace, where 80,000 Moslems thrived, a leftover from the exchange of populations, which was supposed to be balanced by an equal number of Christians in Constantinople. Due to Turkish imposed attrition, the Christian population of Constantinople was reduced, while the Moslem population in Greek Thrace thrived. The Moslem population in Greek Thrace, just like that of Bulgarian Thrace consists not only of Moslems of Turkish descend, but also Moslems of Slavic descend, named Pomacks.[168]

---

166 A. Boinodiris, Book 1, p. 47.
167 A. Boinodiris, Book 1, p. 275.
168 Pomaks constitute a religious minority who are Slavic in origin and recognize Bulgarian as their mother tongue, but who are followers of Islam. Pomaks have fought to maintain a separate identity from ethnic Turks and the issue of forcibly declaring them as Turks has been raised. In Bulgaria, the results from

The attrition was caused when Turkish mobs attacked all Christian establishments in Constantinople, forcing them to a mass exit from that city. From 120,000 Christians there, mostly Greeks, only 5,000 remained. Many of these Greeks that left for Greece, had some horrible stories to tell. [169]

From these Greeks, we learned that while we were fighting the Germans and during and after the occupation, all the way to 1950, the Turks persecuted the Greeks in Eastern Thrace by placing Varlik Verkisi taxes. These were taxes, targeted on the Greeks, requiring them to show how they received any property or money before purchasing a property. They forced them to pay heavy taxes on inheritance of any businesses. Those that could not pay, they confiscated their property right away. In the early years of the War, the Turks dispersed the Greek minority to the region between Tigris and Euphrates. The Turks also gathered men of Greek descent from 18-60 years old and sent them to the Russo-Persian front as conscripts.

If the Russians lost the war, Turkey was ready to join the Axis and with 600,000 soldiers, they were ready to move to Baku and Batoum, to acquire the Russian oil fields. In the process, they were getting ready to use these Greeks as unarmed reconnaissance, ready for sacrifice, like they did in the First World War. If the allies won (like they did), they would switch sides and join the victors. The Turkish policy was always to subjugate all minorities, Armenians, Kurds and Greeks at any cost, including ethnic cleansing. Evidence is the 1.5 million Armenians slaughtered by the Turks. To achieve this, they used their geographic location as a bargaining chip. During World War I, they used Dardanelles and Bosporus as a trump card very effectively.

The Greek Cypriots revolted from England. Instead of bringing up political opposition to what was happening, the tall but stupid King Paul, buckled under the pressure from abroad and built Turkish high

---

the 1992 census were invalidated in two towns due to charges that Bulgarian Muslims were pressured into recording themselves as ethnic Turks.
169   A. Boinodiris, Book 4, p. 24.

schools on the Moslem communities of Western Thrace, named after the Turk President Tselal Bayar.[170]

In 1949, the Parliament decided to form the Social Security Group for all Technicians and Business People (TEBE), of which I become a member. [171] In 1953, the Social Security organization for Tobacco workers (TAK) was abolished. People got a payoff and joined the consolidated Social Security Organization for all workers (IKA). My wife Elisabeth, who worked in tobacco factories, was now protected by IKA.

While we were trying to recover, Urania Aslanides dies in July1949. Michael Aslanides is left a widower. Being very young, he soon remarries Katina in 1951. Next year he has a son, Michael (1952).

Unfortunately, Michael Aslanides does not have the fortune to enjoy his new son. He is diagnosed with lung cancer and he dies in January 1953, after a long ordeal, having his mother Makrina take care of him by his bedside for almost a year. He was not a smoker, but worked in tobacco factories and sold paints which may have contributed to his ailment.[172]

The long ordeal of occupation and the torture of losing her son in such a painful way had an impact on Makrina Aslanides (Tsekmezoglou), who also died in April 1957 from lung cancer.

She was not a smoker. [173]

The World, in Relation to Greece

Turkey, led by President Tselal Bayar, along with Prime Minister Menderes and Foreign Minister Koprulu, the DP controlled the Turkish government from 1950 to 1960. The Turkish economy expanded rapidly during this time because of the new economic liberalism and the large-scale foreign assistance, principally from the United States, that followed Turkey's entry into the Western alliance. Ultimately, however, too rapid economic growth and poor management led to

---

170   A. Boinodiris, Book 4, p. 26-27.
171   A. Boinodiris, Book 1, p. 50.
172   A. Boinodiris, Book 1, p. 141.
173   A. Boinodiris, Book 1, p. 139.

severe economic and social strains and increasing political discontent voiced by the CHP, which the Democrats began to repress. In 1960 an army coup overthrew the government, hanged Menderes and a few of his associates on charges of corruption the next year. At this time, they installed a new constitution based on modern economic and social principles, with provisions to prevent the kind of repression the Democrats had inflicted.

The economy in Greece was so bad, that Greeks started immigrating abroad immediately after the war. After the total desolation of its infrastructure, this country of 132000 square kilometers, with three-quarters of it being non-fertile, mountainous rocks could not support its population of 7 Million. Germany, Australia, Canada and the United States were some of the destinations of choice.[174] Most of the migrant workers from Drama went to Germany. At its peak, Greek migration to Germany reached about 200,000, consisting mostly of young people.

While Greeks were migrating to Germany, the Russians, under Stalin built the monstrosity of the Berlin Wall in 1959. The Eastern Germans, who also wanted to migrate there, were prohibited by the fencing up of a whole city. [175]

News from America (Anthony's Diary, Drama, 1950)

Pandel Mayo's silence was interrupted in 1950, when a Greek-American came to Drama alone and ill with tuberculosis, to die under the care of his family. He brought news of Pandelis and his address. It was then, that I sent a letter with roughly the following message below:

"I do not know what bitterness resides in your heart with my parents, but you should consider the following: What did I do to you to be so bitter against me and my family? My father left me when I was seven; I had to provide for the survival of my mother and myself. My mother is dead. My father is an old coot, who is more of a burden to me than help, causing me a great deal of anguish. We just came through the ordeal of

---

174   A. Boinodiris, Book 1, p. 277.
175   A. Boinodiris, Book 4, loose attachment A1.

a World War, a bloody Bulgarian occupation and a bloodier Civil War. We are in desperate need of friends and help."

The response was a package with clothing and photos from Miami.

Growing Up (Stavros' Memories, Drama, 1950-1960)

Elementary School Experience (Drama, 1950)

When the package from Miami arrived, among the items in it was a leather hat with a wool fleece lining (an item that children in the northern United States wore at that time). After Pandel moved to Miami from New York, the hat served no purpose. Yet, for me it was God sent. I wore that hat to school in the subsequent cold winters until it was in shreds.

My elementary school was Ekpedeftiria, near my father's grocery store. My first days there in 1950 were nightmarish. I seemed to be the shortest child in the school yard, surrounded by teenagers who had missed school due to the War. The dangerous conditions of the years before 1949 did not permit schools to operate. Teachers were executed, or exiled. Schools were used as barracks or temporary quarters for refugees. Children had no school from 1940 to 1949. Those that had some education and wanted to finish it started going on an accelerated program with facilities, teachers and students that could not keep up with normal programs. Teachers were few, schools were overcrowded, and students had become like starving wild animals. Survival tactics through theft and beating of the weaker kids made these children a menace to six and seven year olds like me.

School lasted from 8 AM to 2:30 PM. After giving me hot goat's milk with stale, left-over bread crumbs for breakfast, my mother decided to wrap in my bag a slice of bread and some cheddar cheese from an UNRA can.

I went to the elementary school with a neighborhood boy, named Totos Boskou. One day, as we climbed the stairs to the schoolyard, we separated in the crowd. I found my way in and waited for instructions.

A big child appeared, his yellow legs towering in front of me. I raised my head to discover that he was skinny and yellow, all the way to his teeth. He probably had a severe case of jaundice caused by an unattended disease, like malaria or glucose deficiency in his diet. His face was very close to that of a skeleton. He seemed to be around fifteen years old. He wore shorts, several sizes bigger, made from long pants after they were cut with scissors and tied around his waist with a rope. His top was made out of a cotton sack of sugar, bleached to take out the letters, which were still visible: "UNRA" and "MADE in CUBA." These sacks were from United Nations Relief Association (UNRA) and included sugar, paid by the USA Marshall Plan, purchased from Cuba.

The yellow teen grabbed my bag. He fumbled inside, until he found my food. He took it out and put it in his pocket. He searched some more. Frustrated, he turned the bag upside down, spilling my pencil, notebook and textbook on the ground. Then, he dropped the bag. He grabbed me and pushed me to the ground.

"Tell your mom to put some more food in your bag. This is not enough."

He disappeared around a tree and ate the bread and cheese. He reminded me of the neighbor's yellow cat, eating food, after she stole it from our table. I picked up my bag, filled it with its contents and followed the smallest students that were forming in line.

Teachers had to be tough in those days to cope with 30-40 children in a class, most of them standing up. Those that were teaching the older kids were men and were even tougher. Eventually, months later, the older kids were separated to go to school at night, since most of them worked during the day. They liked the night school, since they did not have to go to school with seven year olds. They found that to be demeaning.

Corporal punishment was as common as breathing. If you were not on time, you were whipped. If you were not prepared, you were whipped. If you talked before being asked, you were whipped. If you were caught fighting with someone, both were whipped, no questions asked.

One teacher, a woman called Roula carried a very straight rod of willow wood, which was used on the palms of all her students. Most students in her class had swollen, or marked wrists. Older students would see a younger kid with these marks and say:

"Oh, you are in Ms. Roula's class." They then would show us their marks given to them by their male teachers.

Some teachers were outright cruel. One of them, whom I encountered when I went to high school, was named Iliades. He forced all his twelve year old students to carry five gravel stones in each pocket. He called randomly some of them on the board to orally examine them about the previous day's lessons. If they had not studied, he would force them to lay the gravel stones on the floor, raise their hands and kneel on the rocks with their bare knees (we all wore shorts then). At the end of the class, he made all other students pass in front of them and spit on them. Such humiliation caused many children to either change schools or to abandon school altogether.

The Shell (Drama, 1952)

I had just returned from my elementary school, when I noticed a peculiar object lying on the retaining dry stone wall of my father's yard. Bethlehem, my neighbor from across the street, was yelling at some villagers that were riding away in their mules towards Drama.

"Those accursed dogs left it there," she said. "Who knows where they found it? It looks like a bomb."

The object was an unexploded 105-mm howitzer shell. Soon a number of children appeared, to look at the object of death. My brother also appeared. He was eleven years older, and just came out of the army.

"Don't touch it." He ordered everyone. "I don't like it where it stands. It can fall, hit a stone below, and explode."

Then someone said, "let us call the police."

"You," he said pointing to one of the teenagers, "go to Papadopoulos' bakery and call the police. Tell them we need someone that is an expert in explosives."

The teenager disappeared around the corner. As we sat there waiting, my brother got impatient.

"You call a rookie policeman and he will blow himself sky high. I don't know how long that will take and I don't like leaving the shell here." Then he looked at me. "Stavros, I want you to move it very carefully and place it on the ground, under those thorny acacia bushes."

I looked at him.

"Trust me, you will be fine," he said.

I moved slowly towards the shell and lifted it. All the other children scattered, leaving me plenty of room. Slowly I lifted the shell and walked towards a thorny acacia bush. I laid it on the ground next to its roots.

"Push it under it, so that no other kids or animals disturb it," my brother said, standing ten meters away from me. I did as he said and returned. It was then, that I noticed that he was shaking. As for myself, I did not realize the danger at that time.

About one hour later, while I was indoors I heard commotion outside.

I ran out and discovered that three explosive experts, wearing uniforms were inspecting the shell. The children had showed them where it was and one of the experts was leaning under the thorny acacia bush. He had a large, white bundle next to him. He pulled the shell out and opened the bundle, which revealed nothing inside other than soft wool. He placed the shell inside the wool and tied the white linen back into a bundle. He raised the bundle and placed it on his shoulder. Then, he and the rest of the soldiers started walking towards the open fields, away from our subdivision. About two hours later, a great explosion shook our whole neighborhood. Several windows shook and some broke. A little later, we saw the soldier walk back towards Drama, carrying his now empty bundle with him.

"Was that explosion the shell you took from the bush?" a neighbor asked.

"Yes," he replied. "If anyone finds any more such things, I suggest that you do not do the stupid thing done here. Don't move it. Just call us, leaving it where you found it."[176]

I still wonder why my 21-year old brother chose me to carry the shell. Was it because he knew that my ignorance helped me carry it in a steady manner, more than he could do so? On the other hand, was it something else?

From that time on, I would see shells like that and urge others to leave them where they were found. One of the neighbors found exploded mortar shells and wanted to sell them as scrap iron. Among these was one that was half-intact. I urged the neighbor to let it be and the scrap-man refused to carry it.

Another time, during a high-school picnic another 105 mm shell was found. It was open and seemed to contain part of the explosive in it. We immediately notified the army. We later heard the explosion and the fireworks. It was a dud phosphorus shell.

The Christian Circle Group Summer Camp
(Livaderon,[177] August, 1956)

I crouched behind a bush, hiding and trying to listen for the enemy. I had my heavy, woolen vest sweater over my head trying to hide my face and peering through one of the short sleeves. The referees who were supervising the "war game," told us that the enemy was less than fifty meters away, concealed in front of us. A few of them were on top of a huge rock, camouflaging their features with masks and weird clothing. One of them, presumably the leader, wore a pith hat, someone's

---

176 Memories of S. Boinodiris
177 Another name for Livaderon is Mokros.

shirt worn backwards, and a large red handkerchief covering all his face, except his eyes. He was holding a flag and shouting names, as he pointed with his finger towards us. He nailed our leader, who was immediately removed by one of the referees. The objective was to knock out through recognition as many of the opposition as possible, without revealing who you are.

I recognized the voice of one of the opponents because he slept in the same tent with me. "Eleminoglou," I yelled, pointing towards him as I raised my body. The referee instantly yelled for Eleminoglou to get out of the fight. Then I yelled the name of the boy who owned the pith hat of the flag carrier. Nothing happened. A second later, I heard my name called by another of my tent-mates that was on the opposition, and the referee came and told me that I was "eliminated."

The "battle" lasted for another fifteen minutes. About thirty to forty boys on each side were playing this war game. They were led by their college-age leaders. The boys were between the ages of thirteen and sixteen. One side was a somewhat larger attacking team, trying to capture a fortification defended by the other team. The boys were selected, by randomly splitting the population of each tent in half so that the opposing teams knew each other well. Then, without any notice, they were taken to two different locations and told the rules as well as being allowed to camouflage themselves with whatever the teams had on them. The end result of this war was that the only person standing was the masked leader of the defending team wearing his pith hat. When the referees declared them winners, he revealed himself. His name was Constantinides, a medical student from the University of Thessaloniki who was spending his summer vacation working as a camp director for the Christian Circle Group.

The summer camp was primarily funded by the Christian Circle Group through donations from various groups, including the Greek Army and many other donors, including the Orthodox Church of the United States. We had to pay only a token of 300 drachmas for three weeks. The Greek Army went on a remote hill near the local elementary school, opened up a road and cleared a campsite. It was a short distance from the village of Livaderon, North of Drama. They also provided the material for building ten, portable plywood shacks and equipped them with eighty cots. Two canvas tents were also provided for the camp leaders. An army truck brought all of these supplies, dumped them on the opened site together with US-donated food which they stored in the local school near by. The eighty boys of the camp spent their first day building their shacks, securing their cots on the dirt and storing their suitcases under them. There was no light during the night, other than the light offered by the hand-held flashlights that happened to be in the hands of a few boys.

During that first night, a rainstorm tore through the area. The roughly prepared shacks were all flooded, suitcases floated and the tents were wind swept. None could sleep. Lightning lit up the otherwise dark skies and all we could see and hear among the thunder was our camp leaders trying to hold their tents. We lifted our wet suitcases on our cots and sat, listening to the commotion outside, as we planned repairs on our shacks. The following day, we started serious work. It took another five days to dig drainage dykes and anchor tents and shacks, so that we had better shelters. We brought electricity from the elementary school via a cable and we even built an operational water fountain, which was lit at night. Every day, volunteer cooks prepared food, made from American powder milk and eggs, canned cheddar cheese, spam, and for special treats we were introduced to Ovaltine, the favorite chocolate milk of that time. The last day, as we were ready to leave, we saw two buses full of girls waiting to occupy our quarters. Some boys started complaining, "…Why didn't they come in first, to put all the work needed to prepare the camp?"

Constantinides replied, "…Because you are boys and they are girls. Chivalry is part of our Greek-Christian tradition."

The Christian Circle Group was an ingenious plan, thought out by some local business leaders and supported by the Archbishop of Drama, to provide an affordable after-school activity environment enriched with Christian moral upbringing. It was an environment where I learned to be patient, earn my respect from others and above all, respect everyone around me. Constantinides was one of a handful of these "teachers," that shaped our spirits, simply by monitoring our interaction with each other. When one child expressed boredom, the reply was, "the devil's misfortune comes to people who are bored, find life uninteresting and complain. If you want to find success on anything, use your brain and patiently make your own life interesting, the way you want it." They always stressed "patience," "humility," and "courtesy to others."

The need for such a social environment was deemed necessary as Greece had just gone through an occupation and a civil war, leaving deep mental scars on most Greek children.

Most of these children saw their people being starved, persecuted, wounded, or killed. They experienced fear, to the point that their natural survival instincts kicked in and they turned into what we used to call them: "wolves."

These children learned how to steal, cheat, and use violence instinctively to satisfy their survival needs. For them morality was not an option. They were always afraid of strangers and formed street gangs. The gangs were led hierarchically. The meanest, strongest member became a leader, respected by the rest. The rest tried to build respect by their deeds, or by showing their mean nature through their foul language.

To curb the growth of these gangs, the Greek Orthodox Church came to the rescue. With the help of local business leaders, like a clothing store owner called Antoniades they purchased a house with a large yard and turned it into the Christian Circle Group Headquarters for boys. A similar facility in another neighborhood was established for girls. They gathered a dozen volunteers, and through donations, they equipped the facility with various games, like chess, ping pong and others, as well as some furniture. A basketball court made the place a haven for boys who had not seen such an environment before. Regular classes on Christian Moral Values taught by volunteer teachers of the local high school, or college age students, like Constantinides (the young man with the pith hat defending his fort), brought many children living in the gang morality of "wolves" back to a civilized world of Christian morality. Regular theatrical plays were organized, allowing each child to build their own self respect and regain confidence in their abilities. The children were organized in neighborhood teams which competed in sports.

Wars are very destructive in human behavior. Every war generates scars that last for many years.[178] We, the children that this group tried to help, owe a great deal to these people. They thought out the situation and with the scarce resources they had, turned the tide of losing generations of children to an abyss of psychological problems. They could only provide cover to those that were young enough, and mentally flexible enough to be helped. Those that were older and inflexible, still carry those scars of their experience with them. Many of these "wolf" people, although they gradually changed in time, left their mark by exhibiting abusive behavior towards their spouses, children and neighbors. Their scarred children in turn continued this behavior to a lesser degree, but the psychological damage of war, regardless of who won, destroys many families for many years.

Personally, I was a timid child, often being pushed around by other children. It took me some time to build my self-confidence and I never volunteered for anything. Most of the other children looked at me as someone to be used in a "backup team," rather than the "first team." Within a year, that perception changed after a soccer game between neighborhoods. Our neighborhood had more players than the opponents, so they sent me and another "backup" player to the opposing team. To their surprise, the opposing team won. The only goal scored by the opposing team was a goal that I scored. Henceforth, the children of my neighborhood did not repeat the mistake of underestimating one of their own, no matter how timid.

---

178 Late studies estimate that these war scars can last two to three genera-tions. See recent report "German War Children Begin Facing Suppressed Trau-mas," by Deutche Welle - Society April, 2, 2008- http://www.dw-world.de/dw/article/0,,3106411,00.html?maca=en-jamaby-1550-rdf

Figure 15 Recent Photo of Mokros (or Livaderon) North of Drama

Figure 16 Class Photo of 1960 - Paraskevopoulos is
shown at the center (right-bar coordinates). [179]

---

179 The author is at the far left (leftmost bar coordinates).

Paraskevopoulos (Drama High School, September 1958)

"I am here so that I can help you to provide positive change, and survive by using education as your primary weapon. Education is the ability to listen to almost anyone on anything, without losing your temper or self-confidence and respect. We, you and I, are nothing more than another kind of the many organisms that live on this planet, a speck of dust in the universe. I tell that to anyone who thinks that they are something special. By calling you an organism, does that make you lose your confidence or self-respect?"

Some students nodded. The philosophy teacher in Drama High School paused with a grin. His eyes sparkled with a peculiar glint of insight. All the students, about seven girls and twenty-eight boys, sat on their desks gaping at what was thrown at them. Paraskevopoulos was a teacher they enjoyed, because he treated them like adults, inspired them and made them think with his fiery lectures. Originally from Pontus, Asia Minor, he was fired up and made it his life's work to inspire the youth to form a better tomorrow. He taught Ancient Greek, Modern Greek, History and Latin, but all his lectures included the basis of Philosophy.

"Those of you that nodded 'yes,' need some education so that your self-confidence and self-respect stay high. The main purpose in the life of all organisms like us is to survive. Ever since we humans climbed down from the trees (more than 4 million years ago), we are going through an incredible Odyssey. Every one of us attempts to survive better than the dinosaurs did and to pass onto our children the sense of working as a team with past and future generations. I will put you in contact with past generations, by teaching you history, the history of human experiences that our ancestors documented for us to read. Does anyone know what the biggest contribution to making human survival possible was?"

The class was silent. The teacher smiled.

"It was the invention of leaving someone's thoughts and experiences for future generations- the art of writing. Our Greek ancestors, through logical reasoning understood the importance of documentation. In fact, they tried to document everything they could. The world knows what they thought because they wrote things down. This helped everyone in the world. We know very little of other, important civilizations like the Visigoths or the Avars that left little or no documentation. We know about them from others that, in a biased manner, wrote about them. The documented message to you by your ancestors is that you represent their future. And, as with every generation before you, you owe it to your species to help future generations learn from your experiences. Unless you can document your life experiences for someone else to follow, you present a limiting factor to our survival. All we have is the short and very precious time of a lifespan. We are driven by many instincts- curiosity, thirst for knowledge and beliefs that take us through our lives. No matter what are someone's beliefs, I hope they enjoy their life's Odyssey, utilizing it in the best and possibly most useful manner to the survival of our species."

"Humans, like other organisms are in a state of continuous change as part of our evolution. Yet, we cannot change physically and mentally faster than allowed by our own natural abilities. Our evolutionary speed limit may be higher than other known organisms, because of our capacity to learn and our inventiveness in finding new ways to pass information to future generations. Yet, no matter how much I want to teach you to go faster, both you and I have speed limitations."

"Another aspect of evolution is the breadth of change. We cannot change for the better until we all can change, both physically and mentally. Documentation that travels to all points of human existence helps others learn from your experiences. History teaches us through repeated lessons that if we leave someone in the human species behind, they will eventually cause us (through war, or rebellion) to slow down so that they can catch up. We must help everyone in this world catch up and, by everyone, I mean every person from the jungles of New Guinea to the Eskimos of the North Pole, to the high societies in Athens, New York and London."

At that instant, one young man sitting in the rear raised his hand. He was an older kid, somewhat of a rebel, who lost a few years in class advancement because of his rebellious behavior. The teacher nodded in acknowledgement.

"Does that include the Turks too?"

A surprised Paraskevopoulos pondered for a few seconds and then smiled. "If you really want to approach the world through the power of logic as the ancient Greeks taught us, then the answer is most certainly yes. That includes the Turks. Our civilization is based on that logic. As I stress to you in all my classes, the Ancient Greeks were the ones that taught us to use organized rules of logic to solve our daily problems. Logically, we, as human beings, cannot survive until everyone survives. If Socrates was around, and heard your question he would say- 'don't worry about being a Greek or a Turk. Worry about acting in a human way.' Some groups get isolated into their own closed world and start believing things that are illogical. They isolate the rest of humanity and treat them as aliens. Neither you, nor I know how valuable a Turk would turn out to be to a Greek, no matter what some did in the past. If some people are excluded, then we lose the benefit of their intelligence for assuring our survival and have less of a chance to survive. There are some people at times that think that 'winning over others,' is tantamount to 'their survival.' These bullying people and countries may win now a short, bitter victory only to have others hate them forever and work against them and willing to sacrifice everything to straighten them out. That is not 'survival;' that is a 'long-term suicide for all of us.' When a country, feels stronger than its neighbor, it tends to breed bullies within its government- bullies that are willing to show their superiority over their neighbor. We faced the bullying Turks for four hundred years, trying to show them not to put too much stock on military victories and to use logic and 'teamwork' with other cultures. Unfortunately, we failed. This failure was in part because they still do not understand these logical concepts of 'universal survival' and 'inter-cultural teamwork.' It could also be because we were poor teachers or, because most humans have learning limitations on what is good for our species."

"Every time such a failure occurs, there is war. We can logically rationalize going to war in order to help universal survival, because war will shock those that seek self-centered short-term gains. Our armed resistance forces them to rethink the error of their ways, and our mutual losses remind both of us not to repeat such mistakes. Yet every time we humans go to war, our progress suffers. Logically, the preferred way would be to wait someone out and let them realize on their own the error of their ways. I am from Pontus. I lost many of my relatives because the Turks went on a rampage and slaughtered them. Yet, I do not want to exclude the Turks, or anyone else from the human family. Such a decision is nothing less than our certain demise."

The student in the back raised again his hand. "What do we do with the Turks if they do not realize the error of their ways and instead want to change us? Do we keep on fighting? Is that a way to help humanity survive?"

"If your neighbor does not want to do things the way you do, let him be. If he tries to change you by force, resist him with all the might of your convictions. That is why my relatives died. They fought for what they considered to be right. Do not try to force anyone to change their ways. It is not rational to say that you must actively seek to change or destroy certain people, so that you and others can survive. You do that only when these people are out to eliminate you or your family and you have no escape. The rational thing to do with adverse people, families, societies and countries is to wait them out and give them time. Yes! Wait them out. In time and through dialogue, either they find the error of their ways, or you will."

"That would take a very long time," yelled the rebellious student.

"You are right. Humans take a very long time to be properly trained. Look at you! How long have you spent on these desks refusing to spend adequate time and concentration on your homework?"

The whole class went up in a roar of laughter. Paraskevopoulos smiled, but then raised his arms, became serious and silenced everyone with his demeanor.

"Today we experienced significant progress from one of you, a very smart student, who on his own realized what it takes for someone to improve. You can also realize how tough the job of an educator like me is. For survival reasons, we are all different. We originally started with instincts that helped us perform primitive personal survival and had to find out different ways of doing it. Now, we need time to adjust to speedy, logical learning. And, by the time we show some progress, our bodies become old and refuse to keep up with our minds."

"Because we have a limited time on this earth, many of us become impatient. Speed becomes so important, that we make short-cut decisions, which end up in tremendous disasters. Impatience drove Turks to eliminate Greeks and Armenians and Nazis to want to exclude a number of 'undesirables' from human existence, in order to speed up change. The result was a human bloodbath. Indeed, our lifetime is very short. Most of us act around our daily life and most of our acts do not have much of an impact beyond our life span. We make short-term plans, that benefit us alone, or very few people around us. We also use brute force, violence, or even wars to achieve a goal, rather than the more painful, patient process of logical persuasion and instruction. Even within our families, there are many parents that use corporal punishment as the primary motivation in instructing their children. You can see lots of that if you pay attention around you. The smart people learn, not only in class, but also by carefully observing things around them."

"We can really comprehend many things, by sharpening our powers of observation. Traces exist all around us, representing our evolutionary history throughout all ages, if we only take a notice of them. We must examine and learn from our past successes and failures. We must occasionally look at the forest, rather than be entangled in the daily routine of life, focusing on the bark of a single tree. Over our human timeline, our limited lifespan organisms evolved from apes, coming down from trees about four million years ago. The anthropologists tell us that Neanderthal hunters lived from 200,000 to 30,000 years ago. The Cro Magnon hunters became prevalent around 40,000 years ago, taking some attributes from the Neanderthal. These Stone Age humans managed to invent copper and bronze around 6,000 years ago. They also invented iron 3,500 years ago. Ever since then, we started inventing all sorts of intricate things."

"Our survival instincts and our mental limitations find it comforting to believe in external forces other than our own. We believe in a Supreme Being, politicians, friends, or even fate. Yet, we find difficult to believe in our own capabilities. We lower our brainwaves into meditation because we cannot stand the mental stress associated with life's decisions. We find it difficult to cope with the increasingly higher speed change required for our survival. Humans have to face continuous dangers. Wars, earthquakes and storms are routine events in history. Other dangers, like global annihilation by a nuclear war, a pandemic, humanity-destroying disease, or a huge asteroid like that which befell on the dinosaurs, require a lot more in order for humans to be able to overcome them. Humans require long term global unity, planning and effort- some things that we are by far unprepared to face. Yet, in order to survive, we must prepare for our survival even in that event. It is up to us to prove that we are capable of surviving on earth, or maybe life on some other planet. There are some optimists, like me, who think that we can if we put our minds to it. The Russians, with Sputnik, have shown us that we can escape from earth and possibly go to some other place, where some of us can survive a massive catastrophe.[180] Otherwise, all our efforts in human history would vanish in a few seconds."

"One frontier that we have had difficulty tackling is the moral and legal-enforcement in uniting humanity. This frontier requires teamwork between diverse humans. The first accomplishment was the formation of a basic family more than 10,000 years ago. Then around 3000 years ago, moral governing laws appeared, in the form of the Ten Commandments. About 2500 years ago, these rules were followed by institutions of governments taking a two pronged approach. The Eastern thought preached by Confucius was based on a single, trustworthy, selected benevolent ruler making decisions on behalf of a nation. At about the same time, a completely opposite notion of Democracy appeared in ancient Greece. There, humans were urged to trust none except themselves in forming democratic alliances for shaping the direction of the government and

---

180   Sputnik (later to be named Sputnik 1) was the first artificial satellite to be put into outer space by the Soviet Union on 4 October 1957. In those years, news about human potential in outer space was been discussed in all the media.

the opinions and actions of their neighbors. That is how they envisioned they could rule their own lives and destinies. These humans had to be their brother's keeper. This was a much more difficult concept for humans to comprehend for many years. We still have difficulty putting our arms around such a task. It was hard to implement because it required extraordinary effort on the part of each ordinary person. Yet, after several painstaking improvements, it proved to be most promising. Anyway, we are still working on it. Then, concepts like world treaties, international conventions and organizations came about. The first concepts upon which the Geneva Convention and the United Nations are based started appearing only about 400 years ago. That gives you an idea in terms of our human existence on how recently we started treating other people and groups of our own kind with a degree of respect."

The teacher paused, looked at his watch and raised a book. "This is your history book for this year. It covers only a small instant in time. This week we will cover the first chapter. Learning your history is a small, but important step towards planning your own human survival. We, Greeks tried to set some guidelines since the time of Socrates on how to survive. Just like the Jews, with their ten commandments, Socrates stated seven articles that define what constitutes an educated Greek." He turned to the board and started writing:

AN EDUCATED GREEK IS:

1. One who controls difficult situations, instead of being controlled by them,
2. One who faces all events with courage and by always using logical thinking,
3. One who is honest and truthful in all dealings with others,
4. One who can face bad events and bad people with grace,
5. One who controls personal urges and pleasures,
6. One who never gives up because of failures or misfortunes,
7. And finally, one who is not corrupted, or become arrogant because of success or glory.

The bell rang. Paraskevopoulos turned to the class and said,

"I want you to think and in the next session discuss the similarities and differences of Socrates' teachings and that of the Ten Commandments."

He then picked up his book and notes, opened the door and walked out. None in that class of note-taking students moved, until he opened the door. Even then, some were still staring at a wall in deep thought. As for me, I recalled all the fears that I had accumulated during my young years. They were now almost completely gone. Education and training with good teachers like Paraskevopoulos could have quite an effect on any youngster with traumatic stress. I was becoming braver every year, brave enough to take a long plunge across the Atlantic Ocean.

Preparing for America (Stavros' Memoirs, 1960-1961)

My brother John had married Efthimia in 1960. In the early 1960's, a great number of Greeks left to work in Germany, since that was the place where jobs were available. Among them were my brother John and his new wife. He went to Stuttgart where he worked in various jobs as an electrician while Efthimia worked in the SKF ball bearing company. John finally settled to work for an industrial rubber glove manufacturer named IGETRO, building and maintaining the ovens required in curing the latex gloves. The owner rented a flat near the factory to him, where they could live. There, they had a baby boy named Anthony in 1961. Since they were both working, the couple had difficulty taking care of the boy, so Anthony and Elisabeth Boinodiris agreed to take care of Anthony with the stipulation that John would help me economically to finish my schooling. As a result, in 1963 John took little Anthony to Drama to be looked after by his grandparents. Soon later, the couple had a baby girl that they named Elisabeth. Again, they had difficulty in keeping the baby girl. As a result, John took her to her grandparents who took care of her.

The year of 1960 started as a year of hope. I received news that Pandel Mayo was willing to bring me to the United States to study. In reality, Pandel needed help. He had invested all of his retirement money in nine apartment complexes in Miami and he needed help to maintain them.

His son John was doing a good job until he married and started his own family and business. Paying a maintenance crew was too expensive. Selling them was an option, but a much better option was to rent them to the newly arriving Cubans who desperately needed shelter in Miami after the Cuban revolution by Castro.

Pandel immediately thought of his young great nephew who could help him out while he was trying his luck at the local college. As Pandel Mayo admitted later, he never expected me to succeed. He expected to have a resident maintenance man, until he decided to sell the apartments. Pandel knew the cards were stacked against his nephew. I had very limited knowledge of English and I needed to pass a comprehensive entrance exam, including a language exam. Greek high schools had English in their curriculum, but in protest to the English occupation of Cyprus, all English courses in Greece were stupidly cancelled around the late 1950's. I knew that my father could not afford private lessons, but after the letter from Pandel arrived, Elisabeth persuaded my father to scrape enough from his savings to pay for a tutor.

The tutor was Michael Mavrides, an ex-Greek-American from Rochester, N.Y. who had to return home at his late fifties after his only unwed sister ran into health problems in Drama. He was an introvert with psychological problems of his own. He had a short period to prepare me, but even that little help was welcomed.

Pandel expected me to try school for a couple of years and then, after Pandel got his return on his investment, he would be ready to send me home. He was getting old and had enough of his own problems, to undertake the support of an unknown relative he had met only once.

Both, Pandel and I were about to be surprised.

In the spring of 1960, I prepared my passport. At age 16, I traveled to Thessalonica by bus and visited the American Embassy to get a student's visa. Having limited funds, I visited and stayed with Katina Bostantzoglou, the widow of Basil Bostantzoglou who was killed by the Bulgarians during the Bulgarian occupation. Katina was living at the Votsis Avenue, several kilometers east of the White Tower of Thessalonica.

In the American Embassy, I became acquainted with a sixteen-year old man, named Theodoros. He and his whole family were immigrating to New Jersey. The father was already there and Theodoros and his mother were making the trip to meet him. I compared notes and discovered that the two were both traveling on the same ocean liner from Piraeus. The liner was OLYMPIA, leaving on August 10 and arriving in New York on August 21. Theodoros was a bundle of energy.

After many days of going back and forth to the Embassy and staying in cheap hotels with beds full of bed bugs, I finally received my paperwork.

The year 1961 arrived with the imminence of travel only months away. I had excellent grades, but I kept my pending plans for America a secret. I did not want my teachers to know what I was planning to do. My father asked me,

"Why don't you tell them about your trip? They may give you an edge to the American reviewers, by raising your grades somewhat."

"Father, please stay out of this. If I cannot get these grades on my own, any grades they give me by favoring my situation are of no use to me."

He laughed.

"I don't understand your generation. You must try to get the most out of life, because others will beat you to the punch. It's a dog-eat-dog world out there."

"I don't care what others do father. What matters to me are not grades, but ability."

The high school went to visit Athens, Delphi and Peloponnesos for a field trip. This was the first time that I visited these areas within Greece.

Mental Preparation (Stavros' Memoirs, Drama, 1960-1961)

My life up to now was somewhat sheltered. My early years were full of fears, some real and some imaginary, caused by my experiences during the civil war years. Like most children in their pre-teens, I felt extremely vulnerable and dependent on others, including my parents. In those years, I found comfort in the arms of my parents who loved me dearly.

My older brother was almost an outsider. He was over eleven years older and had grown up and gone on his own before we could really understand each other. He grew under different, rather predatory conditions than I. He learned these methods surviving the Bulgarian occupation. He knew how to survive using techniques that I considered unethical and abhorrent. These techniques included oppression, blackmail and beating. During my teen years, I found many of the older people around me with the same predatory tendencies. Even in the early high school years, beating was a daily act by students and a few of my teachers as well. The exceptions were limited to a few, select, educated people, like most teachers and a good number of my fellow classmates. Soon though, thanks to my educators, all my fears about my survival disappeared.

When the news came that I was to leave this environment, I did not have to think twice. Being free from this environment was "a dream-come-true." Yet, I knew that liberty meant responsibility. That is why most men dread it. Being free means that I had to be on my own, in a land that I knew nothing about, speaking a language that I did not know. I thought about this for a long time, and prepared to be on my toes for any surprises.

What made me so anxious? Simply put, it was fear of the unknown. Fear that I was very familiar with as a child. I was ready to abandon my restful sleep at night and dependence on my parents to worry about everything. For the next seven years, my sleep would be anything but restful, having to think about possibilities and contingencies about my own well being. Yet, I had some powerful weapons. I had a well-adjusted personality formed by my loving mother and special people around me. One of them was Constantinides, the "big brother" of the Christian

Circle under whom I spent countless hours of my time along with other children. He provided a fairly good education which, although deficient in many ways, was well rounded where it mattered. Finally, I had a young brain that was curious and ready for all the adjustments it had to undergo, and was relatively healthy, able to undertake the punishments that were waiting for me.

Figure 17 Stavros Driving his Brother's Motorcycle (1960)

Figure 18 Elisabeth, Stavros and Anthony Boinodiris
in front of their Home in Drama: Spring 1961.

America (Stavros' Memories, August, 1961)

S.S. Olympia (August, 1961)

S.S. Olympia left Piraeus on the morning of Thursday, August 10, 1961. Olympia was a large ship with all the amenities. I had the cheapest cabin, one that was shared with three other passengers. I did not care, since I spent most of the time on the deck. I teamed up with Theodoros from Thessaloniki and the two of us were inseparable.

The next morning, Olympia docked in Naples, Italy for a few hours stay. I disembarked and started walking around the city near the port. There, I almost lost my life. A driver with a left hand signal and a stop light made a right turn on a pedestrian crossing at 60 miles per hour, barely missing me. I saw him with my peripheral vision and jumped back, just in time. If I did not, I would have been killed. I returned to the ship and stayed put, vowing to avoid Naples forever as a pedestrian.

The passengers boarded the boat and we left Naples with a group of new passengers from Italy. They were families visiting relatives or migrating to the United States.

"They're almost as loud as the Greeks," commended Theodoros.

Among these passengers was a family consisting of a woman from America, traveling with her 14-year old daughter and 10-year old son. They were also escorting a 16-year old niece back to the United States. The 10-year old was annoyed by the "foreigners" and called them stupid because they could not converse. After some consultation with Theodoros, I responded in perfect English:

"You are not as clever as you think young man."

The girls were taken aback, chastising their brother and apologizing. They did not think that these Greeks spoke English at all. We were acquainted with the family and on a couple occasions, we were allowed to dance with the girls on the dance floor of Olympia, trying to practice our English with them. Theodoros was good in comprehension, but could not speak very well. I spoke reasonably well but could not understand the words, as they were spoken fast by these American-born girls. Theodoros and I made quite a pair. One spoke, while the other listened.

In two days, Olympia docked in Lisbon. It was an impressive city, full of parks and statues. Most impressive was the Magellan statue, representing Portuguese exploration. After a few hours in Lisbon, Olympia left for the open Atlantic Ocean.

Up to now the trip was exciting. After the fourth day, it started becoming boring. The crew was trying hard to entertain us with movies, games, music and delicious, plentiful food. My favorite dish was turkey and chicken cordon bleu. Around August 15, the seas became choppier by the hour. Then, we heard the news: a hurricane was in front of us, traveling north. We had to change course and slow down to let it pass. Between the 16th and 19th of August, the rather large Liner Olympia was tossed around in very high seas like a walnut shell. The crew had strung ropes all over the passageways. The waves exceeded 30 feet (10 meters). Food was served, but few people showed up. Most of the passengers were vomiting all day long and had lost their color. Theodoros and I did much better than average. We threw up only once or twice per day.

Arrival to America (New York, August 21 1961)

On Monday morning, 21 August 1961, Olympia passed by the Statue of Liberty and docked in the New York harbor. I had my instructions. I was to meet my great uncle Pandel Mayo at the pier. If something went wrong, I was to go to the dental office of Kominos in Astoria, where a Greek American community thrived. The dentist was Pandelis' brother-in-law.

As Theodoros and I were waiting to disembark, exchanging addresses and saying our good-byes, we were watching the skyscrapers nearby and looking at the "lucky Americans," at the pier. Then, among the people that were waiting there appears a gay transvestite black man making passes at some of the men in a loud manner.

"God help us," said Theodoros. "I wonder. What country is this that we came to?"

We both laughed.

I disembarked with my suitcase, passed through customs and searched for Pandel Mayo. He was nowhere to be found. Following my instructions, I decided to hire a taxi.

"How much does it cost to go to this address?" I asked the taxi man pointing to a circled address at my uncle's letter. The man looked at the address.

"Ten dollars..."

"I do not have ten dollars and I am stranded."

"How much do you have?"

I double-checked my wallet. I had six dollars and ten cents.

"I only have six dollars."

"That will do. Get in," responded the taxi man.

The taxi man had to pay his way through the tolls of the bridges and took me to Astoria. I paid him, thanked him for the help, grabbed my suitcase and climbed up to the office. A nurse got a glimpse of me.

"Are you Stavros?"

"Yes."

"Oh, my God, you are here. Wait here."

In a few minutes Mr. Kominos appeared and started talking in Greek. He shook my hand.

"Hi. Your uncle and your aunt left for the pier. I will tell them where you are if they call."

"Thank you."

In about an hour a call came in and Pandel found out where I was. A bit later Pandel and Katherine Mayo walked in, upset for having traveled all this time for nothing.

Trip to Florida (August 21st – 24th)

The three of us boarded a 1956 black Ford and took the road to Newark, New Jersey to meet the older brother, Nick Kominos and stay there overnight on that Monday night. Nick had a nice home. He was a mechanical engineer. The stay at his house was pleasant. At the dinner table, I picked up a piece of bread. It was not like the bread I knew, but it was a sign that I would not starve in hunger.

"Thank God for this bread," I said inadvertently. "If America has bread like this, I am going to survive here."

Pandel and Nick laughed their hearts out.

"As you will find out, there is plenty of bread here. America feeds the world." said Pandel.

Nick gave Pandel a few bushels of apples, which were loaded in the back seat. I had apples to eat on the trip to Florida. We left New Jersey and went to the home of Harry and Dorothy. Dorothy was Katherine Mayo's sister. She had a young son Eddie and a younger daughter. Eddie was a nice 17-year old, well-built teenager that loved football. He immediately wanted to play football and soccer with me.

I had not seen an American football until that time. I was awkward at it and could not throw it at all. Eddie was quite happy to teach me. When it came to soccer, I had the upper hand. Having played soccer in high school as a goalkeeper, I could use both, hands and feet with a round ball. The next day Eddie took me and a couple of his friends to Philadelphia to watch a professional football game. I was surprised to see Eddie drive his own Chevrolet car. I was also dazzled by the color and beauty associated with the football stadium. Up to that time, no spectacle was that dazzling and exciting to me as the football stadium. In that game, the Philadelphia Eagles were playing the Washington

Redskins. Yet, my greatest surprise was seeing how Eddie was so open-handed in spending money. Eddie had spent over ten dollars for hotdogs and drinks that day in addition to the cost of the tickets. Ten dollars was to me many day wages and an unbelievable waste of money. What I did not realize then was that I was viewing middle class Americans with the eye of a poverty-stricken family that just came out of a devastating war.

We had a good time, but I was uneasy and speechless. We returned home and I got some of my answers. Harry was an electrical engineer, who had his own factory making special diodes for government contracts. He showed them to me at his basement, where he had his workshop in which his invention of diode manufacturing process was conceived. Harry made lots of money and his son could afford to spend it.

After spending the second night in Pennsylvania (a little town to the northwest of Philadelphia), we left for Florida. We entered the home of Pandel Mayo on the night of Thursday, August 24, 1961. The house was located on NW 45th Street, between First and Second Avenue. It was a three-bedroom home, but I was placed in the back porch, which was turned into a sun-room, surrounded by jalousie windows that opened up for ventilation. A couch, which unfolded into a single bed, was located on one corner. A table was in the middle. I spent most of my next three years, sleeping and studying in that room.[181]

Paraskevopoulos on Stavros' Departure
(Anthony's Memoirs, Drama, Fall, 1961)

During the fall of 1961, after the grades were issued and Stavros had gone to America, Paraskevopoulos visited me at the grocery store to deliver Stavros' certificate with his final grades.

---

181   In the early 1960's, air conditioning units were a luxury that few could afford. Considering the Florida heat, few schools were equipped with AC units. The Mayo home had one window AC unit, mounted on the family room, which was turned on only when the family had guests. There was a central, oil-fired heater that heated the whole house except the sun-room. The room that I stayed in was the sun-room, which had neither heating nor AC. Yet, the house was quite comfortable for a seventeen year old young man, like me.

"I want to congratulate you Anthony. Your son did very well. What does he plan to do?"

I started laughing.

"He has not told you, but you might as well know it now. He has left for America to study."

"What? Why did nobody tell us?"

"I don't know. He…"

"We could have been a little more lenient with his grades. He did very well, but instead of 18, I could have given him a 20."

"That was exactly why he did not tell you. He said that if he cannot get these grades on his own, any grades anyone gives him by favoring his situation are of no use to him."

"Knowing that, I'd like to congratulate you even more. You have a special child Anthony."

Years later, Paraskevopoulos was talking again about Stavros' behavior in his classes. I know that because my grandson Anthony, who also had Paraskevopoulos for teacher and superintendent, took the brunt of it and came and told me. Unfortunately, my grandson took these lectures as an especially hard criticism on him, since he could barely pass his classes.

The Worst Time of My Life (Miami, Florida, 1961-1962)

The first six months were so frustrating, that I consider them the worst time in my life.

A few weeks after my arrival, my uncle and I visited the administration offices of Miami Dade Junior College. The college was then at its infancy, located on 95th Street of NW Miami, a year before moving to an old airport at Opa Locka on 125th Street, where it grew over a few years into being the biggest Junior College in the United States. I attempted to communicate with the woman in the admissions, only to verify what I knew all along: how limited my English was. Since I could not attend classes in any college, my education in English took primary priority.

I soon realized that my great uncle was not doing me a favor by bringing me to America. I would have to pay dearly for this privilege. It did not take long to discover that Pandel Mayo was a born dictator and bully to everyone around him. I did not know it then, but I now realize that he had acquired some of these traits from his own father, who ran his household like a railroad. Pandel expected to be informed on anything going on with anyone under his roof. He screened all mail, in or out of his own household. All visitors to his home had to get permission, a day in advance. Expenses must be screened, scrutinized and registered by his wife to the penny. For example, my great uncle would send me to a barber college, instead of a regular barber, where students learned how to cut hair. It cost 25 cents per haircut, rather than the usual $1.50. The first thing that one of those students told me one day was:

"Did you make your will before coming in here?" I gulped, because he was holding an open razor in his hand.

Dental care meant that teeth were pulled out when cavities appeared, because Pandel did not want to pay for the extra expense of filling cavities. Years later I would pay a lot more to straighten my teeth, warped because of this cost-saving practice.

I was to work for no pay, in return for the loan of money for room and board and any school fees. The job assigned to me was to maintain all of the nine houses and apartments that Pandel Mayo owned. Half of these, near Miami Avenue were old apartment units, rented to recent Cuban refugees. The Cubans were making fun of the young "Griego"[182] that fixed their electrical fixtures, sprayed under their homes for red ants and termites, fixed torn screen porches, and patched roofs, cut limbs off palm trees and numerous other tasks. Tree-cutting and trimming work was my typical daily task. The insect-infested, hot and humid Florida weather was new to me, but after awhile I learned to live with it. These

---

182   Griego in Spanish means Greek.

tasks were taking place whenever the need arose during the week. I also started doing odd jobs for John Mayo, securing some limited allowance at 50 cents per hour.

Food was good, but limited, especially to a hard-working young man like me. I could not have my usual milk that I grew up with. It was substituted by water. The worst of it was that I felt alone and without any friends. Several evenings, especially during weekends when the Mayo family left me at home, visiting their friends I found myself crying, feeling sorry for my condition.

Then, I started thinking about my situation. Pandel was not singling me out. He treated his wife, his son and his son's family almost as rudely. Not knowing me at all, the Mayo family justifiably treated me as a stranger, working and living in their home. By the time they found out who I was, I had already made my move.

After a few miserable months, I made my decision. Instead of crying and feeling sorry for myself, I decided to fight and win. My goal was to get educated on my own. I could do that, if I could bear living in the prison that my uncle set for me for a while longer.

To do that, I needed to get access to schools without having my uncle taxiing me around. I persuaded my uncle to purchase me a bicycle and lots of tire patches. Pandel was very happy to do so, in order to avoid transporting me to work locations. With my limited allowance, I purchased a plastic raincoat, so that I could bike in the rainy weather of South Florida. I carried that raincoat on my bike all the time, going back and forth to work.

Next, I found out where the public libraries were. I discovered one at Biscayne Bay Park. During every weekend, holiday, or days that I had no work, I was there reading everything I could lay my hands on, from novels, to dictionaries.

Soon, my uncle realized that I was serious. He volunteered to enroll me in a night-class at Jackson High School, together with Cubans, most of them working during the day. There, I practiced comprehension. I soon found out that I had less difficulty in comprehending Cubans than Americans and realized that a better way to learn English would be to attend an actual High School. There was only one that offered day and night classes: the Lindsey Hopkins educational center. This center was in a 15-story building, I believe around 14th Street, used as a public school. This school was set to provide high school degrees to grown-ups and slow learners, but now it was doubling up to teach English to Cuban immigrants. It also happened to have a great library. I biked back and forth to the Lindsey Hopkins, most of the days from January to June of 1962.

I probably read most of the books in that library. I had two goals in mind: one was to pass the entrance exam; the second was to improve my English comprehension, by being able to understand the CBS news on television, as broadcasted from anchorman Walter Cronkite.

I realized that my duty to myself lay in being useful, not according to my desires but according to my capability at that particular time. The methodology of learning English soon became apparent. I started from what I knew, science and mathematics. These were my first books and the first classes at Lindsey Hopkins. They built up my vocabulary of words associated with the known science and mathematics terms of Greek roots. Then, I wrote and translated all unknown words I encountered. The greatest difficulty in attending the science classes at Lindsey Hopkins was the distraction caused by the other students, who had zero interest in being there.

In Lindsey Hopkins I met some Greeks. One of them was a woman from Kozani, a newcomer called Polyxeni, calling herself Jenny. Jenny was around thirty years old, and was trying to learn English, like many of us. She was a real beauty and attracted men as honey attracts bees. Among these men was a disturbed jealous bully, who threatened to beat me up, if I did not stop talking to her. My response was:

"Don't worry Jimmy. I keep company with her because she has adopted me. Can't you see that she is old enough to be my mother?"

I had no intention of getting into any scuffle with Jimmy, for I had nothing to gain by it. Jimmy was a Greek-Jewish American, as his mother was Jewish and his father was Greek. Their son, a 250 pound, six-foot man had problems which some that knew him attributed to his environment at home. In spite of my intentions to stay out of trouble, trouble came to visit me anyway.

"What do you mean by saying that I am old enough to be your mother?" Jenny said to me one morning, as her veins were popping out of her forehead. It seems that Jimmy was more than a bully. He was also a rat fink. "How old do you think I am?"

I had to explain to Jenny how Jimmy tried to bully me. She became red:

"I will fix that bully well!"

A few weeks later, I noticed that Jimmy was not around Lindsey Hopkins any more. When I asked Jenny, she responded:

"My brother took Jimmy to the police. I was told that the law put an injunction on him. He cannot be closer than 50 feet from me."

I love the legal system in this country, I thought.

By May of 1962, my English preparation time was expiring. In June, reluctantly, and knowing very well that my English was not good enough, I took my entrance exam at Miami Dade Junior College, now having moved to Opa Locka. [183] Although my mathematics grades were 97%, I passed with a grade of 76% in English.

---

183   Opa Locka is a small suburb township of Miami. In 2007, it had over 15000 residents. Opa Locka was named the city with the highest violent crime rate in the United States by the FBI in 2003 and 2004. Despite major drops in crime, it still remains among the most dangerous places in the United States. Destiny had it that I had to travel 16 miles every day (8 miles each way) from 45th Street to Miami Dade Junior College for two whole years to a notorious place. Opa Locka gained this notoriety when it was discovered that the 9/11 Hijackers trained there, on the airport where the college is located.

Miami Dade Junior College (Miami, Florida, 1962-1963)

My first semester at Miami Dade was full of surprises. I registered at the pre-Engineering school and managed to secure excellent grades. Naturally, my best performance was in science and mathematics.

I had to bike 8 miles each way to school every day to the campus from 45th street to 125th street and take a shower at the gymnasium after getting there. I always had two sets of clothing, deodorant and soap tucked in a bike bag with me, one for the road and one for class. The probability of a rain shower on the way to school was greater than 50%. Flat tires were also common. I simply pulled to the sidewalk and fixed the flat with my portable tools and patches. I also became good in avoiding careless drivers.

It was in Miami Dade Junior College, that I was told that I had to take a swimming test for a gymnastics qualification. The State of Florida required that all young men had to know how to swim. I forced myself to jump into the pool, knowing that I could not swim. I wanted to see if I could learn to do it, just by necessity. Naturally, since I had never been in a swimming pool before in my life, I could barely keep myself afloat. Fortunately for me, a black female gymnast dove in and saved me from drowning. She then proceeded to chastise me and told everyone not to repeat my stupidity in the future.

During my first semester as a freshman, I had an English teacher, who assigned us a composition. I was surprised when my composition received an "A" grade. In fact, the teacher made me stand up and read my composition to the class with my broken English.

"I gave him the 'A' because his grammar is better than most of your compositions," she said with a smile.

I made some good friends in that college. One was Bill Curran, who was brilliant. He was a musician, ham radio operator, mechanic, awesome tennis player and electrician all in one. Some other friends were Vince, Steve and a Vietnam veteran named Hoper Lamar with his friend Terry. I saw Hoper again, because we both graduated from the University of Florida. Terry (whose name I forgot) was a Vietnam veteran as a helicopter pilot. He was continuously being offered a commission to return to Vietnam for another tour of duty. He told us that he wanted to stay out of the war, get educated and live a peaceful life.[184]

Another friend was a young man named Forrest Lehman, who wanted to become a pharmacist. He was a young man that liked practical and obscene jokes. He laughed, snorting viscerally after blurting them out, in the most disgusting manner. Deep down, he was good-natured, and because he had a car, he often asked me to come along with him to the movies or to his home.

One evening, Forrest invited me to his home, where we had dinner with his parents. The Mayo's were notified but they were not there when Forrest came with his car to pick me up for dinner.

The Lehman family was a typical American family of that time. The father was a middle class salesperson and the mother a homemaker. They were curious about their son's Greek friend. They asked me to sing a Greek song. I sang the song "Pote," or "Never" by Stelios Kazantzides. They were disappointed to hear that the words of the song were so depressing.

A discussion started about why I decided to come to America.

"I wanted to get educated. After the war, economic conditions in Greece were tough. You should feel very fortunate that you live in America."

"We are," said Mrs. Lehman. "Are you listening to this Forrest? I wonder if you would do what Stavros did if America was in the same situation."

"America would never be in that situation," said Forrest. "We are too smart to allow it to happen."

---

184   One day Terry came to class all shaken up. Someone pulled a gun at him because he did not like the way Terry was driving on the I-95 highway. A year later, I saw Terry in crutches. He was involved in an automobile accident. In 1966, Hoper told me that Terry lost his life in another automobile accident. Poor Terry could not realize his dream of staying out of harm's way.

Mr. Lehman looked at me.

"What do you think? Do you think that America could ever be a poor nation?"

"Of course it can," I responded. "If Americans turn out to be arrogant, they can be in as bad shape as other countries. People in other countries want to improve their condition. The question is how much they want to sacrifice to achieve it, in relation to how much Americans want to do to retain their wealth. If Americans relax and waste their wealth, other countries would be hosting American children, just like you are hosting me."

The Lehmans looked at each other. Forrest was eager to change the subject of discussion.

One day Forrest made the mistake of appearing at the Mayo house unexpectedly, without notice. The Mayos were at the grocery store, so he parked in the entrance of the carport and rang the bell. As Forrest and I were making plans on a future outing, the Mayos arrive.

"Who is the son-of-a bitch that parked in my driveway, not allowing me to come in?" Pandel Mayo started yelling at the top of his voice. "Steve! Get out here, now!"

The Mayos called me Steve. I jumped up and rushed to the front door, followed by Forrest. My aunt Katherine was aping Pandel's yelling.

"How dare you allow a stranger in the house?"

"I am sorry. He is a classmate; he is the same classmate who invited me for dinner one evening. He dropped in unexpectedly to talk to me."

Forrest quietly drove his car off. He never drove his car again to the Mayo's house.

I tried to get a permit to work, but the immigration and naturalization service denied my application. After a year of stay, I was permitted to work only a few hours per week. This was the worst obstacle that I had in making ends meet.

My uncle's rude and suspicious behavior was routine. Yet, I always saw in him a benefactor and was very grateful to him. Even when others, within his own family tried to badmouth him for his behavior, I responded: "I will always be thankful to him. He, at least did something about us, his Greek relatives. I cannot say that about others."

Regardless of his shortcomings, he had taken a leap of faith and offered me to come to America. Others would not bother with a poor great nephew, grandson of a lost sister that disappeared in Cappadocia and caused his family all sorts of aggravation.

Change in Plans (Miami, Florida, Spring, 1963)

By springtime of 1963, I got a clear indication from my uncle that he did not need me any more. This meant that I could no longer earn my keep. His houses had appreciated in value and he started selling them, one at a time. Eventually he would not need me to maintain them. I knew this would happen and I was getting prepared for it. I had worked a little over a year to get into college and do well. I also knew that if my uncle did not need me, he could yank me out of school and ship me back, regardless of how I did.

As I was seeking the solution to my problem, I received verification from my brother John in Germany, telling me that he could send me some money if needed. This was verification to my father's letters, describing his agreement with my brother as a payback for their baby-raising services. My parents agreed to help with my tuition by working it off. They were willing to raise John's children in Greece. I had to communicate secretly with my brother (by sending mail without Pandel's knowledge) and ask him to put his money in a bank, because I would soon need it. I explained how Pandel screened my letters and asked him not to write a response and wait until they were told when and how they could help.

John was surprised and discussed the matter with his wife Efthimia. According to John, Efthimia had no intention of helping at all, but my mother Elisabeth, after finding out what was going on, persuaded John to keep his commitment, in exchange of taking care of his young children. "Otherwise," as she quoted herself later "come and pick up your children and take them back to Germany."

When Pandel told his son John that he was planning to send me back, John Mayo suggested that I stay at his home and work for him. Consequently, around April of 1963, I moved in with John Mayo and his wife Christina to their house in North Miami. I was assigned to work with him before the semester was out. John Mayo was in the construction business and had his own roofing company. The good thing about working for John Mayo was that John paid me a minimum wage salary (about 75 cents per hour), salary that I saved for emergencies.

In order to accommodate me, John had to modify his large garage and make an extra room there for me to sleep on a cot. He was good with his hands and within a week he built the partitions with insulation and sheet rock.

John Mayo had troubles of his own. He was a good-natured young man. He had to deal with his despot father, who managed to control him and his mother all his life. John was a good athlete, a tackle on a football team in school and a very strong man that could flatten anyone.

His father found him a bride and John married her. Yet, when the bride stepped in, she discovered how unbearable his father was. A war was afoot between them, and I stepped in it without knowing it. She became irritable with me, connecting me as one of the relatives that Pandel Mayo unloaded on her husband.

The Roofing Business (Miami, Florida, Spring, 1963)

The construction company that John Mayo ran had its own roofing crew, in which I was assigned. I worked there all my weekends during school season and throughout all vacation days. John Mayo's business came from various sources, including Sears Roebuck. A foreman with a heavy Georgia accent managed the roofing crew initially. Later, a Puerto-Rican man called Manuel took over.

One day, the Georgia foreman said to me:

"Bull ofr them nails," pointing to a set of new nails on the roof.

I understood that to mean: "pull off them nails," because of a possibly mistaken placement. So, I started pulling out the nails. The foreman yelled something I could not understand and raised his hand to stop me. He immediately showed me what he meant by "bull."

"Bull" was a black, tar, patching compound for sealing nail openings in roofing slogan. All my co-workers were laughing at my mistake. Among them were habitual drunks, illiterate, hard-luck blacks and people that had foul manners and language.

One of the blacks, a 300-pound big man named Willy, got very drunk every night. He was in such a condition, that he was falling asleep on the job. One day, I had to tie him to the truck's railings because he was so sleepy, that he was about to roll off the truck in the middle of the highway while the truck was speeding at 60 miles per hour. All these men were supposed to bring or buy their own lunch. After drinking all their money the previous night, many did not have a dime in their pockets for lunch. They were begging me to share a sandwich with them. I did so on occasion, even though I found out where all their money went.

The work on the roofs was hot and tiring. The temperature often rose to above 150 degrees Fahrenheit to the point that I had to stop and pour water on my thick shoes to avoid my feet from being cooked. Men had to drink water very often. The water was brought up on the roof with ice in an ice cooler. Since we had no cups, all the men had to share this water by drinking it using the same tin ice cooler cover. It may not have been healthy, but when you are thirsty at over 150 degrees, you don't care.

Manuel, the Puerto Rican boss was married to an American wife and had two daughters, but his marriage was on the rocks. He liked and praised me for working with this bunch of people without griping, while I was going to school at the same time.

Some of the jobs included a fire station building in North Miami, houses at Kendall and Coral Gables and some complete roof renovations in two hotels in Miami Beach. Several notable events occurred during that period, some of which I will present.

When I was working in building the fire station of North Miami, I had to travel by bicycle from John Mayo's home to the site. During those times, most of that area was newly built and many Everglades animals still considered the land as their home. Wildlife was teaming all over the place. It was not uncommon to see wildcats, wild turkeys and other Everglades creatures all around us. As I was rolling down a long downhill with my bicycle, early in one morning, I saw two huge rattle snakes blocking my road. I had too much momentum to stop and I was also afraid that a sudden breaking could cause the bike to slip on what I noticed to be a very sandy road. I decided therefore to go on. As I closed the distance to about five yards, I saw one of the snakes raise its head and ready to lounge at me, as both snakes rattled their rattlers aloud. Now I had no choice but to go through with my decision to pass. I swerved slightly away from the snake with the raised head and lifted my feet off the pedals and placed them on the handlebars.

It worked. I was not hit.

Another time, working in the center of Miami, near the railroad tracks, I took a shortcut to work, only to come up to a dead-end street in a black American neighborhood. As I realized my mistake, I made a U-turn. As I did that, I saw that there were about 8-10 teenage boys on the street, staring at me as they were now trying to block my road. Their leader had a round object in his hand and was giving directions to the rest to encircle me. Immediately, my instincts kicked in for self preservation. I stood on the pedals and started pedaling straight through them. My only option was escape and the only weapon I had was my bike. Then the leader tossed the round object at me, which I discovered was a bowling ball. I went straight towards the leader, to minimize his probability of hitting me. The ball partially hit my front wheel, but I controlled my fall and kept on pedaling towards the leader. When they saw me not stopping, they opened a path, to avoid being hit. I fled as fast as my feet could pedal. It did not take me long to realize that Miami had some tough neighborhoods. These are neighborhoods, which most people avoid. They do not go roaming alone in those streets on bicycles, regardless of whether they are black or white.

Another time I happened to have a flat tire close to Opa Locka. When I tried to fix the tire, I discovered that I was out of patches. I started walking my bike, when I saw a convoy of movie making vehicles filming in front of me, near a Kentucky Fried Chicken restaurant with a black Oldsmobile as the main object. I later saw that same scene on the movie "Goldfinger." The black Olds was carrying "poor Mr. Solo," to his fate.

For Some a Paradise; For Others, Hell (Miami Beach, August, 1963)

I started unloading the truck, carrying rolls of tar paper up the stepladder. If you happened to be in that hotel, you would see a nineteen-year old, wearing some of the dirtiest work clothes imaginable, weaving through the pool area of a luxurious Miami Beach hotel. I wore a tar-stained long sleeve shirt, a dirty straw hat, and heavy work shoes with two pair of socks. The summer sun was beating on the concrete pavement, forcing the pool servers to water it, so that the barefooted tourists can walk on it. If they did not pour water, its temperature could reach over 140 degrees.

As I walked through the half naked tourists, both men and women glanced at me with discomfort. These people came to Miami Beach to have fun. Some were newlyweds. Others were making out on the pool chairs. This was a paradise for them, with one exception: they had a very dirty youngster unloading roof supplies among them and this was spoiling their fun.

"How long are you going to take to unload?" asked a man, dressed in whites.

"Just a few more minutes," responded John Mayo, who was watching me and the rest of the roofing crew. After unloading the paper on the roof, we rolled the tar heating unit to a remote back side of the hotel, so that we did not fumigate the guests. We also rolled a trash disposal container next to the roof.

"I want you to hurry up, and take that truck away from the access road," said the man in whites, who was probably a hotel manager.

I climbed up and together with the rest of the crew, started tearing up the old roof, throwing pieces into the trash disposal container. By noon, we were nailing new tar paper on. Then we applied the hot tar sealing, by mopping hot tar over the tar paper. At that time, the thick soled work shoes, with two pair of thick socks became so hot, that I could not stand it. I went to the IGLOO water cooler and filled the cover, full of ice water and poured it on my shoes. In less than a minute, all that water became steam, but it cooled me off.

"Good idea, amigo," said a Cuban co-worker.

"What we need is a dozen eggs," said Manuel. "We can use this tar paper as a skillet and make an omelet for us."

I did not doubt that at all. I now wish I had a thermometer to measure the temperature on top of that roof. I can only guess that it was fairly high.

Kennedy (November 22, 1963)

**Figure 19 Miami Dade Junior College (1963), WW II
Opa Locka Airport Barracks, Used as a Library**[185]

---

185   Noticeable is the lack of any air conditioning units. Miami heat and humidity took a toll on students during summertime in those years.

During the fall of 1963, I registered again at the Miami Dade Junior College, for my sophomore year. I was living at John Mayo's garage. I worked in various projects, including one that was right in the college itself. John received a subcontract to renovate an old building and turn it into a college cafeteria. I now worked in between classes, by supporting the construction, including the breaking of old concrete slabs using an air hammer.

One November day, as I was working on top of a ladder, placing anchors on the newly constructed concrete wall, I hear a girl crying below. The girl was the girlfriend of Bill Curran, one of my classmates. Bill was next to her and looked dumbfounded, staring at a television in the adjoining room. Others were also teary-eyed.

I came down the ladder and asked Bill, "What's wrong?"

"Someone assassinated our president in Dallas. We just heard it on television."

News about the J.F. Kennedy assassination started pouring in. For most students, the day was shot, as they could concentrate on little else, so they spent it watching the news. Most of them found it useless to work and achieve, when the highest achiever in the country is assassinated.

I distinctly recall what went on through my thoughts that day. America was a democracy, one that evolved over time from the concept of ancient Greek democracy taught to us in school. Yet, something was wrong here. Immediately, the words of Paraskevopoulos came to mind:

"Humans, like other organisms are in a state of continuous change as part of our evolution. Yet, we cannot change physically and mentally faster than allowed by our own natural abilities. Our evolutionary speed limit may be higher than other known organisms, because of our capacity to learn and our inventiveness in finding new ways to pass information to future generations. Yet, no matter how much I want to teach you to go faster, both you and I have speed limitations."

It all made sense. I concluded that the American Constitution is dependent on the premise that all its citizens are intelligent enough to control their destiny. Yet, the irrefutable "axiom of reality," as stated from ancient times is that all humans have mental limitations. In America, freedom of expression is defended by the First Amendment. Unlike some European countries, the freedom to bear arms is also protected by the Second Amendment. [186] This creates a constant conflict in America. Freedom of speech allows people to express themselves, but also allows pundits and demagogues to sway people and incite rage. Freedom to bear arms allows people to hunt freely, but also gives them the easy means to act violently when in anger, or to fulfill ill conceived thoughts as viewed by their limited intelligence. I sensed then that the United States was in a continuous war-like state. In the front lines were certain brave people, whose job is to interface with the rest of us, understand us, control us and educate us. These are the police, justices, and public servants, like John F. Kennedy. The whole country is involved in a continuous balancing act. Do you curb certain freedoms, or do you face the violence brought by these freedoms in cases of ignorance and mental limitations? [187] Why is that? Is it because they got so used to it? Is it because they do not know what it means to be without fear of your life when you walk the streets? The answer to that question still haunts me today.

Classes were cancelled on that day of November 22. I finished my work, climbed on my bike and returned to my bedroom that evening. By Christmas of 1963, I had to move back to 45th Street with my uncle Pandel. Christina expressed her need for privacy, after losing the baby.

In the last semester at Miami Dade Junior College, I asked my uncle Pandel if I could remain in America provided I pay my own way, starting the summer of 1964. A surprised Pandel agreed to do so. I applied for a transfer to the University of Florida in Gainesville and accepted. I

---

186   In 2008 and 2010, the Supreme Court reinforced the Second Amendment by issuing added Second Amendment decisions. In *District of Columbia v. Heller* (2008), the Court ruled that the Second Amendment protects an individual's right to possess a firearm, unconnected to service in a militia and to use that arm for traditionally lawful purposes, such as self-defense within the home.
187   Unfortunately this "war-like state" continues to be a scourge in America, but the people do not seem to care enough to draw limiting lines for free speech, or for the freedom to bear arms. The latest victim was Rep. Gabrielle Giffords of Arizona on January 8, 2010.

then wrote to my brother, asking him to line up a monthly support of $200 for me.

At the end of the semester, after receiving my two-year diploma in pre-Engineering, my uncle drove me to Gainesville with my old suitcase and dropped me off at the curb, across from College Inn, the campus restaurant. I was on my own now, having only the money left from the meager wages, earned while working with John Mayo. I had not heard from my brother, and I was worried. I boarded in a dorm and started thinking about my new options. It was the end of May 1964.

University of Florida
(Stavros' Memories, Gainesville, 1964-1966)

The Hungry Summer of 1964 (Gainesville Florida, August, 1964)

I had a few dollars to secure residence in a dorm, namely the Rawlings Hall and I was supposed to share bunk beds with another student, but during this particular summer session, I had no roommate. I later found out that students avoided these dorms because they were non-air-conditioned and extremely hot and humid in the Central Florida summer. I stayed there because they were cheap.

I had very little money, no work permit and after paying for summer school registration, my food budget was averaging about $30 per month. After repeated pleas to my brother, who had promised me financial support, I received no support. I had to study in a new school, manage to learn my new environment and survive on less than $1 per day. My daily diet, at $1 per day was one can of beans and a peanut butter sandwich. I could not afford fruits or vegetables, because that would take me over my budget. I knew though that I could not drag on like this for too long, because I would get sick from malnutrition, or scurvy. Yet, in spite of all the difficulties I faced, this was the best and most memorable summer of my life. It was the first time I experienced freedom. During that summer, I registered and got some electives out of the way.

Those summer days, I learned how to play chess, taught by two fellows in the dorms.

The summer was coming to its end and I needed a less costly residence for the fall semester, when dorm prices go up. I saw a notice at a bulletin board and contacted a student named Jim who found a "house," but needed a roommate. The rent was $25 per month.

The "house," if that place could be named so, was a two room tin roof, wooden shack, with boards on its sides, boarded both inside and outside, totally without insulation from heat or cold and having adequate cracks on the wallboards for roaches to come in at will and call it a home. This shack had a shower and toilet, and one of the rooms had a sink and a gas stove. It had two kerosene stoves for heating.

An ex-attorney named Smiser owned this shack as well as many adjoining shacks of this sort. In fact, as I found later, Smiser was a millionaire, but he lived like a bum. He had property in Gainesville, Hawthorne and Jacksonville, amounting to many millions of dollars, but he lived in an old home on University Avenue containing old furniture that someone could have tossed at the side of the road. Smiser was always in need for cheap undeclared labor and I found a means of earning some extra money. During breaks, I could work more than 10 hours per week and Smiser would not care because he paid wages that were well below minimum wage for the skill of his worker. I had lost a lot of weight and energy, being malnourished during the summer of 1964 and I needed the cash to get some fruits and vegetables.

My first work, cutting tree limbs for one of Smiser's homes was memorable. My malnourished body was relatively weak to deal with the demands of this work. As I was up a tree, I cut my little finger with an axe. I managed to come down the tree, went inside the house and asked a carpenter that was working there if he had a band-aid. Then, I passed out, presumably from the loss of blood and my condition. I soon recovered and bandaged myself, drank some orange soda that the carpenter offered me and went back to work.

I soon had enough money to eat a descent meal. I remember it very vividly. It was liver with onions and mashed potatoes with lots of gravy and a salad, prepared at the College Inn cafeteria. I also managed to gather enough money to purchase a used DUNELT bicycle, pump and tire patches. I was almost on my way, except that I had no money to register for the next semester.

**Figure 20 One Typical Building of the University
of Florida, Gainesville, Florida**

The Kokkinos Girls (Gainesville, Fall, 1964)

The first check from John arrived in September, barely in time to pay for the fall semester tuition. It was a $200 money order. After paying tuition, very little was left. I had to work with Smiser on weekends to eat. What I had missed the most was green salads. Salads, priced at about a dollar were expensive, considering my budget was $1.50 per day.

My grades suffered, but they were still above average.

Then, something unexpected happened. I received a letter from my godmother Kyriaki Zoumboulidou (who was also my mother's oldest sister) and in it was a folded note of five dollars. That evening I enjoyed a salad at College Inn made of green lettuce. Kyriaki Zoumboulidou, from the Aslanoglou family was indeed my second mother. In fact, all of my aunts helped me a lot when I was growing up. I grew up in their home, ate there, slept there and played there. Now, reaching from across the ocean, Kyriaki sent me the best present I could ever hope for: the money for a green salad. Ever since she was a little girl she could sense when someone she cared for needed something badly.[188]

One day I met with a Greek post-graduate student, called Alexis Stasinopoulos. Alexis was there with his wife Lea and their baby. He was a graduate assistant in Chemistry and his wife was working on her Masters and PhD as well. Alexis told me of other Greeks. Among them was a Cypriot, named Dinos Athanasiou, and some Kokkinos sisters.

A few weeks later, one Saturday morning I took a bike ride near a neighborhood north of University Avenue. It was then that I heard some women screaming in Greek. I approached a driveway adjacent to a house and behind the house I saw an apartment over a garage, with its own entrance on the side. The whole garage unit was separate from the main house. The windows were open and the screams were coming from the upstairs windows.

"You have turned this place into a pig sty," screamed one girl in Greek.

"Leave me alone," yelled another in the same language. "I stayed up all night for you."

I walked towards the entrance, when a girl appeared at the door. She was still yelling, as she was sweeping the stairs and dusting the floor mats with a stick.

---

188   Kyriaki Aslanoglou – Zoumboulidou was a lady of immense compassion. She has been mentioned in the previous book, "Andros Odyssey – Liberation," pp. 69-71 when she fed a stray Turkish boy a meat pie. Years later I would meet that boy in his nineties at Guzelyurt, Turkey. In September of 2010 the prefect of Akserai, Mr. Ramazan, (shown in Figure 10 of the above book) informed me of that man's name. It was Veysel Tas. He also informed me that Veysel had passed away the previous year.

"Get off your butt and help, otherwise you are in trouble."

She had not noticed me coming and staring at her, right in front of her.

"Hello!" I said in Greek.

The surprised girl was flustered and stopped dusting the floor mats.

"I am Stavros Boinodiris. I heard Greek and came to introduce myself."

The girl started chuckling. She pulled the cloth from her hair, dropped the mat and the stick and tried to take the dust out of her clothes. She came forward.

"I am Despina Kokkinos."

"Very happy to meet you; I was told by Alexis that there were some Kokkinos sisters somewhere around here. I think that I found them."

"Come on in."

The girl went up a staircase, and I followed. The top of the landing reached a tiny kitchen with a wooden bench table and a bench chair situated below an east-facing window. A corridor-living room was on the left leading to two bedrooms over the garage. In front of one of these bedrooms was another girl, somewhat younger.

"I am Vasso Kokkinos," she smiled.

The two girls were happy to chat and exchange information. I was even happier, for I had no other acquaintances in Gainesville. We talked into lunchtime and Despina suggested that we have lunch.

"Would you like to stay and have lunch with us?" said Despina. "We don't have much, so I could understand if you went to eat elsewhere." I saw that she was hoping that I would decline.

"I was planning to make spaghetti, but we only have a tiny amount of hamburger for three," echoed Vasso.

I smiled. They thought that they had nothing; if they only knew what I had to eat these last few months.

"Let me see how much spaghetti and hamburger you have," I said. Vasso showed me. It was about one pound. Then I saw some stale bread on the counter.

"I accept the invitation, with the provision that I cook the spaghetti," I said. "It is more than enough."

The girls were dumbfounded.

I rolled my sleeves, picked up the stale bread and made breadcrumbs. I mixed the breadcrumbs with the hamburger, added basil, and garlic, salt, pepper, and after sautéing some chopped onions, I stirred the hamburger mix in the pan. I added canned tomatoes and made enough sauce for a pot full of spaghetti, which I prepared a few minutes later. As I was preparing all this, the girls were transformed too. Instead of yelling at each other, they were cleaning up the place and themselves, without any complaints.

"Lunch is served," I declared.

The table was set and we had lunch. After we ate, there was enough spaghetti and sauce left for at least another four servings.

All three of us talked some more after lunch. The Kokkinos family was consisted of the father (John), mother (Efthimia) and five daughters. Olga was the oldest, graduate student in Chemistry and living in Gainesville. Sophia was next, living in Monroe, Louisiana. Despina followed, who lived with Vasso in Gainesville. The youngest one, Marlena was still living with her parents in Greece. The girls explained how they ended up in the U.S., with the help of a great uncle from Louisiana. I told them about my background. We found that we had a lot in common. Vasso was at that time a senior in an experimental high school, named P.K. Young, whose faculty consisted of students in the College of Education at the University of Florida.

After al lengthy exchange, I thanked them and departed. I felt strangely at home around these girls.

"Was I too obvious in showing that I liked them in my first visit?" I thought.

One Friday evening, as I was studying inside the shack, I heard a call from outside my door. When I opened it, I saw three girls on their bicycles: Despina, Vasso and Olga.

"Let's go to the CI (College Inn) for a soda," Despina said.

I joined them.

Jim (Gainesville, Winter, 1964-1965)

Jim was a strange, but interesting roommate. He was majoring in history.

He had a brown dog, named Ben who also resided in the shack with us. Ben was always getting into scuffles with other dogs. One day he came home with Jim, full of bites, made by a Doberman. I got my first aid kit and patched him up. Since then, Ben thought of me as a best friend.

Jim was a Jewish-American young man who detested going to the synagogue. He did not think much about the Jewish community of Miami Beach, regarding them arrogant and indifferent to the needs of the poor.

He was an activist, wanting fast results, even through violence. His rebellion was against the war in Vietnam and against the white supremacy policies of the South. He wanted Goldwater to win in the November 1964 elections against Lyndon Johnson so that more people would become activists like him and have a revolution. Like many young men, he was impulsive, wanting to change the world in one swoop.

He was not without means, but he worked his way through school. He worked in auto-assemblies in California and managed to gather enough money to buy a station wagon and to go to school for a year. While in Gainesville, he had a part-time milk run job.

Jim said that the wife of a famous Hollywood comedian was his aunt. He had another brother, teaching at the University of Syracuse.

Jim had at least three girlfriends at the same time when we lived at the shack. To avoid conflict, he dated them in sequence. One weekend, he ran into a snag. One of his girlfriends (we will call her Betty) moved in with him to sleep in his bed overnight, while he was expecting the second (we will call her Amy) at 6:00 AM on Saturday morning as she was planning to drive with him to the beach and the third (we will call her Sue) also on Saturday morning, around 10:00 AM, to go on a picnic. Before going to bed in the next room with his girlfriend, Jim approached me, pulled me out and whispered:

"Can you cover for me?"

"What do you mean?"

Jim laid out the unfortunate wrong scheduling of his girlfriends.

"Tell Betty in the morning that I had to leave on an emergency. When Sue comes, tell her the same, but do not tell her who was here, or with whom I left."

"OK." I said shrugging my shoulders. Jim smiled. He took a step, then stopped and added.

"Also, make sure that Betty gets out of here before 10:00 AM. Thanks. You are really a good pal."

The two slept in the room next to mine. Jim got up at 5:30, got dressed and waited for Amy outside, while Betty was fast asleep inside. At about 7:30 AM, I got up and got ready to go to work. I heard Betty snore in the kitchen-area bedroom, where Jim bunked. I went in to make sure that Betty got up, before locking the place and also to get some milk for breakfast. I looked at Betty and my jaw dropped. As I stood there, I watched a spectacle.

Betty was sleeping on her back and snoring loudly. She had a shoulder-length red hair, on top of which there were two roaches. A third one inched its way on her nose and approached her half open mouth. As the roach approached her upper lip, Betty would blow harder and throw it up in the air, making it land on her hair. As the second roach crawled doing the same routine, Betty jumped up, tossing the roaches about and shrieking on top of her voice.

I started laughing loudly.

Betty stopped and looked at me holding my aching tummy from laughter.

"What were those things?" Betty asked.

"Roaches," I responded, barely able to catch my breath.

Betty got up and went to the bathroom to get dressed, fussing about those "disgusting beasts."

When she returned, she looked at me.

"Jim left early this morning. Was that Sue with him?"

It was my turn to be surprised. "I don't know."

"Don't worry. I know all about Sue and Amy. I am leaving now, so that you can lock up."

"Have a nice weekend Betty," I said. I wondered how much Betty knew, but did not care.

On New Year's Eve, (December 31, 1964) Jim invited me to one of his meetings with an activist group. I was told that the group was called Students for Democratic Society, or SDS. The leader of the Gainesville area was a woman who was a good leader, but a lousy cook. She prepared eggnog that had eggs that were not well beaten and were closer to a raw egg, than eggnog.

Those early members of SDS felt that the United States was a democracy that never existed, or rather that it was transformed into a representative system after the constitutional convention. SDS felt it is crucial for people to have a part on how their society is governed.

SDS understood the need for a communications medium to make it possible for a community of active citizens to discuss and debate the issues affecting their lives. While not available in the 1960s, such a medium had to wait until the 1990s. The seeds for the revival of the 1960s SDS vision of how to bring about a more democratic society were some of the driving force behind the computer and the Internet. These seeds were thought to be an important element in the battle for winning control for people, but the remaining controls of government were not well understood.

Some objectives of SDS at that time were the stopping of the Vietnam War, the Civil Rights of blacks and some whites who were under persecution and discriminatory harassment by the FBI for being against government policies.

The SDS leader wanted to accomplish this change through peaceful non-cooperation, through publications, sit-ins and demonstrations. Jim was considered a lot more violent, suggesting destruction of property of storeowners who refused to serve to blacks. She chastised him and excluded him from many such activities.

Over the time I spent with Jim as a roommate, I tried to calm his anger on society, by suggesting that he first joins up with those that he despises, learns why they think the way they think and then try to change them. I do not know if my words had any effect, but one day he approached me and asked me to join him on a mission to a Daytona Beach High School, to see if we can motivate and enable black students to apply and be admitted at the University of Florida.

"You can be a great motivator!" he said. "Here you are, a penniless foreigner getting your Engineering Degree, while most of them are unable to even get a High School Degree."

The next morning, we were off to Daytona Beach. He had already contacted the High School Principle, who was waiting for us to give us a tour. His High School was brand new, with a superb football and basketball courts. Several of his select students joined us. I took a hint from Jim and I actually introduced myself as a "penniless foreigner from

Greece," who was working my way as I was trying to get my degree. I then asked them why they have not applied for an Entrance Exam. I received a variety of answers, but their overwhelming numbers were saying to me that they did not think they could pass an Entrance Exam. After telling them about my story, and the fact that four years ago I spoke no English, I suggested that they use willing tutors and take tests repeatedly with study periods in between, until they either pass, or their number of permitted attempts runs out. But, giving up should not be an option.

The problem with that facility was not evident to me, until I took a tour. We walked in a huge, brand new library and my mouth dropped open. Here was a huge room full of shelves, with less than fifty books in it. The rest of the shelves were bare empty. The principle saw my expression and nodded.

"We ran out of funds this year," he said as his eyes penitently stared at the floor. "Maybe next year we can get some more books."

"I would sacrifice all of the brand new buildings and fields for a shack, full of books and some good instructors," I said. "That is the only way these students will ever get a chance to compete."

He nodded smiling.

As we drove back Jim said, "I don't think that the principle was giving us all the facts on their library."

During the next semester, I discovered that three graduates from that High School were successful in the Entrance Exam and were attending the University of Florida.

Smiser's Shack (Gainesville, Spring, 1965)

In the spring of 1965, during my junior year, I kept working on my course work for electrical engineering. I was keeping company with Despina, now a sophomore, who was questioning herself as to what field she should take. As time went on, we started feeling increasingly more comfortable around each other.

Jim's brother arrived in Florida early that spring and took Jim and me for a ride to Flagler Beach. He was a professor at Syracuse University and a very smart fellow. He looked at me and asked, "I will tell you a word. Can you tell me without hesitation what is the first thing that comes to your mind?"

"OK," I responded.

"The word is 'SYSTEM.' What does that mean to you?"

"...a set of N algebraic equations, with N unknowns."

He laughed.

"You are truly an engineer, or a mathematician."

During one weekend, a couple arrived from Daytona Beach and met with Jim. Jim introduced them to me. The husband showed interest in electric motors for his hobby mini-racers. I borrowed a set of books from the University Library and loaned to him. After they left, Jim told me that the wife used to be his girlfriend.

"Does the husband know that?" I asked.

"Yes, he does."

"How does he feel about that?"

"I don't know, but they invited me to their home for Easter break."

"Are you going?"

"Sure; why not?"

"Because every time her husband sees her close to you he may have doubts about her faithfulness to you, you dummy. Do you really want to do that?"

"I never thought of that."

After thinking a bit, Jim responded.

"You must come also. We have to go together, otherwise it would look bad. If I do not go, he may think that there may be still something going on. Can you come?"

"Sure," I responded.

At the Easter break, Jim and I were at the couple's home in Daytona Beach. The couple had a lovely 2-year old girl that charmed everyone. We slept there for a night and returned the following day. We had a wonderful time.

The Vietnam War (Gainesville, Spring, 1965)

I was in continuous contact with students and non-students that were coming and going to Vietnam. Most of them were veterans that saw war firsthand, returned and used their GI funds to better themselves by going to college. They were very conscientious and quite capable, especially in the laboratories. A good number of them had a great deal of previous experience with electronic equipment, mostly because they were in the Army, Air Force or Navy communications maintenance corps.

They were silent about their experience, as if they wanted to forget it. Among the students were also a few Vietnamese men. They were all brilliant, all of them with scholarships from the Vietnamese Government. One of them named Tin was my laboratory partner. He was actually born in North Vietnam, but his family moved south. He was initially very silent, but later on, he opened up to me. His family was writing to him about the bad news and he felt as if he was helplessly imprisoned in the University, not being able to help them. He saved part of his assistantship and sent money to his family, a ten dollar bill at a time by a postal card, which he split in half and glued it back again with the bill inside. This trick was invented by necessity, because all postal package handlers there watched for mail from abroad and stole anything of value. One day, Tin walked into the lab very upset.

"What's wrong Tin?" I asked.

Tin hesitated.

"They found out about the card-splitting method," he uttered. "I lost fifty dollars before I found out what was going on."

I felt sorry for Tin. I knew very well the results of civil strife from my early days in the 1940's. I shared some of them with Tin. Tin was unimpressed.

"Things are very bad there. Nobody here understands how bad things are."

A number of anti-war movements were going on around the University. The University Foreign Student Center was advising all foreign students to stay away from any demonstrations. One day, a radio station crew was on the campus. A young woman stopped me on the way to my class.

"Is the United States justified in fighting the War in Vietnam?"

"I am not qualified to know if it is, or isn't," I responded. "I do not have all the facts. You, as a news media have an obligation to inform us properly of these facts. We depend on the U.S. Government that has the information to let us know if we must be there or not. If you have facts that point to another direction, you have an obligation to make those facts public, no matter how unpopular they are."

International House (Gainesville, Summer of 1965)

Jim and I split up that summer of 1965. I moved to a house on Gainesville's SW 2nd Avenue, owned by a sheriff, named Marshall. The sheriff lived there with his wife and family (a boy and a girl) and maintained a large eleven-bedroom house. They rented eight bedrooms with some limited kitchen and living room privileges. The rental money provided the additional income required by the family to pay the bank's mortgage. They liked to rent to diverse nationalities from abroad and for that reason the house was nicknamed the INTERNATIONAL HOUSE.

When I moved in, there were three Indians, a post-graduate student in biology from Kashmir, a post-graduate math major from New Delhi and a low class tiny man from Bombay, named Zaki, majoring in industrial engineering. In addition, there was a French man and a French woman, a Japanese woman and an American man.

It was a very educational summer. Two of the three Indians showed the discrimination problems of far-off India. A big, burly Asian Indian getting his PHD in Biology was from an elite Sheikh class. The Hindu Sheikh would repeatedly and openly beat up poor Zaki who was a Moslem, and considered to be of lower class by other Indians. We reported the incident to the sheriff, asking him to intervene. We literally ganged up on the Sheikh and threatened him with expulsion if he ever raises his hand on Zaki. College students can define their own laws of fairness, blind to class and religion distinctions practiced in India.

At the end of that summer, the young American man ran into trouble with his fiancée and his ugly temper. His fiancée cheated on him. He caught her and in his anger, he beat her up. Her family sued him and he was facing a long prison sentence, unless his sentence was commuted by volunteering to go to Vietnam. In that case, the district attorney through the intervention of Sheriff Marshall negotiated the dropping of charges by the family. He was gone within a week.[189]

The summer of 1965 was hot and exhausting for me. The classes were intensive and short (only five weeks). What made it worse was the fact that Despina had gone to work in the New York World's Fair that summer. I realized how much I missed her company.

The Church of Hate

During the summer break in August, I went to work with Smiser on a hotel that he owned at Hawthorne, Florida. We had with us a 15-year old child, who wanted to help. On the way to the hotel, Smiser asked me if I could cook so that we could shop for a few things for dinner.

---

189   I would see that young man again in 1968. One 1968 noon, I was driving my Volkswagen beetle from Florida Atlantic University in Boca Raton, Florida and would recognize a hitchhiker, whom I picked up immediately. He was my co-resident from the International House.
"What happened in Vietnam?"
"It was hell. I should have stayed home and gone to jail," was his response.

"I can make you tomatoes and eggs," I responded.

We stopped at a country store and Smiser negotiated the purchase of a whole bushel of ripe, rotting tomatoes for fifty cents. He bought margarine, eggs and cheddar cheese according to my instructions.

On the way to Hawthorne, the teen saw a couple of blacks on the road. He immediately started throwing the rotten tomatoes against them, calling them obscene names.

"What's wrong with you Billy?" I yelled, surprised that Smiser did not make the slightest attempt to stop the kid.

"I hate niggers. They are a menace. I want to kill them all."

"Why? What made you hate them?"

"They are trying to annihilate us here. They are against Christ and the Church."

"Who told you that? What in God's name made you say that?"

"What's wrong with you man? Aren't you a Christian? Even our preacher tells us so. They are trying to inter-marry with us and become white."

"...Preacher? What church do you attend?"

"...The Church of Christ."

The teen kept on yelling obscenities against blacks, an indication of how much hate was being seeded in those backwards churches of Central Florida at that time.

The truck pulled into a three story hotel driveway at dusk. It was completely empty and gutted. It sustained fire damage and needed a new roof. As I found out, Smiser had bought it. We found some kerosene lamps and portable gas stoves. A carpenter pulled in with his car as well.

I made dinner at the hotel with a gas stove. We ate and went to sleep on the floor.

The Hawthorne Hotel Stand

The next day was a scorcher. As the hours moved into noon, clouds formed, creating a hot-house effect in Central Florida. This raised the hotel roof temperature to over 150 degrees Fahrenheit. I helped tear the old roof and prepped the top for the new. The material had to be taken to the roof by long, unstable ladders. Smiser became nervous.

"We have to move fast before the rain hits us and gets the interior wet. No more drinking water breaks."

I looked at him.

"This is a hot day. You stop people from drinking water and one of us will faint and fall down three stories. Stop and think man."

"You are sissies. We must finish before the rain starts. I said, no more water breaks," Smiser insisted, sitting on top of the water cooler.

I threw down my tools, climbed down the ladder and walked away.

"Where are you going?" yelled Smiser.

"I just quit."

"Come back here. You cannot abandon me now. The rain is coming."

As I was asking directions for a bus stop from the carpenter below, I heard Smiser yell all sorts of cuss words towards me.

I had to find another means to subsidize my income. I was getting $220 per month now from my brother, but after paying tuition ($420/trimester), books ($80/trimester) and rent ($200/trimester), I was left with $45/month, or about $1.5/day for food, clothes and other miscellaneous needs, like laundry, soap and toothpaste.

Despina returned early that year and she suggested to me to seek work from Dr. Armenakas, a professor, who could use an assistant for grades and research. She herself was teaching his children Greek. Dr. Armenakas, a mechanical engineering professor had three children: Alexandra (11), Manolis or Noel (7) and another three-year old female toddler. The children were brilliant. I contacted Dr. Armenakas and received 10 hours per week worth of work at about $2 an hour. This helped a lot.

Dr. Armenakas was a very proud Greek from Lesbos. He wanted the best education for his children, including Greek. He registered his children to so many schools that they hardly had time to play. Besides their normal schooling, they were taught Greek, French, dance and piano. His wife was much younger and quite a beauty. She was extremely tender and loving to her children and very proud of them.

During the summer of 1965, another Greek student appeared in Gainesville, by the name of Dimitris Petropoulos. He was a brilliant civil engineering student, enrolled to get his PhD degree. He had a Fulbright scholarship and a University of Florida teaching assistantship. He talked to the Kokkinos girls about finding an apartment. A two-student apartment became available for graduate students and Dimitris applied, while looking for a roommate. Despina suggested to me to become his roommate. I had to pay $75 per month instead of $50, but I accepted, basing my decision on some of the Smiser savings and my new job with Armenakas.

So, I left the "International House" and moved in with Dimitris Petropoulos into the Graduate Student Housing.

Falling in Love (Gainesville, Fall of 1965)

During the fall of 1965, Despina and I realized that we are in love. We started dating each other full time. Despina decided to become an electrical engineer herself. Maybe, I was one of the motivators that steered her career in that decision. The other motivator was her first cousin, George Lyras, who moved into a fraternity house near the campus a few years earlier and entered the School of Engineering. George joined the fraternity and shortly thereafter became the fraternity president. He had an old Lambretta scooter without breaks which he used for transportation. He went through many shoe soles while breaking that beast.

Despina's decision to enter the Electrical Engineering School at the University of Florida was a record breaking event. She was the only female student in the school of Electrical Engineering. She had to sustain a certain degree of harassment from male classmates, especially from certain older students, Vietnam veterans that used their GI benefits to get a college education. Even her professors told her that she was out of place. As one of them said, "The place of a woman is at home, raising babies."

They often left tampons on her desk, during class break. This made Despina more determined to go on with her plans, in spite of all the rude behavior of students and professors. In the 1960s, most women were going into education. For some strange cultural reasons, engineering was completely dominated by men. Strangely, this attitude made Despina even more determined to stay the course.

Despina and I were walking in the campus at around dusk, visiting a screened alligator pen next to the University Tower. The alligator was the mascot of the Florida Gators, the university's football team. The team was doing very well then, having as a quarterback the Heisman trophy winner Steve Spurrier. During the previous game, the South Carolina Game Cock fans managed to abduct as a prank the poor 10-foot alligator from his pen. He was now back and he was quite an attraction.

I do not know how, but I found myself kissing Despina near the pen. Suddenly, I could hear or see nothing. I was so focused on her kiss that the whole world had disappeared. I found out later, that as I was enjoying her kiss, a fraternity was initiating their new members by making them march through the campus dressed only in pampers. About thirty, half-naked men, passed next to me and I did not see them. My mind was elsewhere. We did not see them until Despina, and I came up for breath. We saw the men in their diapers going away from us, towards the Architecture School Building, which had a water fountain. It seems that the typical procedure of initiation included a water-born baptism.

"What was that?" I said.

"It looks like that a bunch of half naked fraternity men have just passed us by."

We looked at each other and went back to enjoy our kissing.

By Christmas of 1965, I realized that I could not sustain my budget. The high rent, added to the shared expenses in cooking for high-class meals (like meats) required by Dimitris, depleted all my savings. Despina again came to my rescue.

Her sister Vasso now was out of her apartment and she subleased half of the garage apartment to a girl from Pensacola named Claire. Claire had a steady boyfriend, named Harry who wanted a roommate after finding a house near Highway 401, or 13th Street. I talked Harry into being his roommate. The rent dropped back to $25/month.

The Snake Shack (Gainesville, 1966)

The house near 13th street was on a high plateau overlooking the street, one of three structures inside a lush, thick forest of trees and bushes. Two of the houses were one-story duplexes, while the third was a two-story duplex. The houses were run down and needed continuous repair. They had wood frames and tin roofs. The owner lived in Miami and had no time to spend on their repair. What characterized these houses was the fact that everywhere around them there was a real jungle; and in that jungle, there were always moccasin snakes, slithering in the open, climbing the wooden steps and sunning themselves at the porch. During the spring of 1966, Harry and I had double dates with Claire and Despina. After a few bicycle visits to the house Despina, named the place the SNAKE SHACK.

Harry had arranged with the owner, so that all materials used in repairing the homes can be subtracted from the rent. Only one section of the duplex in each single-story house was rented, the other being in such disrepair that it became a storage place for unused furniture. The two-story house was fully occupied.

I had no money to spend on such expensive luxuries as movies, so Despina pitched in most of the time. We spent most of our time together at the Catholic Church Center, enjoying such simple pleasures as talking, watching television, playing chess, or table tennis. We were both very busy with our work at school and at the Armenakas office and home. I often helped Despina with her homework, especially in her Engineering Drawing classes, where she admitted that she could not do well.

The oldest Kokkinos girl, Olga got married, and after she, and her husband, Alan graduated, they moved to Stamford Connecticut in May of 1966, where Alan got a job with Cyanamid. As a result, Despina was left alone, without any sisters to help her. [190]

Harry Dewberry and Claire left after their graduation in May. I kept the "snake shack" all alone, now paying $50 per month.

Despina decided to stay in school during the summer of 1966, not because she liked the idea but in order to be close to me. She left the garage apartment she had leased with Claire and found a dormitory. By summertime of 1966, we started dating more frequently and the strict dorm rules started to annoy Despina. She was not about to get indoors at 10:00 PM, or face expulsion. After a month of that, she changed locations and leased room and board from a family. After a few late appearances, she was told to stop being late there as well. By the end of that summer, she had enough. She found a student-housing shack of her own and found herself a Cuban roommate named Vicki.

By the end of the summer, I had a new roommate, a Cypriot named Dino. My rent dropped again back to $25 per month. Dino turned out to be a superb roommate.

Then, a Korean PhD candidate named Kim moved to a near-by home. He was married, but his wife was in Korea. Also, in a two-story duplex lived a pair of rowdy young men at the bottom floor and a pair of single girls upstairs.

---

190   Alan stayed in Stamford until 1970 and then took a job as a professor of chemistry at Eastern Connecticut State University in Willimantic, Connecticut.

One day, I came home and found Dino upset.

"What's wrong?"

"I was robbed."

"…How?"

"Two young men barged in here uninvited, looking around the bedroom and before I could react they left. Within seconds I realized that they stole $10 that I had laid on my dresser."

"Do you know them if you saw them again?"

"Yes, I believe that they live next door."

"Let's go see them."

We rushed out and I started knocking at the door. One of the neighbor girls from upstairs appeared. I explained what happened.

"They took off, the minute they heard you coming."

"Dino, it is up to you to file charges with the police. Do you want to go now?"

"No. Forget it. I cannot prove a thing, one way or another."

I was very upset with Dino's attitude. A few days later, the two rowdy men came during the peak class hours and emptied the place. They tried to rape one of their neighbor girls and after Kim and I rushed out, they took off like rabbits. They were not seen again.

The fall trimester of 1966 was my last one, prior to receiving my Bachelor's Degree in Electrical Engineering. During this last trimester, I had a class on Creative Engineering Design. I was involved in two designs that were extremely creative. One was the complete design of an automated electric wheelchair for the handicapped. The second was a variable focus antenna. Both of these were realized years later by enterprising industries. Drawings of these designs were decorating the wall of my "snake shack."

"What is that?" said the next-door girl, after seeing the drawing. She dropped in unexpectedly.

At that moment I had a "Control Systems" study session with Larry (another classmate) when she knocked and entered. She was barefooted, walking in the muddy ground. It had just rained.

I introduced her to my friend.

"It is a variable focus antenna. It can be used to focus communication from deep space onto a very large antenna. Can I help you?"

"I just wanted to see what this place looks like."

I pointed to her feet.

"You may get a cold in the process, unless you wear some shoes. Do you know that there are snakes all over here?"

"Not in the cold months. Thank you for caring. I have to go now."

She departed and Larry cracked laughing. I did not.

"This girl is a nut," I declared.

On Despina's side, her roommate Vicki was a shy woman that studied industrial engineering. The two women found out that they had something in common: the harassment, by men, for trying to become women engineers. Despina found the courage to fight back with an occasional lecture. Vicki did not. The more they teased her, the shyer she became, causing the teasers to tease her even more.

By the end of 1966, I was about to graduate. Immediately I registered for the graduate school to get my Masters Degree and applied for a teaching assistantship. My grades were good, so I received it. I had no choice but to continue my schooling. If I stopped school, my visa would expire and I would be forced to exit the United States and go back to Greece, away from Despina. On top of that, by late 1966, political conditions in Greece worsened.

In 1964, the Center Union of George Papandreou was elected, and governed until July, 1965 when King Constantine II dismissed him, causing a constitutional crisis. A group of George Papandreou's dissidents, led by the politician Mitsotakis, then also member of the Center Union, crossed the floor to bring about the fall of his elected government in favor of the King. This group was called the "July apostates." It was followed by a succession of unstable coalition governments formed by conservatives and rebel liberals, bringing Greece into a chaotic state.

Graduate school was more of the same. I found that Kim was quite helpful with some of the advanced mathematics that I was now learning. Meanwhile, Kim had arranged for his wife to come from Korea. He was sick and tired living alone in that shack, surrounded with Playboy centerfolds.

One Sunday morning I saw Kim kneeling next to a bush with a large kitchen knife in his hand.

"What's up Kim?"

Kim turned, smiled and then started giggling, in an oriental manner showing his embarrassment.

"I got a head cold and do not feel well. In Korea, when someone has a cold they serve him snake soup. You caught me as I was hunting snakes."

"Go for it Kim. I hate snakes. When does your wife arrive?"

"Next month," he responded with a wide smile.

Later that afternoon, I visited Kim.

"How are you feeling?"

"…Much better. Thank you. These black snakes make an excellent soup for colds."

On April 21, 1967, just before scheduled elections, a group of right-wing colonels led by Colonel George Papadopoulos seized power in a coup d'état establishing the Regime of the Colonels. Civil liberties were suppressed, special military courts were established, and political parties were dissolved. Several thousand suspected communists and political opponents were imprisoned or exiled to remote Greek islands. Alleged US support for the junta blamed to be the cause of rising anti-Americanism in Greece during and following the junta's harsh rule.

After listening to such news, I was glad that I decided to stay in Graduate School. If I had returned, I would be drafted into the Greek Army under the regime of the hated and unpredictable Greek Junta.

My other option was to apply for a United States residency, upon which case I would become equally eligible to be drafted and be sent to Vietnam. My goal for the next few years was to walk on top of that sharp fence, without losing my educational goals. My father Anthony was pleading with me to return. I refused to do so, balancing myself on a tight rope.

The spring of 1967, Despina and I decided to announce our engagement to friends and relatives. Instead of rings, which we could not afford, we exchanged beer top lids. To keep with tradition, I wrote a letter to Despina's father John, asking for his daughter's hand. The Kokkinos clan had a number of meetings and decided that it was best not to object to Despina's engagement. They knew that we were in love and would go through our relationship, regardless of what they say.

They set the wedding for the end of summer in 1997.

After that decision was reached, John Kokkinos took his wife Efthimia and his daughter Marlena to Drama to meet with Anthony and Elisabeth. My parents were worrying about the decision of their son to marry and repeatedly wrote me to change my mind and return to Greece.

At the same time, I thanked my brother for the economic help up to now and declared that I would not need it any more. To collect money, I tried to get a summer job as an engineering graduate. By finding an employer, I could get my student visa extended and converted to a work visa. I managed to get a summer job with IBM in Kingston, New York.

At the end of that spring semester of 1967, I got my Bachelor's diploma (one trimester late, since at that time, all graduation ceremonies were scheduled in May). Pandel and Katherine Mayo attended the graduation.

**Figure 21 Despina and Stavros, Pandel and Kathryn
Mayo at Stavros' Graduation (May 1967)**

Wedding (Summer and Fall of 1967)

The first thing that I did after graduation was to visit IBM and secure my job. Right after the end of the spring semester, I arrived at Kingston, N.Y. by bus. Then, even before I had a place to stay, I walked to the IBM building carrying my suitcase with me. The project manager at IBM (Jim Greeson) was quite surprised to see me. Nevertheless, he immediately gave me my assignment. I was to assist an engineer in the design of a high voltage power supply for a Model 360-40 monitor. I excused myself at noon in order to get settled. The people there probably thought that I was a nut, when I asked the receptionist if I could leave my suitcase with her.

The second thing that I did was walk from the IBM building to the local Montgomery Ward department store in order to purchase a bicycle.

With it, I found a boarding house. An elderly woman who rented rooms to IBM employees owned it. There were four rooms. One was rented to an Indian Sheikh, another to a young Jewish American from Brooklyn, the third to an Italian-American from New York City and the fourth I rented. By 5 PM I retrieved my suitcase on my bike from IBM and got settled in my room.

I found summer work at IBM very exciting and rewarding. On top of that, I had some fringe benefits. As I was moving into Kingston, Despina had found herself a job with an architectural firm in Stamford, Connecticut, near her sister. We made it a point to see each other during weekends by alternating locations between Kingston and Stamford.

The young Jewish American from Brooklyn was quite helpful. He gave me a ride to New York a couple of times, dropping me off where I could take the subway and the commuter train to go to Stamford. Other times I had to take the train to New York Central and from there go to Stamford.

These rides were lengthy, but for an inquisitive mind watching the various people milling in those trains, very interesting. One day, I was sitting in the New York subway train next to a soldier who just came back from Vietnam. A middle age commuter with a suit, a tie and his work briefcase was busy drilling him with questions on how it was there, trying to determine his morale.

"We hear that your M16 rifles jam a lot. Is that right?"

"That is a lot of bunk," responded the soldier. "The rifle is excellent. If soldiers use it as they should, it is a superb weapon. Anyone can jam any rifle if they misuse it."

Then the commuter turned to me, as I was listening intently.

"What do you do?"

"I work for IBM."

"What do you do there?"

"I am a small gear in a big machine. I make parts for computers."

"How do you like your job?"

"I love it."

The commuter smiled and turned back to the Vietnam soldier, drilling him some more.

Our wedding date was set for Saturday, September 2 in the Greek Orthodox Church of Stamford, Connecticut. Monday was Labor Day and the University of Florida registration was on 11 September.

The IBM workers found out about my plans and gave me a combined bachelor's and departure party. My line manager (Dave Bell) tried to talk me out of getting married.

"Why do you want to do a stupid think like that?"

I smiled. Dave smiled too.

"I am trying to talk you out of it because I know what it's all about. I am married and know that no matter what I tell you, you would not listen. Good luck."

A civil ceremony at the Stamford City Hall prepared the paperwork a few days before the church wedding. I arrived in Stamford on Friday night. I had a suit, but no shirt. Joe and Alan (my future brothers-in-law) helped me buy a shirt on Saturday morning, a few hours before the ceremony. On the way back, they tried to get me drunk by passing through a local bar. It would have been easy if I had more than one Tom Collins since I had nothing to eat that morning.

The wedding was simple. It had only nine attendees other than the priest, the five Kokkinos sisters, their mother, Alan, Joe and me, the groom.

Despina and I were driven into central Manhattan for our honeymoon. The hotel was overlooking Times Square. We rested there on Sunday and Monday (Labor Day). On Tuesday, both of us were back at work.

We needed the money to pay our expenses in school. I sold my bike in Kingston, packed my suitcase and went back to Gainesville, Florida by bus.

We came back to Gainesville to complete our education. I was going to complete my studies for my Master's degree and Despina had another year for her bachelor's degree. We rented an apartment for married students, retrieved our bicycles from friends and started bicycling to school.

Meanwhile, we hear that Joe, my brother-in-law, left for another tour of duty to Vietnam, leaving his wife Sophia alone in Monroe, Louisiana.

I now started a teaching assistantship program and to supplement my income. I gave Ancient Greek tutoring lessons to students of theology. Despina kept on teaching the Armenakas' children. For some peculiar reason, our grades peaked to the highest level ever.

The Black-American's Struggle for Self Respect (Christmas, 1967)

During the Christmas vacation of that year, Despina and I took a Greyhound bus from Gainesville to visit Sophia Ashley in Monroe, Louisiana. This trip was memorable.

A black man in the bus heard us speaking Greek and turned to me:

"You are Greek. I just came back from Greece."

"...Really?" I said smiling, "... where ... from?"

"I was serving in the Air Force in Crete."

"How did you like it there?"

"I loved it. The people were so friendly and the food was out of this world."

The black man was full of enthusiasm. Despina and I moved to his seat in the rear as the soldier shared his experiences in Crete, occasionally bursting into laughter, Greek-style.

The bus kept on traveling somewhere in northern Florida, when a uniformed white man gets in and asks for tickets. Immediately the soldier's laughter froze.

"I suggest you get back to your seats folks," the bus inspector said rudely to me.

We all had our smiles frozen; our faces were like those of children caught stealing cookies.

"Why?" said Despina. The people in the bus stared at us as if we were criminals. We had heard of these practices in the South, but the reality never sank in, until that moment. *Are we going to be lynched because we are talking in a friendly manner to a black soldier?* I thought. I did not know how far to push, but I certainly knew that that bus inspector brought us from our ideal, happy clouds of Greek indifference to a person's color, to the realities of this segregated Greyhound bus in the South.

"Go on to your seats," said the soldier. "Unfortunately this is not Crete."

We moved back to our seats, leaving the now sullen soldier in the rear seat, looking very frustrated. Here he was, serving a country as a soldier abroad, and in his homecoming he was being treated as a second class citizen by those that he served. We considered the incident as a possibly isolated case, until we arrived in the Tallahassee Greyhound bus depot around 8 PM.

All passengers disembarked and during the hourly wait for the next bus, we decided to have something to eat at the depot restaurant. We went in and sat on the counter, not realizing that the place was void of any white people. Suddenly it seemed odd that the black server was not coming to take our order. White passengers passed us by, looking at us in a weird manner. Then, we noticed the toilet.

"Toilet for blacks," was written on the door. We got up from our seats and started walking, only to find out another section of the restaurant, behind a wall, full of white customers. The toilets were marked: *"White Men Only"* and *"White Women Only."*

"This is sickening," said Despina in Greek. "When will these people start accepting blacks as human beings?"

We discussed how blacks had to fight for the respect they rightly deserved. To an outsider, like a European like me this respect was a given. However for many people in the South it was not. After going through the struggle that they went through, we concluded that they earned that respect the hard way because the two groups did not comprehend the strength of each other's culture. The greatest battles for respect were fought and won not on battlefields, or street riots, but in music halls, jazz bands and theaters, athletic competition, the integrated armed forces, integrated schools, integrated work places and integrated church gatherings.

Three years later, I would have a discussion with a German industrialist in Stuttgart and I would defend the struggle that was taking place in the United States. "At least, the United States is actively dealing with the discrimination problem among the various minorities, by instituting legislature for their protection," I said. "Sooner or later Europe has to step up and do the same. Wait until other, non-European nationalities start invading Europe."

The trip to Monroe was long, and with the exception of this incident, pleasant. We returned in the same manner back to go to school.

During the spring semester of 1968, I taught the Armenakas' children. Despina was due for graduation and applied for work on a permanent basis. She received a job offer from IBM at the Boca Raton, Florida location.

How did I view America in the 1960s?

To me, the United States of America was not just a country, whose interests encompassed its own survival. It was not like Greece, France, or England, focusing on parochial issues of the survival of their citizenry.

The USA was formed from immigrants, just like me, who came here with bitterness in their soul about how things worked out in their own homeland. These immigrants founded this relatively new country on democratic principles and to me it represented an incubator of ideas on how to change the world for the best.

When you gather all these people in a country, the sum of their interests under such a democracy becomes global in nature. The immigrants that suffered from oppression of speech and lack of free press fought hard to make America a country with freedom of speech and open press. Similarly, the immigrants that suffered from religious prosecution, fought hard to make America a country with religious freedom and the separation of church and state. Others, suffering from a continuous economic oppression based on nepotism, fought hard to make America a country of opportunity to all. Some that suffered from prosecution of minorities, (race or national origin) fought hard to make America a country that protects minorities. And the immigrants that suffered from time consuming bureaucracy and governments which were blackmailed into hiring public servants that served none, fought hard to make America a country that speeds up operations, eliminate permanent jobs and bring competition into the workforce and global open markets.

All these immigrants can in turn bring changes to the government of their own countries for improving this world.

There are countless stories of immigrants from various countries abroad that merged in the United States to improve their world. These people had to face all the others, who had a different view of what is best for the world, confront them and get their approval. This struggle was ongoing and continuous. People's emotions ran high in the streets, factories and meeting halls. The inevitability of this "melting pot" is a continuous high energy, "internally violent change."

For me, violent change equals war. It may not have all the known attributes that we saw in the World Wars, but it is a war nevertheless. The main difference is that this "violent change" is working under "internally" controlled conditions. Another name could be the violence associated with the "American Melting Pot." This violence had many victims. New York based immigrant Greeks had to fight with the "previously established immigrants" in 1911 to gain usage rights of Central Park. Irish immigrants had to fight earlier, to abolish signs on store windows saying "Irish need not apply here." Every minority had to fight in the streets and city halls to assert their rights. And now, since 1963, Martin Luther King was saying that, "I have a dream" because he wanted to change the oppressed lives of blacks through the civil rights movement. We saw part of that struggle in our Greyhound bus ride to Monroe and in the high schools of Daytona Beach, as the teachers were struggling to find resources to teach black children.

Violence and wars are the result of one underlying reason in human beings: the lack of patience. Americans are characterized as the least patient people with neighbors, or even rulers that try to exert any unwanted pressure on them. They will simply not stand for it. They will fight back in any way that they can.

Anyone that came from abroad and saw what was going on in the 60's could not escape noticing the electrified tension of violence in the streets of America. Containing this "violent change" was a big challenge. The opposition was fierce, but so was the determined force to seek a just change. The legal system of the United States had to be revamped, to take care of all that "violent change." Eventually, those relentless opponents like those priests of that Church of Christ near Gainesville that spread fanaticism in the hearts of children, were silenced. Riots in colleges and universities, anti-war rallies, bussing, sit-ins, and numerous other events were happening almost every day. The various police forces, the FBI, and the richness, complexity and speed of the legal system were part of the evolutionary process that had to happen to contain this "violent change."

The people in other countries abroad only saw the results caused by the melting pot in America mostly through the movies. They saw these results, some with envy, some with mistrust, and on rare occasions with gratitude. In spite of world opinion, these results of change continued to come. Yet, no matter how envious the people abroad were, they reaped a definite benefit out of it. Their own societies improved, attempting to duplicate some of the benefits of change proven in the USA. And yes, most of these duplications were carried back by returning immigrants. Unfortunately, they also carried back some non-beneficial American attributes.

This "violent change" of America started way before World War I. In those days, countries that understood its benefits and were strong started providing support to the United States because they knew that they would get it back. This support came in terms of capital investment and political and military pacts. The weaker countries sent immigrants, immigrants that the leaders of these countries knew they could help their mother countries by bringing back cash and the know-how to improve conditions there from lessons learned by the "violent change."

The United States saw an unprecedented amount of support from many countries between World War I and World War II. Having that support became a foundation upon which the United States economy was built. In return, it was this economy that managed to help the US finance World War II and mend the destroyed economies of Europe and the Pacific after the War.

To me, the USA was identified as a gathering, mixing and weighing of world interests, requiring proper, reliable representatives and support from all nations of the world to function fairly. Its existence aided in making the world a better place to live, by first evaluating and trying things out experimentally in the USA. Its mission was to abolish violence and suffering in the world, by first abolishing all reasons that cause it here. It must be the laboratory upon which remedies are tested before being applied to the rest of the world. The influence to other countries comes through diplomacy, logical persuasion, economic means, political influence, and if nothing else works, by organizing many nations into an armed intervention.

There is no other nation on earth that can honestly claim that they have every nationality of the world living in it, which is free to express their national and religious preferences and opinions on how USA is governed. The people of the world will have their hands full with the

United States Experiment for as long as the USA continues to assume the "violent change" role.[191]

Can the USA do this job alone, without support from other countries? No.

Is the role of the USA to be a police officer for correcting all wrongs in the world through war? No. War is something to be abolished and never to be considered as a beneficial tool.

Then, why is the United States fighting in Vietnam virtually single-handedly?

I had no answer to that question.

The United States of America became my second homeland, but the first in my future dreams.

It is a vibrant, dreaming, struggling and indomitable country. It uses diversity as its strength, encouraging people to thrive, allowing for dissenting opinions, as they are expressed freely. Agreement is reached mostly through peaceful discourse and understanding of dissenting ideas and their consequences. Force is used to preserve this openness and the process of reaching agreements.

Laws are set to make things work, only to be changed based on when the people decide that a new law may be better than the existing one.

In the 1960s I thought that America embraced everyone, as long as they are willing to embrace other cultures and ideas in a continuous frenzy of change, good or bad. Those that do not tolerate variety and change suffer.

---

191   The "violent change" role of the US was difficult to understand by Europeans in the 1960s. At that time most European countries had relatively homogeneous populations. Wherever there were minorities, they were "bypassed" through oppression, or exclusions. Recently, with the influx of tremendous numbers of immigrants from Eastern Europe, Asia and Africa, the European Economic Community is experiencing what the USA had experienced in the 60's. Riots by immigrants are commonplace everywhere. Through "violent change," they are trying to assert their rights in the EEU.

Those that do, contribute to the tornado of change by fighting or working with others like them, in a continuous struggle of competition in the streets and the countryside. This is the country where people live and die for new ideas and ideals.

That concept was the driving force behind America's attractiveness to youngsters like me. Over time, this ideal society would lose somewhat its luster by my day-to-day experiences.

I discovered that many Americans became intolerant of other cultures, ideas and religions through sheer ignorance or misinformation. The only means to discourage them is through education and the slow moving legislature and law enforcement of the democratic process.

Yet, I have yet to find another country in the world that fares better on that score. There are societies, like Singapore that seem to be faring better, but they do that through a strong, authoritative dictatorship. The people of Singapore all work harmoniously together, they are zoned to live in mixed society housing, but deep down, there is still a lot of intolerance. They are just not allowed to voice it, because it is illegal, but the hate is still there. Some believe that that technique may work. In that country, the government is the parent, treating its citizens like children. The US on the other hand tries to enable an environment for its citizens to work it out themselves the democratic way.

Most people in the United States are type "A" people, namely self driven. They are very impatient in reaching a goal, and then, when they reach that goal, they are impatient in reaching a much higher one. Such impatience creates violent people. The only speed control is when people fall from bullets in the streets and from mental agony in psychiatric wards. When that happens, others pick up where they left off. Ideas are born to create riches, only to die soon, crash into oblivion, and create room for new ideas. When the country is in danger from internal or external threat, the "once foreigners" become patriots, fighting for their newly acquired freedom. The country thrives on challenges.

Space exploration was a challenge. It was met, worked upon and went into a slump.

The Vietnam disaster was a challenge. It was met, worked upon and will be slowly forgotten over time.

The civil rights of black Americans challenged America. It was met, worked upon and will also be slowly forgotten.

The exciting innovations created by traveling to outer space will eventually be sidestepped, and replaced by new innovations.

Values treasured in other countries are set aside here. Tradition, religion and customs can be nurtured within a family or even a group, but they are neutralized and equalized by all government, from local to federal. Language is chosen as English, but this choice was done at random. It might as well have been Swahili.

You see some of the worst crimes here, but they are also the cause for bringing out some of the best in humanity, ready to counter them.

If you see a child suffering and crying here, watch out. You may be looking at a future country President and a World Leader with an agenda in mind.

If you see a distressed immigrant, discriminated by citizens who immigrated earlier, you are seeing a fighter who might one day lead an anti-defamation league for other citizens.

Dissent and crime is high in America, the pace of life is fast and mental illnesses and divorce rates are high. The Americans move so fast that most of the people abroad tend to hate them. The United States, with less than 5% of the global population, uses about a quarter of the world's fossil fuel resources. [192] Most people of the world want America to stop this frenzy in spending and give the rest of the world a chance to grow as well and feed the less fortunate starving masses. They want to stop

---

[192] As of 2003, the U.S. had more private cars than licensed drivers, and gas-guzzling sport utility vehicles were among the best-selling vehicles. Also, the US burn up nearly 25 % of the coal, 26 % of the oil, and 27 % of the world's natural gas. New houses in the U.S. were 38 % bigger in 2002 than in 1975, despite having fewer people per household on average.

all the advertising campaigns[193] to sell unwanted products in the US markets, and put some money on the side, that can be loaned to poor countries to buy irrigation pumps for clean drinking water. In many instances, America is viewed like a big brother that stunned the growth of younger siblings by not letting them express themselves.

In spite of what the rest of the world wants, this is a vibrant country, not because of the land, but because of the people that by strange events in history, ended up here. The Americans are made of people who will not sit still and be content with less than their neighbor. They will fight, maneuver, change, go elsewhere, but find an environment where they will do better than some idolized consumer, even if that greedy action takes them down to bankruptcy.

You can sense when part of America is not doing well. People leave. They sell homes like they were shirts and seek a better place to start all over again. Nowhere in the world, except in some nomad societies, are families as mobile as in the United States of America.

There is only one enemy of the United States. This enemy is called stagnating tranquility. Any peaceful, non-diverse, utopian contentment can undermine this society. Anyone that wants to slow things down, whether it is in the economy, transportation, immigration, communication, or creativity is contributing to the destruction of this country. It is exactly this lack of patience in status quo that makes Americans be at war almost every day of their lives.

Is this why the United States is at war in Vietnam virtually single-handedly? Maybe...

Ever since I stepped my foot in America, I wondered what these hundreds of millions of people would do if they had to face an occupation, or starvation conditions like those that the Greeks faced in World War II. This may happen eventually; possibly because a better choice made

---

193   The US advertising market continued to sputter at the end of 2007 and finished the year with measured spending of $148.99 billion, up 0.2% from 2006, according to TNS media intelligence.

its appearance in the world. How would we know that America is in trouble?

My belief is that when you see Americans move "elsewhere," to better "hunting grounds," that would be the beginning of the end for America. After all, America was built by people who did not hesitate to pioneer a better place for them, even if that meant great initial sacrifices. But until a better "elsewhere" becomes available, America has a serious role to play as an impatient, greedy, violent, pioneering, self-balancing, test case society that currently contributes its services to humanity.

Epilogue (1970-2000)

Cyprus (Anthony's Memoirs, 1970-1980)

In the mid-60s my father George decided to go to Russia. It was then that my brother Paul treated me with treachery. Secretly he pressed my father to sell the house, the house that I bought with my money. He did not even have the decency to give me my share. I even had to pay the last payment of 3400 Drs for that house to Manouseli and Emorfiades the development manager. He took even the old icon, which I personally carried over, all the way from Asia Minor. I never acted in a treacherous way and that is the reason why I attribute that God protected me all these years.

In the early 1970s, the Greek junta restored some civil rights that had been suspended after the junta took power. On June 1, 1973, it abolished the monarchy, proclaimed Greece a republic, and named Papadopoulos to the presidency, to serve until 1981. After his inauguration in August, he proclaimed a broad amnesty for political offenses and promised new elections in 1974. A civilian cabinet took office in October.

Student antigovernment riots in the fall of 1973 led to the re-imposition of martial law.

On November 17, 1973, many students of the Polytechnic Institute of Athens took to the streets. They barricaded themselves inside the Institute and fought off police and the army, until tanks were called in. About 400 students lost their lives. Ever since then, the November 17 terrorist group was organized in a vengeful killing spree against the Greek Right Wing politicians, NATO and American interests. [194]

On November 25, the military removed Papadopoulos, for failure to maintain order and named Lieutenant General Phaeton Gizikis president. Encouragement of a coup that only temporarily removed Archbishop

---

194   A. Boinodiris, Book 4, p. 31.

Makarios from the presidency of Cyprus, followed by the Turkish invasion of the island, led the junta to step down in July 1974. [195]

"General Davos of the 3rd Army sent a note to the Gizikis government, that with the current preparations we have we cannot go to war with Turkey, because the junta had weakened the army; simply, the Greek defenses were insufficient at the border of Thrace and the Aegean Islands. It was then, that Gizikis recalled Karamanlis from exile to form the first civilian government since 1967. His first task was to reinforce the Greek defenses. The islands started getting airports and new weapons were ordered. [196]

The junta took out Makarios and made president of Cyprus someone called Sampson (called a terrorist by the English and the Turks, but a liberation fighter as far as the Greek Cypriots were concerned). This caused Turkey to react and attack the island, occupying 40% of the island. Two thousand people were missing in Cyprus, some of them believed to be prisoners in Turkey.

The only good thing about the junta was that they got rid of the blood sucking Royal Family. The worst was that the Turks invaded Cyprus, because the Americans made sure that Greece was weakened in armament, while Turkey was strengthened, even though the junta was initially set up with the support of the Americans. The West changed their mind later on, but that did not correct the situation in Greece. It simply changed the parameters of armament between Greece and Turkey, letting Turkey take advantage of a weak Greece with the barbarous ATTILA attack on Cyprus. [197]

After an election in November, Karamanlis headed the New Democracy Party and formed a new government; Gizikis resigned in December. A referendum on the restoration of the monarchy was defeated in December, and a new republican constitution was approved in June 1975.

---

195   A. Boinodiris, Book 4, p. 31.
196   A. Boinodiris, Book 4, p. 31.
197   A. Boinodiris, Book 4, p. 31.

Karamanlis legalized the communist party and went through political means to fight Turkey through the United Nations. For him, the only one that would gain from a fight between Greece and Turkey would be the Eastern block countries, especially Russia and Bulgaria that would gladly occupy a weak Greece or Turkey.

In November 1977 the government called a general election in which the main issues were Greece's future entry into the European Economic Community and its strained relations with Turkey over Cyprus and offshore oil rights. The New Democracy Party won, but had a smaller majority in parliament. The Pan-Hellenic Socialist Movement (PASOK), under Andreas Papandreou, was the second largest party.

After the 1974 Cyprus crisis, Greece withdrew its troops from NATO. Terms for the continued presence of U.S. military bases in Greece were renegotiated in 1975 and 1976. In 1980, the country rejoined NATO's military wing.

When we returned to Drama from our USA trip on 17 May, 1973 we went to St. Constantine's church with Jordan and Kyriaki Zoumboulidou, Anestis and Makrina Zoumboulidou and Aristodimos and Fevronia Rousakis. A few days later, Jordan, Kyriaki and Makrina went to Constantinople for a tour. In 1974, Jordan Zoumboulides was diagnosed with heart trouble. On 6 February 1975 he died. We got very tired during that winter, watching over Jordan. As a result, Elisabeth started having respiratory problems in 1976. [198]

Cyprus (Stavros' Memoirs, Summer of 1974)

Early in 1974, I was working for IBM and was responsible for the development of the analog output module of a process control system, named the IBM System 7. Testing of that system was in process on various customer locations. One of them was an Italian tanker belonging to Maersk Company, which wanted to upgrade its navigational system and be capable of using the now new Global Positioning Satellite, in conjunction with System 7's Automatic Pilot software. The system was

---

198   A. Boinodiris, Book 1, p.151.

to use an automatic steering on a large tanker, guided by the System 7 software, using the analog output, to perform the steering controls.

I was due for vacation, but planned to board the Italian ship in Naples after my vacation, around the first week of August of 1974. I took off for a month's vacation to Greece with my family on July 1. I also purchased a ticket from Athens to Rome for Wednesday, July 31.

This was the first time I had returned to Greece since 1961.

The reasons initially were economic. As a student, I had difficulties paying for my tuition, let alone for trips. After I graduated, I had to face two draft boards for military service. By delaying my going to work and staying in school, I reached my 26th birthday which made me exempt from the draft. Yet, the Greek government would still draft me, regardless of age and US residency or citizenship, unless I compensated the Greek government monetarily for evading draft. The sum was small, but the government must issue eligibility for my age group. This eligibility became available in 1973, which prompted me to pay the sum (about $2000). Now, with white discharge papers I could travel to Greece.

As soon as Despina, my 2 year-old baby (Phaedra) and I landed in the Athens airport, John Kokkinos (Despina's father) greeted us and brought us home to his house in Kipseli. This was a special occasion. I was meeting John for the first time and John was seeing Phaedra, his granddaughter for the first time.

My family left for Drama around July 7. Another welcome was waiting there, all relatives wanting to see us. I returned to Athens on Thursday July 18, 1974. A trip to Schinias followed on the 19th. We were planning a trip to the beach house at St. Theodore and the Peloponnesian home at Steno.

On the morning of Sunday, July 20, John took me to his office at the Justice Department. Even on Sunday, Athens was crowded and full of life. As we exited the building to return home, weird news swept throughout the streets. People started talking to each other in restaurants and café stores.

General mobilization was declared; Greece was at war with Turkey.

Radio stations had no news, just military marches.

As we boarded the trolley, streets were being deserted. Everyone was withdrawing to their homes. By the time we reached John's home in Kipseli, Athens had lost its noisy breath. We were glued onto the radio, trying to pick up BBC, since no Greek radio was saying anything.

News trickled in. The Turks invaded Cyprus. They captured Kyrenia, the city of my Gainesville house mate Dino Athanasiou. I started thinking about his fate, because I knew that he had returned to Kyrenia with his uncle and his two young, American-born nieces that were there for vacation.

From the news we learned that many Greek soldiers were dying there. Several soldiers, attempting to reach the island with a transport plane, were shot down. No traffic was allowed in or out of Greece. Borders were sealed.

The Greek station reported news on types of men that were called to arms. Different color codes were called. All other eligible men should stand-by for further orders. I was advised to stay in Athens, until further news on my draft disposition came through. Night fell.

Most men went to the Kipseli Square, called Fokionos Negri. There, people shared news. A man with his American nephew from Chicago wondered when his nephew would return home. He had lost his flight that afternoon. He was also told that his nephew could be drafted too, even though he spoke not a word of Greek.

Monday morning of July 21 was not shedding much light on the question of the future of Greece. Then, around mid-day, we heard the news that Karamanlis was returning. More calls to arms for men, but all of them were not covering me. That night, Karamanlis took over the government.

Tuesday morning of July 22 was decision time. We decided to exit Athens and go to St. Theodore, at the family beach house, where all the rest of the relatives were vacationing. We used a small, white English car. As John was driving, I saw the results of mobilization. The coast was dotted with destroyers, protecting the Isthmus of Corinth. Few vehicles were on the roads, mostly military.

We stayed in St. Theodore until the general mobilization stopped, on Thursday July 24. More news started trickling in. None could travel, but businesses were coming back to life. Plans were made and we drove back to Athens on Monday, July 29. That same day I went to the Athens IBM office.

"Can I help you sir?" said the receptionist.

"I am with IBM, from Boca Raton and need to send a message to my manager on my disposition," I said as I showed the receptionist my badge.

"One minute sir," said the young woman.

She called a number and two young men stepped out. Meanwhile, I had already written the IBM Network address and message on a piece of paper.

I handed them the paper.

"Can you please send this message as soon as possible? I am due to board a boat in Naples for System Test and as you know, I cannot make it."

"Of course," said one young man, reading the note. "I will do it in the next 5 minutes."

"I appreciate it."

"Good luck."

"Thank you."

The message was sent to my line manager for System 7 at the IBM facility in Boca Raton. In a few minutes, all his management was reading my message:

"Due to circumstances beyond my control, I cannot make the trip to Naples. Please make backup arrangements."

Air traffic was restored by mid-August, 1974. My family returned to Boca Raton, Florida. Around mid-September of that year, I went again to Italy with another colleague.

I traveled to Rome, took a flight to Brindisi and drove to Taranto. There, after meeting with my Italian counterparts we boarded the tanker Sardinia where tests were conducted on a short trip to Ancona, Italy. With System 7, ships saved fuel, because the computer avoided steering in zigzag patterns, which most human wheel handlers could not avoid. Fuel consumption of 10-15% meant a great deal of savings for the any tanker company.

The Last Years (Anthony's Memoirs)

My son wrote to me that he was moving to Raleigh for his Doctorate program in Electrical Engineering at North Carolina State University starting in the summer of 1975. On September 14, 1977, they had another daughter, named Ismini. They came to Greece the following summer to baptize the infant. On Sunday, August 7, 1978, Ismini was baptized on Phaedra's birthday. She was baptized in the monastery of St. Silas in Kavala.

A big party was held with all the relatives in the village of Mikrohori, in the Tavern of Savas Mavrides. On Tuesday the ninth of August, her baptism was registered in the Kavala archives of the church.

Elisabeth then started having lung complications between August 10 and August 20. After Elisabeth came home from the hospital, news arrived that John Kokkinos (Despina's father) was dead.[199]

---

199   A. Boinodiris, Book 1, p. 331.

On April 17, 1979, Elisabeth went to Raleigh, North Carolina in America. She spent Easter there and had her health checked at Duke Hospital with a general examination. They found that she had an extremely high level of diabetes and was set on a diet regime. She returned home at the end of June after spending time with my son's family and the two grandchildren Phaedra and Ismini. She returned in good health, keeping up her diet.[200]

We then hear that my son's family moved again in 1981, finding a place in Connecticut.

Then, their address changes to a place in Saugerties, NY.

At the end of 1985, we received news that my son's family was moving back to Raleigh.

In 1985, Elisabeth went to Athens for a gallbladder operation. She was eating raw vegetables as part of her diet prescribed to her by Duke Hospital due to the diabetes. When I asked her about her health, she responded,

"If I do not eat, I am fine, but when I eat I hurt. Can someone live without eating?"

---

200   A. Boinodiris, Book 1, p. 331.

Figure 22 Boca Raton, FLA, USA: Anthony, Elisabeth,
Phaedra and Despina Boinodiris (1973)

Figure 23 Elisabeth, Despina and Anthony
Boinodiris at Cape Kennedy in 1973

Elisabeth's Death (Anthony's Memoirs, May 11, 1986)

Today I lost my wife. She went like the light of a candle in a light breeze. She was ill, having heart deficiency since 1976 after the death of my brother-in-law Jordan. We had to develop multiple x-rays in the hospital. In addition, she had diabetes, high blood pressure and gallbladder problems. She was constantly on medication.

In her youth, she had rheumatoid arthritis. Since 1933, at the age of 23 she had to go to hot mineral baths for treatment. What was amazing was that during the occupation she was very well, probably because of her forced starvation diet.

At that time, she could go to the springs of St. Barbara and carry two cans of water to the house. After my mother's death in 1938, she took in the orphans, namely my under-aged baby sister Georgia (7) and baby brother Paul (9) and raised them like her own son John. She managed to raise them in spite of hunger and occupational violence. Finally they were settled, including John who left for Germany where he worked.

In 1943, we had our second son who finished high school and left for America in 1961, after John was married. In 1962, my son John brought us our grandson Anthony, only 100 days old. In 1964, a granddaughter is born in Drama named Elisabeth. These children grew with us, sometimes one at a time, sometimes both of them, until 1976, when Elisabeth had a heart problem. We then asked John to come and pick up the children, because she had no more strength to take care of them. She went to the United States with my son Stavros to Duke Hospital where they diagnose her as a critically diabetic person. She was given medication and placed on a strict diet. She had her gallbladder removed in Athens.

At lent time of 1986, she had severe pain in the stomach, but became better with some medical prescriptions. On Good Saturday, she ate the heart of a lettuce and again, strong pains started. We passed Easter at the hospital eating nothing. The following Friday, ninth of May, she cooked fava beans and stuffed cabbage. She ate very little. The next day she started again with severe pains until the doctors came. They gave her some injections and all through Saturday, she was in pain. Around 7 PM, she fainted.

We called the heart specialist Krikelis, since her main doctor Efthimiades was absent. He immediately took her to the hospital. By 3 AM on Sunday, she was in a comma. They declared her dead a few hours later, on Sunday, May 11, 1986.

We had some problems burying her, because Drama, Kavala, Serres or Xanthi do not have a freezer to maintain a corpse, long enough so that her son from America can come for her burial. John had to take her body to Thessaloniki to a freezer at the AHEPA hospital.

On May 12, Stavros arrives in Thessaloniki by air and they both came to Drama, bringing the frozen body of their mother in the rear of John's truck.

On Tuesday, the 13th of May 1986 Despina arrived with her mother Efthimia and we buried Elisabeth. According to tradition, we did all the memorials; ninth of August for the 40-day memorial; ninth of August, for the six-month memorial and that followed by the 9-month memorial and the annual memorials. [201]

Conclusion of Anthony's Memoirs

Anthony Boinodiris continued to write on events of the day regularly until 1995, when he got sick.

He wrote on the war between Iran and Iraq:

"The war between Iran and Iraq, lasting from 1982 to 1989 caused the loss of life for 1.5 million youths. The crazy, fanatic, religious leader Khomeini and Iraq's leader Hussein caused the destruction of their economy, finally making peace without anyone being a winner. That is why humanity is hoping for peace and the Europeans are uniting into the European Economic Community (EEC), in which Greece is a member. Turkey is jealous, wanting to enter, but nobody wants her until she stops her illegal acts."

---

201   A. Boinodiris, Book 4, p. 125-134.

Here are some more entries:

"17th of August, 1990: Today is the 60th anniversary of my wedding. I married Elisabeth in poverty and economic crisis. We suffered war, occupations, fear, starvation, beatings from occupying forces, without being at fault and being sent on forced labor for six months to Bulgaria. Even after liberation, we had to go through the civil war, fighting our brothers for another six years. I had to wear military clothes until I was 42 years old. With all these conditions I managed to buy a piece of land and open a grocery store, using these resources to build a family and finally go on retirement at 62 years of age. We managed to travel a little, to Stuttgart in 1970 and to Boca Raton, Florida in 1972-73..."

"4th of September 1990: Hussein continues his aggressive behavior. I do not know how he has the guts to do this, but he is occupying Kuwait with Iraqi troops. I believe he has plans to conquer the whole Middle East and raise the price of oil to the West...."

"Today, 16 September 1990, I feel like celebrating my birthday. I got up cheery, drank my milk and walked to the local KAPI (public meeting place for the elderly), in Drama.

The US is getting ready for something big in the Persian Gulf. The UN met and decided to boycott the Iraqi oil after Iraq invaded Kuwait. They could not imagine that someone would attempt to invade another neighboring country and member of the UN. The Greek government sided with the West, since they are part of EEC. Fortunately, the Arab countries sided against Iraq. I do not know what position Turkey will take, since they have borders with Iraq and must be ready. Many Kurds live in the mountains of Turkey, Iraq and Iran. Meanwhile, Iraq shut off the pipelines leading to the Turkish port of Alexandretta. As I am finding out, American ships have closed off the Persian Gulf, while American army have advanced to the Kuwaiti border, not to attack, but to defend Saudi Arabia since Iraq is ready for war, being in a war state for eight years. The King of Jordan went to America to help in the negotiations with George Bush, the American President. Now Iraq turns to Islam, releasing 70,000 Iranian prisoners and dividing the area that was under contest, an area for which a 1.5 million people were killed. So many lives lost because of the stupidity of dictators and fanatics, using poisonous gases that they got from East Germany. The Jordanian King returned without results. Meanwhile, Iraq's Hussein keeps prisoners Americans, English, French and other citizens..."

"18th of September 1990- I had a very weird dream last night:

I was at the market, coming back home. The streets became narrower and narrower, preventing me from proceeding farther. When I decided to come back, I turned to find out that behind me was a torrent of a river. In trying to find an alternate route, I climbed on top of a wall, next to the river. Finally, without getting muddy and wet, I found a way out of the river into an opening where there was a beautiful building. The building door opens and Elisabeth, my wife comes out with a piece of paper asking me to take it to the police. Strangely, she was not an old lady, but a middle-aged one (40-50 years old). I woke up and cried. Then went back to sleep.

I woke up later, went to the bakery, got some bread and went to the old citizen center. There, I went through the newspapers, came home, took my bath, changed my clothes, ate and slept for another two hours. The weather outside is cloudy and warm. I woke up in good mood, drank a cup of coffee and pondered on my loneliness. I told myself that death is unavoidable. I assured myself that I was not a bad person in my youth. I was not greedy and worked like an honest man to support my family and to educate my children. I spent no more than what I could afford. The only regret I have was for my actions during the years of economic crisis from 1931 to 1935, when I was made to face injustice to my family with the violent act of arson. I had a baby and two of my father's siblings to support. I hope the world does not face the mentality of those days, mentality based on the dogma: "your death is my life." It was that thinking that gave rise to Fascism and the results of World War II. With God's help I will spend the days remaining in my life remembering my past life in this fashion."

Anthony Boinodiris became sick from colon cancer early in 1996. Symptoms like his have appeared in many instances to people after the Chernobyl incident of 1986. Northern Greece was polluted heavily with radiation, causing over time the deaths by cancer of many people. It is beyond doubt that Anthony died from radiation poisoning caused by that incident. He and Stavros saw each other for the last time in August of 1996. He died in February of 1997, leaving his treasured notebooks to the author of this book.

During the last meeting with his sons Anthony stated:

"I lived a good life. I may not have amounted to much, but I added a miniscule, but –for me-real contribution to human existence. We may not be improving much in our lives, but we try our best. If we survive natural disasters, and we do not destroy ourselves, we will eventually improve our lives to something miraculous. I am not afraid of dying. In death, we return all that God gave us during our birth back to him. We return all that we are, back to the stuff that makes this thin, changing soup of the universe. We must return our bodies to the microbes that made us all in the first place."

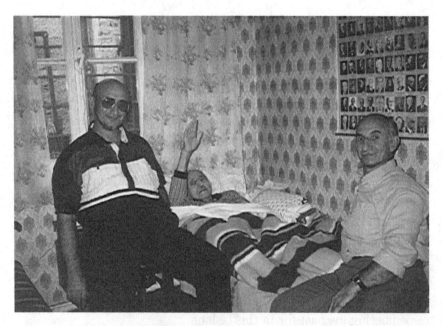

Figure 24 August 1996: Anthony in his death-bed.
He died six months later (February 1997).

Going on a Full Circle - Return to Andros
(Author's Remarks)

Figure 25 Andros, Monastery of Panachrantos as it stands today.²⁰²

This completes my five-part story of the "Andros Odyssey." As I went through my research and my father's notes, I had to relive all those years, both historically, and as a human being, trying to understand how they dealt with their problems during their times. In doing so, I felt overwhelmingly humble by the amount of effort exerted by our previous generations, from Kalinikos Psellus of the early eight century to my father, Anthony Boinodiris.

This 1300-year old story of human endeavor viewed in snapshot events may show to most of us, with our limited time focus of a lifetime how slowly humans have evolved over time. It shows how many of the issues that our ancestors dealt with are still with us. As Dr. K. Wright (my

---

202   It is one of the oldest, remaining monasteries of Andros, built by Nikiforos Focas in the 10ᵗʰ century.

niece) said: "... it is depressing to see how slow our progress has been. Youngsters reading this book must be very frustrated, as they have a gleam in their eye to improve the world during their lifetime. Human behavior is changing, not in terms of months or years, but over hundreds of generations of youngsters, with the same gleam in their eyes." We discovered that what once consisted of ancient Greek thinking lives on, not in a territory which we know as Greece, but in the hearts and minds of many people that follow tenets of Western Civilization. It crossed country barriers and continents through the massive immigration of Greeks, following the crusades. In the 12th century, it crossed religious boundaries, by inspiring Moses Maimonides to bring Judaism to a higher, Westernized level, by applying neo-Platonic logic. Immigrant Greek-educated teachers, in Italy and Switzerland fought for, and taught freedom of religious expression during the dark, pre-reformation years of Catholicism. They even tried to change the Islam-based Shariah law into logic-based Cannon Law within the Ottoman Empire, with some degree of regional success. In their long Odyssey, Greek thinkers spent a great deal of energy trying to improve humanity in the best way they knew. We can only judge them by their results, some of which are visible today.

We are all part of an Odyssey of our own. In it, each one of us represents a lifetime of endeavor trying to achieve something. We know that no matter how much effort we put in our survival and progress, all we can accomplish is a minute step forward to somewhere unknown, as this step compares with the big picture of human survival. We are one of many living organisms, most of which became extinct (e.g. dinosaurs), with a limited lifespan, with limited life on a planet, in a universe eventually doomed to oblivion. Yet, no human, from birth to death thinks of doing anything else but be part of this Odyssey, because we are driven by some strange evolutionary laws, measured in much longer timeframes than we can comprehend. In those timeframes, we may be very fast. I am sure that many asked the question: what evolutionary drive makes us be who we are? Every time a new baby comes to life, it is driven to explore, to learn, to overcome perceived challenges of life and to question. What drives us since birth?

Are we pre-programmed to seek new ways of improving our lives on this world by some evolutionary program?

Are we driven by survival, or pleasures of life, over which we have no control (instinctive rationale)?

Are we driven by curiosity on the mystery of life (thirst of knowledge on how things will turn out)?

Are we driven to selfishly win over other humans and earth creatures, only to discover that some victories lead to a step backwards to actual human intentions? Our whole existence revolves around recognizing "healthy competition," geared to improve ourselves, helping humanity and "unhealthy competition," that can seriously set humanity back.

Are we driven by a belief that somewhere, there is a Supreme Being with a reason for all this and that there is another dimension of life ... after our departure from this world (religious rationale)? Some of us are driven by the desire of "perfection," one that can take us to "paradise," a place none claims to have been yet and be able to describe.

At this point, it is proper to remind ourselves of the story of the "perfect human," which succeeded to meet the strict criteria of perfection that he imagined that God Has set upon us. When the human entered paradise, the paradise was empty. The human became so lonely, that immediately asked: "Can I go where the rest of humanity is?"

Is it worth for some of us to come out ahead, leaving the rest of humanity behind?

I looked around me and met people like you with various thoughts on the subject; many readers described their own experience and beliefs in their own Odyssey and tried to put their arms around what motivated them to do what they did. They all wanted to "achieve something." When they were pinned down as to what was the final object of achievement, after considerable thought they admitted that trying to achieve something in life made them happy, and the happiest they felt was not for their own achievement, but seeing the humanity around them achieve something as a whole. Notice was taken of the extreme emotions felt by the attendees in the stadium of the Para-Olympics event in Seattle, when one boy fell in a 100 meter run. The remaining participants stopped, turned back and helped the boy. They raised him up and went to the finish all together. The stadium attendees still talk about that strange emotion.

I do not have the answer on what motivates every one of us, but does it matter? No matter what motivates us, we have no better option than to cultivate that motivation and live our Odyssey to the fullest. If some Supreme Being programmed us to perform certain functions in our lives, let us find out where that program takes us and do it with zest and versatility. After all, it is versatility that made us survive up to now. As Charles Darwin thought, "it is not the strongest of the species that survive, nor the most intelligent but the most responsive to change." You and I, through some weird events in evolutionary history may be very lucky to be part of our continuously changing Human Odyssey.

We, humans are not much of an entity, if we consider ourselves in the context of the vast universe. But, whatever we are, we have been given the opportunity of life and even more important, the opportunity to discover about ourselves and the universe we live in. This opportunity to discover was a gift that did not come overnight. Each human, since we climbed down from the trees, became human by developing a specific type of brain through evolution. This brain allowed humans to express what ideas were in their brain in a form, so that they or others can experience a form of these ideas, as they appear in the world outside the originators brain. This form we call art. Humans drew, sculpted, spoke, wrote, sang and danced to express their ideas. Such precious gifts as freedom of expression provided us with the ability to discover ourselves and our environment. They cannot be suppressed or wasted, because that would be contrary to our human nature. We are built that way and they are our major tools for human existence. They must be treasured and explored every moment of our lives. Even if our short presence in life does not amount to much, we should be thankful for these gifts in our existence and make the best of it.

The iconoclastic conflicts that started the Andros Odyssey were an unfortunate suppression of certain freedoms of artistic expression, in the name of religious misconceptions. It is also unfortunate that these conflicts are still with us in certain parts of the globe, supported by certain religious fanatics that do not appreciate the value of human freedom for self expression.

By using arts, humans enjoy every minute of life's adventures and through the art of writing they make sure that they pass on that desire to the next generations by encouraging them to play, explore, experiment, and savor life's lurking surprises, curious in search of a purpose. No matter how painful life may be at times, alternative options do not exist. There are no alternatives to our freedom for self-expression, life's most precious gift for curious thinking animals like us.

Why are all of us involved in this Human Odyssey? I do not know. I suspect that there are clues for the reason of our existence all around us, but I admit to have limited intellect and experience to come up with an answer that holds the test of my human logic. I think though that even if many of us do not have the answer, we go through life based on a hope that some of our future descendants may figure the purpose of it all, through their search for Ithaca. Armed with this precious hope, our freedom for self expression and our instinctive curiosity, the Human Odyssey continues through time and space.

Appendix

References

1. **"Ten Notebooks,"** by Anthony Boinodiris, Drama, Greece, 1975-1995 (Greek).

2. **"Interview with General Markos Vafiades, former Leader of ELAS,"** from the Greek Trotskyist paper Socialist Change, 1983, http://www.marxists.org/subject/stalinism/origins-future/1983mv.htm

3. **"Deserter Restored,"** Time Magazine, Monday, Apr. 01, 1957 (Markos Vafiades Restoration).

4. "Foreign Banks in Bulgaria," The William Davidson Institute Working Paper No 537, University of Michigan Business School, Jan. 2003, p. 10.

5. "The Virtue of Selfishness: A New Concept of Egoism," a 1964 collection of essays and papers by Ayn Rand and Nathaniel Branden.

6. "Arvanites," by Aristides Kollias, (in Greek) E. Rallis Press, Athens, Greece, 1985.

7. "The Virtual Jewish History Tour – Greece," by Shira Schoenberg, http://www.jewishvirtuallibrary.org/jsource/vjw/Greece.html#Jewish%20Greece

8. "Vote on Armenian 'genocide' resolution put off," CNN News, Oct 25, 2007. http://edition.cnn.com/2007/WORLD/meast/10/25/us.turkey/index.html

9. "Speaker Pelosi hedges on genocide resolution vote," CNN News, Oct 27, 2007, http://edition.cnn.com/2007/POLITICS/10/17/house.armenian/index.html#cnnSTCText .

Figure 26 Chronology of the Ancestral Family of Characters during the Period: 1925–2000

Boyun-egri-oglu (Stravolemis) Boinodiris	Mayoglou	Aslanoglou	Tsekmezoglou
Paul Boyun-egri-oglu *(1855-1926)* / **Katherine Makisoglou** – potter **Children:** -George *(1882-196X)* -Charalambos *(1890-195X)*--farmer -Katina *(1887-196X)* -Orsia *(1880-196X)*	**Haji-John Mayoglou** *(1855-1919)* – Director of the Railroads of the Ottoman Empire / **Makrina Suzanoglou** **Children:** Pandel Mayoglou/Mayo *(18XX-19XX)* - Evanthia Mayoglou *(18XX-193X)*	**Christos Aslanoglou** *(1856-1919)* Merchant and Church Leader /1st **Wife: Kyriaki** *(1861-1891)* **Child:** -John Aslanoglou (1875-1926) /2nd **Wife: Elisabeth** *(1862-1920)* **Children:** -Prodromos -Jordan -George -Despina -Marika -Calliope	**Basil Tsekmezoglou (1851-1920)** **Married Maria Zopoglou** -Makrina -Martha -Calliope -Stavros -Kyriakos

George Boyun-egri-oglou-Boidaris *(1882-196X)* **/Evanthia Mayoglou** **Children:** -**Anthony** *(1905-1997)* -**Irene** *(1913-1999)*/**Prodromos Topal-oglu /Topalides** -**Paul Boidaris** *(1928-)* soccer player in DOXA -**Georgia** *(1931-)*	**Pandelis <Pandel> Mayoglou <Mayo> / Kathryn Kominos** **Children:** -**John Mayo** (193X)	**John Aslanoglou** *(1875-1926)* merchant / **Makrina Tsekmezoglou** **Children:** -**Michael Aslanoglou** (1906-195X)**/Aslanides** -**Kyriaki** *(19-19)* -**Elisabeth** *(1910-1986)* -**Marianthi** *(1914-198X)* - **Basil** -**Leonides** *(1918-198X)* -**Fevronia** *(1922-)*	**Kyriakos Tsekmezoglou** -farmer -Nea Karvali **Children:** -**Vasilis** -**Vasiliki**
Anthony Boinodiris *(1905-1997)*/**Elisabeth Aslanoglou** *(1912-1986)* **Children:** -**Stavros** *(1943-)* -**John** *(1931-)*	**John Mayo** (193X) / **Christina** *(building contractor -Miami, FLA)*	**Michael Aslanoglou** **<Aslanides>** • 1st wife: **Urania** **Children:** -**John Aslanides** -**Charalambos** -**Christos** 2nd wife: **Katina** **Child:** -**Michael**	
Stavros Boinodiris *(1943-)* Engineer and Author / **Despina Kokkinos** -**Phaedra** *(1972-)* -**Ismini** *(1977-)*			

Index

297

Joseph Nasi xxvii